Re:Cyclists

200 YEARS ON TWO WHEELS

MICHAEL HUTCHINSON

BLOOMSBURY
LONDON · OXFORD · NEW YORK · NEW DELHI · SYDNEY

Bloomsbury Sport
An imprint of Bloomsbury Publishing Plc

50 Bedford Square   1385 Broadway
London   New York
WC1B 3DP   NY 10018
UK   USA

www.bloomsbury.com

BLOOMSBURY and the Diana logo are trademarks of
Bloomsbury Publishing Plc

First published 2017

British Library Cataloguing-in-Publication Data
A catalogue record for this book is available from the British Library.

Library of Congress Cataloguing-in-Publication data has been applied for.

ISBN: HB: 978-1-4729-2559-6
ePub: 978-1-4729-2561-9

2 4 6 8 10 9 7 5 3 1

Typeset in Minion by Deanta Global Publishing Services, Chennai, India
Printed and bound in Great Britain by CPI Group (UK) Ltd, Croydon CR0 4YY

To find out more about our authors and books visit www.bloomsbury.com.
Here you will find extracts, author interviews, details of forthcoming
events and the option to sign up for our newsletters.

For Louisa

Contents

CONTENTS

INTRODUCTION

A Man Walks into a Bar

Many of life's defining moments pass almost unnoticed at the time. It often takes weeks or months or longer for the significance of a chance meeting or an unexpected phone call to become clear. When an unfamiliar girl at college put her head round the door of my room to ask me to turn the music down, it was not immediately apparent that we would be spending the next twenty-something years living together. Instead I scowled and told her that I turned down the towering genius of Leonard Cohen for no one, least of all Abba-fancying philistines like her. She rolled her eyes and slammed the door, and I think we probably both assumed that that was that.

Some pivotal events, on the other hand, are hard to miss. Take what happened to me around lunchtime on 6 June 1999, for instance.

I'd just finished riding a National Championship bike race in North Yorkshire. It was a warm summer day, and it had been a hot race. I was tired and a bit dehydrated. I was also very, very pleased with myself, because I'd just finished fifth, only a few seconds off the podium, which had been my best result in that race to date and had been the result of a very carefully planned campaign and a lot of hard work. I was, therefore, cheerful, satisfied, perhaps even a little smug and generally in the highest of spirits as I walked into the pub where I was staying to collect the key to my room from behind the bar.

I had come straight from the race. To be specific about it, I was wearing a time-trial helmet with a large point at the back and a mirrored visor at the front. I was still in my racing skinsuit, which was exceptionally tight and, in the whiter bits at least, had a pinkish translucence. My smoothly shaved legs ended at a pair of shiny silver cycling shoes, the futuristic-superhero effect of which was undermined by the hard carbon-fibre soles that meant I had to walk in very tiny steps to avoid slipping on the stone floor.

The bar was packed for Sunday lunch. The loud 'clack-clack' that accompanied every mincing step meant that heads started to turn. Then conversations petered out. Forks stopped halfway to mouths. Behind the bar, beer poured unwatched over the rims of glasses and into drip-trays. It wasn't the sort of pub people played darts in at lunchtime, but if it had been, the darts would presumably have stopped in mid-air. It felt like the special video-effect where the people freeze-frame and the camera pans around them.

I clacked across the unnaturally quiet bar, and asked the landlord for the key to room three. He took it off a peg and set it on the counter. Then, in a moment of exuberance, I said, 'And a pint of Theakston's XB, please.' I suppose the idea was that this would break the tension, everyone would laugh and smile and perhaps I'd be hoisted aloft and carried in celebration around the bar.

That did not happen. I still looked the way David Bowie would have looked in the mid-1970s if his alter egos had been designed by a focus group, except that now I had to stand at the bar and drink a pint in a calm, unhurried fashion. People told their children to stop staring at me, even as they held their own gazes on me steady and unabashed.

I still didn't care. For probably the first time in a rather self-conscious life I was quite happy to look the fool. That morning, perhaps during the race, perhaps on the ride back the couple of miles from the finish-line to the pub, perhaps just as I crossed the bar, a real pride in being a cyclist had sprung up in me. I loved what I did, and I loved all the people I did it with. Anyone who didn't like looking at odd strands of my body hair through the pinkish bits of my tight, tight suit could get knotted. I stood there and lifted my pint with an air of, 'One day, my friends, you will all be like me.' I was right, and everyone else was wrong. It felt magnificent.

What can I say? Adrenaline and jubilation can do terrible, terrible things to people. If I wasn't embarrassed then, I certainly was later. But the pride was real. I was a cyclist, and there was nothing else I'd rather have been. That's still very much the case.

I wasn't born a cyclist. I didn't come from a cycling family, nor did I take it up young. I came to it late, and entirely by accident. My girlfriend's father had lent me one of his racing bikes and suggested I might enjoy a spin. Within about ten miles I felt ready to devote the rest of my life to riding bikes. I spent a blissful summer riding it for miles round London's parks, or out of the city into Surrey or Sussex, just wearing a running vest and a pair of old rugby shorts and having the time of my life.

My happiness was only increased when I started racing and discovered that, not only did I like it, I was good at it. I read magazines and books; I went to stand on chilly roadsides to be a third of the two-men-and-a-dog who traditionally watched British races. I went from neophyte to dyed-in-the-wool bikie in about six months. There was nothing about cycling that wasn't exciting, nothing I didn't want to do.

Cycling does this to people, and I'm not surprised. To sit on something as simple and brilliant as a bike is to become a better, faster, nimbler version of yourself. A bike isn't artificial. It doesn't separate you from your surroundings. It is very much whatever you want it to be. There are surveys that claim to have identified anything up to 60 different sorts of bike rider – from full-gas racer to someone riding to a village shop, to an urban cyclist whose idea of a perfect Sunday afternoon is putting on a vintage racing-jersey and going to sit with their bike at a table outside a café. You can even switch from one type to another with nothing other than a change of purpose – I've probably been most of the sixty at one time or another, and often several within the space of a single ride.

I don't think it would be possible for me to stop being a cyclist. Even if I never rode a bike again, I think I'd still be a cyclist before I was anything else. I've made my living in cycling. It was never part of my life plan, but how could I resist the opportunity? What on earth else would I prefer to do? I raced professionally for several years, and when that ran out I started writing for a cycling magazine. The magazine was *Cycling Weekly*, which was first published as *Cycling* in 1891, just as the penny-farthing era was ending and the safety bicycle was taking over.

With all due respect to my colleagues, by some distance the best thing about their office was their archive. Other than the odd Christmas, the magazine hasn't missed a week in well over a hundred years. The copies are bound into large six-month volumes. I used to sink into one of those like a time traveller. I could spend an afternoon that had been earmarked for something a bit more useful working my way through a random interwar year, following the fortunes of the racers, the journeys of the touring correspondents, the arguments about bike lanes, compulsory lights and even helmets. There was something special about seeing the past through the eyes of people just like me, people who were first and foremost cyclists. Their concerns were sometimes very modern-feeling, while their worlds were rather different. It was nice to have a familiar perspective from which to look at the past.

The magazines always referred to their remit as 'the sport and pastime of cycling'. It's an unfussy phrase that crops up again and again. It sounds like it ought to be in the text for some sort of sermon: the two sides of cycling, often the concerns of the same riders, the same clubs, the same writers. It tidily gathers together all that was and is best about riding a bike, both the fury of competition and the pleasure of time wasted well.

That's where my fascination with my predecessors came from, and why I wanted to know more about them. This is a personal history, and I mean that in two ways. I mean it in the normal style, in that it's a history guided entirely by my own curiosity. But I also mean it in the sense that it's a history of people like me. People who raced, people who regarded a ride with a friend on a sunny summer afternoon as something close to perfection, and even people who worked for cycling magazines and managed to pull their noses out of the archive for long enough to actually do some work.

The fascination has been with cyclists, not with bicycles. I'm as keen on a moodily lit close-up photograph of a 1963 Campagnolo Record rear derailleur as any other right-thinking person. I once expressed my admiration for an elderly, monolingual Italian man's beautiful old Cinelli SuperCorsa through the medium of mime and did so with such vigour that he tightened his grip on it and shouted for help at the top of his voice.

I've even ridden old bikes at vintage rallies. I've gone the whole way and done it in period costume. But I still always want to come back to the riders, not their bicycles. On a vintage rally, there is a wondrous sense of timelessness about standing by a country road in a tweed suit trying to repair a puncture with a vintage bicycle pump. You know what it was like for the bike's first owner, you know how it felt, you know just what sort of language he resorted to and you know that however hard he tried, it was impossible to hurl a 30lb roadster far enough to give any real sense of closure.

There are certainly points in the history of cyclists where the state of the technology mattered more than others. It's especially the case in the early years. Things like the change from the penny-farthing to the safety bicycle in the 1880s had profound consequences for who could ride, and where they could go. But, overall, the most remarkable thing about bicycles is not how much they've changed, but how little. If you ride a bike from 120 years ago, the differences are of refinement and cosmetics. So I haven't dwelled for any longer than seemed necessary on the mysteries of different steel alloys or the fascinating and vexed question of who first built a bicycle with ball-bearings.

Cyclists have always been fond of decrying others as 'not a proper cyclist'. I've been happy to accept a sort of self-selection. A cyclist is anyone who calls themselves a cyclist, for whom the sport and the pastime was or is part of their identity. It's a definition that means that I haven't really looked at utility cycling, cycling purely for transport. For most of cycling's history, those who rode for simple transport didn't look on cycling as part of who they were at all, any more than someone who gets the train to work counts themselves a trainspotter. And in this context, I happily accept I'm the man in the cagoule standing at the end of the platform with a flask and a notepad.

It's a good time to be a cyclist-spotter. Numbers are increasing, the sport and the pastime has become a more aspirational activity than it has been for a century. Although over-confidence is a perpetual risk – there's such a thing as a warning from history, and there's also such a thing as a warning from history books. One of the unvarying features of all the cycling histories I've ever read is that they finish with a chapter called something like 'Towards a Cycling Tomorrow!' which confidently claims that cycling is poised to take over the world. I think it's always going to be more complicated than that, but I think it's not too much of a risk to say that things for cyclists are better than they have been for quite a long time.

Another reason it's a good time to be a cyclist-spotter is that there are a lot of people to talk to about it. While there is a bit of uncertainty about the very beginnings of cycling, most of the years of the later nineteenth and early twentieth centuries were very well documented – there were countless books and magazines, accounts of everything from the races to the grand tours of Europe that aristocratic cyclists made. As cycling matured and changed in the twentieth century, these died out. By the middle of the century, other than *Cycling* magazine, there is not a great deal to be found. Happily, since old cyclists never die (that's not the set-up for a joke, they just don't), I've been able to talk to a lot of them about the neglected years.

I've enjoyed every conversation, every hour spent with an old book or magazine or photo album. I've found out more about some of my old heroes, and discovered a few new ones. The experience has made me feel even more like a cyclist than I did before, and prouder to be part of the story. If, when I walked into that Yorkshire pub, I had felt the way about cycling that I do now, I'd probably have declared a round for the whole bar. Which would have made the moment when I remembered that the contents of my skinsuit didn't include a wallet even more memorable for all concerned.

CHAPTER 1
1817: The Big Bang

It all started with a volcano. And what a volcano it was. Every bicycle and every rider that the world has ever seen has its genesis in recorded history's biggest bang. Mount Tambora in Indonesia was the volcano in question. In April 1815 it did not so much erupt as explode – and with such violence that it blew more than 24 cubic miles of rock and ash into the sky. The mountain's height was reduced by almost 5,000 feet. It was an entire order of magnitude bigger than its more famous neighbour Krakatoa. You could have heard it 1,600 miles away, which is further than the distance from London to Istanbul.

As if the event hadn't been hard enough to miss already, it changed the weather. Ash and sulfur dioxide thrown into the atmosphere caused a dramatic fall in global temperatures,[1] leaving 1816 as 'the year without a summer'. Harvests failed. There were food riots across Europe. Red snow fell on Italy. Brown snow fell on Hungary. A disastrous crop failure in Ireland precipitated a typhus outbreak that killed an estimated 100,000 people. There were floods, avalanches, famine, and civil unrest across the world.

Still, it wasn't all bad news. All those wonderful pictures J. M. W. Turner painted with the hazy yellow-orange skies were apparently not the result of his imagination, but a reasonably faithful reproduction of the effects of ash in the atmosphere. At a washout of a summer house-party in Switzerland the guests were reduced to the indoor amusement of a competition to write a scary story. What sounds like the parlour game from hell produced Mary Shelley's *Frankenstein* and a short story by Lord Byron that went on to inspire the modern mythology of the vampire. And in the cold and damp of a German forest, a man accidentally invented the bicycle, or, at any rate, something very close to the bicycle.

His name was by some distance the finest in the history of cycling: Karl Friedrich Christian Ludwig Freiherr Drais von Sauerbronn, which would have been quite a handful to paint on the frames of his machines had it been the custom at the time. He's generally known as Baron von Drais. It's still enough to give you an urge to don a silk scarf and a monocle and start shooting down Sopwith Camels.

In 1816 von Drais was a senior forestry official in Baden – a position of some considerable status. When the effects of Tambora made themselves apparent he was faced with a sudden dearth of horses. They starved for lack of food and were, in their turn, eaten by the foresters, also for lack of food. We don't know whether the invention came about simply because von Drais was looking for an alternative means of personal transport or, whether in the absence of horses to drag felled trees, he was looking for a way to move logs out of the forests, and tried attaching wheels to them, discovering when he did so that if you could steer the front wheel then you could balance successfully on the log.

Whichever it was, the result was the '*draisine*' (also known as the 'hobby-horse', the 'dandy-horse', the 'running machine', the '*Laufmaschine*', or even, in an early swing at naming-it-like-you-want-to-sell-it, the 'pedestrian curricle'). It was, as you'd expect from a machine born in a forest, essentially a wooden beam with two fore-and-aft cartwheels attached. You sat astride it and pushed it along with your feet, in much the same manner as a toddler learning to ride a modern balance bike.

It wasn't, in truth, all that marvellous as a means of transport. Even staying upright on the rutted roads of the early nineteenth century was a challenge. One of von Drais's early rides of ten miles took him an hour – which wasn't at all bad – but he could only manage to ride ten miles at all because he'd sought out the smoothest road his home town of Mannheim had to offer.[2] On most roads walking would be just as fast, and would leave you in a less dishevelled state for doing whatever it was you were planning to do when you reached your destination.

The *draisine* wasn't the very first human-powered vehicle, not by many centuries. It's just that most of its predecessors had even greater issues of practicality. Litters and sedan chairs dated back several thousand years, but really only worked with a ready supply of slaves, which had issues of sustainability as a means of mass transport due to the problem of how the slaves themselves were going to get to work.

An even more grotesque human-powered carriage was the work of a German called Jean Hautsch. In the 1660s he designed a carriage for the King of Denmark that was powered by small children concealed within the structure. It seems likely that it was intended to be no more than a curiosity, and, since its means of propulsion was not visible to an onlooker, maybe provide a bit of a puzzle. A witness claimed it was capable of 3,000 paces in an hour, presumably something in the region of 2 mph, which, given the machine's likely bulk, says something for the stamina of Danish children.

And so it went on. Through the eighteenth century there were numerous carriages propelled by adult servants, jumping up and down on cranked axles, winding with their arms, while their master steered and (perhaps) provided encouragement. They all suffered from the basic defect that they were essentially four-wheeled horse-drawn carriages, retaining all the accompanying size and weight. All that had really changed was that the horses were replaced by a couple of grooms or footmen capable of providing only a fraction of the power, even in the unlikely event that they were enthusiastic about jumping up and down on the axle of a carriage while onlookers stared and sniggered.

Accounts of these machines are not always very reliable. A French inventor called Blanchard said he had used a horseless carriage of his own design to give Benjamin Franklin a ride from Paris to Versailles while Franklin was serving as the American ambassador to France. The inventor claimed it had taken him just an hour and three-quarters for the trip, which would have been an impressive 12 kph or thereabouts. But it seems telling that Franklin appears never to have mentioned his trip to anyone, nor to have expressed much subsequent interest in horseless carriages. The inventor's claims came only 15 years after Franklin had died, which seems, under the circumstances, relevant to any weighing of the evidence.[3]

What made the *draisine* different from all the foregoing was its lightness – it was more like a grown-up's version of a children's toy than an attempt to find a way for a man to do the work of a horse. When von Drais started selling his machines, unlike their ridiculous ancestors they actually enjoyed a certain level of popularity. Von Drais took it quickly to Paris, which was the California of the early nineteenth century as far as getting a fad off the ground was concerned. After a disastrous start, where he omitted to check that the servant employed to demonstrate the machine could actually ride it, he managed to build up a certain interest. He was mocked by some, applauded by others, and he cultivated a take-up of the *draisine* among precisely the sort of young men who two centuries later would buy little fold-up scooters, Segways and hoverboards.

In a foretaste of exactly how popular cyclists were going to be for the subsequent two hundred years, the *draisine* was hated wherever it went. The problem was the roads. Rutted by cartwheels, pocked by horses' hooves, even if it wasn't covered in mud, an early nineteenth-century road was not, with a few exceptions, a very inviting place to ride an iron-tyred lump of wood. So the dandies who bought them moved onto the pavements and the park paths, which were much smoother, and where it was possible to build up more speed. Much more. By 1819, *draisines* were banned from all or part of Milan, New York, London, Paris and even Calcutta.[4]

There was less actual mockery than you might have expected. The general view, even from establishment commentators, seems to have been one of mild curiosity, perhaps even mixed with a little enthusiasm. One Parisian journal let fly with, 'Long live this worthy Baron von Drais to whom we owe such novel pleasures! . . . Be quick to sharpen your pens, you chroniclers of fashion!'[5]

In a way it was the 'fashion' bit of that which condemned the *draisine* in Paris. It never got past being a novelty. You could rent them at the pleasure gardens, and they were ridden in theatrical shows. They were probably closer to a skateboard in terms of practical transport than they were to a modern bike. Baron von Drais continued to earnestly conduct forestry inspections on his, while everyone else who rode a *draisine* was using it for a bit of fun, maybe to impress their friends, and not much more.

The invention was viewed less indulgently elsewhere. When the *draisine* arrived in England, the first thing that happened was that von Drais got royally done over by Denis Johnson, a London coachbuilder, who essentially stole the *draisine* idea, patented it, improved it by making the frame out of iron rather than wood, and made a small fortune selling them to Regency dandies of the type ridiculed in *Blackadder the Third*.

The second thing that happened in London was that, unlike their French counterparts, the English commentators were not curious, nor were they even mildly enthusiastic. Street urchins and newspaper caricaturists and every other variety of opinion-former were of one mind on the *draisine*: they pointed and laughed until tears rolled down their cheeks. There was enough interest for Johnson to start two riding schools, and for the authorities to feel it was necessary to ban *draisines* from the pavements, but the craze was a short-lived one, because no one in London had a skin thick enough to persist with it.

It was the same in the US. The *Baltimore Telegraph* noted the arrival in its bailiwick of 'a curious two-wheeled device called a *velocipede* . . . which is propelled by jackasses instead of horses'[6], and that just about said it all.

There were one or two signs of the machine's possible worth, and of its descendants' glorious future, not least among them the very considerable feat of athleticism that allowed a *draisine* rider to beat a coach from London to Brighton.[7] But by 1819, after just two years, it was all over. In the end, the *draisine* died of mockery.

Von Drais himself died in penury. He kept inventing, and displayed no small talent for it – he came up with the first typewriter with a keyboard, a stenograph, a device for recording piano music onto paper, and a human-powered railcar that he felt might be useful to passengers who had missed a train and wished to pursue it, and didn't care how ridiculous they looked while doing so. But he was commercially witless, and managed to avoid making a living from any of these ideas, including the original *draisine*, which was too easy to copy and too easy to improve. He was in an even more precarious position after his father died in 1839. Politically naïve, he got himself on the losing side of a revolution by renouncing his title to align himself with the republicans, only for the royalists to win. The father of the two-wheeler only avoided by a whisker being locked up for insanity, and died penniless in 1851 at the age of 66.[8]

Unfortunately the *draisine* was almost totally ignored for the next four decades. The development of the steam locomotive and the public railways during the first half of the nineteenth century revolutionised transport, and generated huge excitement in the idea of travel as something that wasn't profoundly uncomfortable, dangerous and totally dependent on horses. The world was so thrilled by the possibilities of large-scale engineering that no one really got back to looking at the simple, lightweight, inexpensive *draisine*. It's a very strange kink in history that the steam train and the railways predated the pedal bicycle in their invention, especially since the bicycle requires almost no technology that wasn't available to the Romans.

It's probably owing to this hiatus that the *draisine* gets fairly short shrift in bicycle history – it didn't have pedals, so it wasn't, strictly speaking, a bicycle. Yet it deserves better, because it was the breakthrough. The key to the bicycle is not really the pedals, because any fool can master that. It's the astonishing, counterintuitive possibility of balancing on two wheels, one behind the other. That's the bit of cycling that's like witchcraft. It makes no sense. It ought, by rights, to be a precarious circus trick, reserved only for those with the dedication to spend months or years learning how to do it. When I learned to ride a unicycle it turned out to be only just this side of impossible. Cycling looks like it ought to be very nearly the same.

Following the death of the *draisine* there was quite a long period of sustained, scatter-gun innovation in the field of human-powered transport that might as well have been conducted with the guiding principle that 'you can invent anything you like, and as batty as you want, as long as it's not a bicycle'. Substantial engineering was very much in vogue – the locomotives, the factories – and light, simple things didn't really get the attention they deserved.

The *Mechanic's Magazine* and other journals featured numerous machines designed to bring the revolution of the railways to the horseless carriage. For the most part the machines were the work of amateur British tinkerers and artisans and not professional engineers. And almost without exception they repeated the mistakes of the servant-powered carriages. There was heavy ironmongery, and plenty of it. Few of the machines devised ever got as far as being built, which allowed flights of fancy to run unencumbered by considerations like mass and the consequent difficulties huge amounts of it might cause with gravity and inertia.

'Mr Merryweather's Pedomotive Carriage' of 1839 was not atypical. It was a tricycle, with a front wheel not much bigger than a modern bicycle wheel. But the two rear wheels were appreciably taller than a man. The whole machine appears to have been over 12 feet in length. It was powered by single rider, who stood up between the rear wheels to operate treadles. God alone knows how much it must have weighed. It would be unwieldy if you reproduced it in carbon-fibre, never mind iron and wood.

Treadles were the most common means of propelling one of these carriages – they had the advantage that they could, in effect, be geared up. The downside was that they were clearly decidedly tiring to operate. In the same year as Mr Merryweather offered his machine, his fellow mechanic Mr Baddeley designed what he called his Manumotive Exercising Carriage. It was on a similarly heroic scale, but powered by a seated man operating hand-cranks in the rear axle. The logic was that continuous cranking in a circular motion would provide a smoother, more efficient application of power than jumping up and down on treadles. There was force to the argument; the problem was that powering a machine of (wild guess) more than 100 kilograms over rough, rutted roads by hand must have been almost impossible. With hindsight, it seems odd that Mr Baddeley didn't make the leap to circular pedalling.

A man who did was Mr Williams. He was among the first advocates of what we now recognise as conventional pedalling – but still managed to incorporate it into a bizarre festival of engineering. Williams's machine had two riders, one of whom pedalled standing up on the front axle, steering with his hands. His partner, well over six feet away at the machine's rear extremity, sat down and hand-cranked the same axle via a substantial transmission-belt arrangement, while steering the other axle with his feet.

This whole riot of innovation was topped with a revolving parasol, for no reason that is even remotely clear – maybe it was supposed to be a cooling fan, maybe it was intended to be a stab at some sort of slipstream-driven perpetual-motion component, maybe it was meant to make the whole thing fly. You wouldn't want to rule anything out where the fertile brain of Mr Williams was concerned. The whole thing was a marvel. In *King of the Road*, historian Andrew Ritchie describes the Williams

Passenger Propelled Locomotive Carriage as 'fantastic', and he clearly means it in every sense of the word.[9]

Speed claims for these machines ranged anywhere from practically nothing to 30 mph. The former seems a lot more believable than the latter, at least on a level road. They would have gone faster – a lot faster – down a hill, but anyone who wanted to try that with only nineteenth-century braking technology between him and a spectacular arrival in the next world would have required more balls than the astronauts on the *Apollo 11* moon mission.

There was no shortage of invention and effort, and machine after machine was proposed. But the actual bicycle? Two wheels, a saddle, handlebars and some pedals? *Draisine* plus pedals was all we were looking for, and given both bits of technology existed, and existed together in the minds of exactly the right group of tinkerers, it took longer than you would believe to put them together.

Exactly how long is, however, surprisingly unclear. Nor do we know exactly who was responsible for the magical union. It's the grand frustration of cycling history that no one really knows when, where, and by whom the pedal and the bicycle were brought together. There have been any number of claims and counter-claims, and any amount of evidence, but when it comes down to it, we just don't know, and it seems unlikely we ever will.

The truth has been obscured by jingoistic myth, family loyalty, fraud, revisionism and, perhaps most of all, by the fact that whoever did first build a pedal-powered two-wheeler was not the kind of person in whom history usually takes much interest. It was not a nobleman, an aristocrat, or an inventor of the grand and documented style. It was an artisan somewhere: a blacksmith, or a carpenter, or a wheelwright. In an era before mass communication, who would ever know what an ordinary person playing around in their workshop had produced, especially if the ordinary person wasn't worldly enough to realise what they'd created and patent it or market it?

I like this very much. There is a lovely irony of the world's greatest invention being the work of someone who history didn't so much forget as never even notice in the first place. The bicycle is a deeply democratic object, and it's fitting that its invention belongs to no one. (Leonardo da Vinci had nothing to do with it, by the way. He may have invented everything else, but he didn't invent the bike. A famous sketch of a bicycle, and a relatively modern one at that, complete with a chain transmission, was found among Da Vinci's papers in the 1970s and widely publicised. It was very quickly overturned as a fake, drawn around two pre-existing circles with a brown crayon by a forger sometime during the sometimes-chaotic restoration of the papers by Italian monks in the late sixties or early seventies. It was a strange design, owing to the forger having to work around other lines on the drawing. The machine in the sketch couldn't be steered, and so couldn't be balanced, which suggests the forger wasn't even especially familiar with a bicycle, which would be especially embarrassing for, of all people, an Italian.[10])

Even if we don't know for sure who it was, there are two or three leading contenders. The British have always promoted the idea that the inventor in question was a Scottish blacksmith called Kirkpatrick MacMillan from Courthill near Dumfries, and that the date was around 1840. The alleged machine was essentially a *draisine*, adapted so that the rear wheel was driven by two rods attached to treadles mounted beside the front wheel. There are two bits of evidence for this, and, frankly, they're both pretty shaky.

The first is (and there are some out there who will want to classify this under 'they started as they intended to continue') a court hearing in Glasgow where 'a gentleman' was fined five shillings for knocking down a child while riding on the pavement.[11] Two pertinent questions, then. First, who was this gentleman? The newspaper report is silent on the matter, other than to say he had ridden to Glasgow from Old Cumnock, 40 miles away, in just five hours. Old Cumnock is, to be fair to the MacMillan camp, a plausible stopping-off point for a man riding the world's first bicycle on his way to Glasgow from Courthill. On the other hand, several critics have questioned whether a Victorian court reporter would refer to a blacksmith as 'a gentleman' instead of 'a blacksmith'. And that's about as far as that discussion has ever got.

The other question is, just what exactly was this gentleman/blacksmith sitting on while he rained down terror on the pedestrians of the Gorbals? The newspaper is vague. It refers to 'a velocipede', which 'moved on wheels, turned with the hands by means of a crank'. The gaping 'with the hands' anomaly is normally explained away as a reporter writing 'hands' when he really meant 'feet', or misunderstanding an account of a machine he'd not actually seen personally. It seems like a stretch you're only going to make if you're already convinced about MacMillan's bicycle. To me it sounds a little too much like it might be a non-mechanic's description of how the front wheel of a *draisine* is turned for steering – 'handlebar' was hardly a word in common circulation. It certainly seems a brave leap from whatever the reporter was trying to describe to claiming proof of a bicycle.

The second bit of evidence for MacMillan's machine is some drawings, made many years later by one of his descendants who claimed to remember the bike, and a replica machine, which the same relative commissioned for a bike show in the 1890s. It's clear that this was done largely with the intention of staking a claim for the family, for Dumfries, and for Scotland.[12] It might have been entirely legitimate, but it's impossible to ignore the conflict of interest.

The replica was commissioned from a Thomas McCall, who had built several very similar machines in the 1860s. There were claims that those were 20-year-on copies of MacMillan's work, and even suggestions that the true inventor was McCall himself, despite his never having made any such claim himself. To say that the situation is confusing would be an understatement.

At the same time as Kirkpatrick MacMillan might, or might not, have been inventing the bicycle in Scotland, a man called Alexandre Lefebvre might, or might not, have been inventing it in France. The date, again, was around 1840, and what Lefebvre is alleged to have invented was remarkably (not to say suspiciously) similar to MacMillan's machine, a wooden *draisine* of more or less equally sized wheels, with a treadle arrangement to drive the rear wheel.

Lefebvre emigrated to San Francisco in 1860 at the age of 55, taking, so the story goes, a bicycle with him, a machine that was subsequently donated to a San Francisco museum. Interviewed in the 1890s, one of his old apprentices back in France claimed to have seen the bicycle built and ridden in 1843, and drew a reasonable sketch of it.[13] But that's about as far as it goes. There's no way to prove that the bike that ended up in San Francisco wasn't built after Lefebvre arrived in California, other than the pleasingly empirical observation from one historian that it appears to have been too heavily used to have been the velocipede of a man over the age of 55.[14]

Even by this point we're still not nearly done with people who may or may not have invented the bike. The French have at least two more dogs in the fight, three if you want to count both of the father and son team of Pierre and Ernest Michaux. In around 1860 they attached pedals to the front-wheel axle of a *draisine*-type machine, and christened it the '*Michauline*' – a name that, happily, didn't last for very long.

You'll know what a Michaux bicycle (I point-blank refuse to call it a *Michauline*) looks like – they're the things that feature at the stone-age end of those twee little 'ages of the bicycle' illustrations you get on birthday cards and mugs. There were dozens of design innovations and improvements, but none of them did much to fundamentally alter them, or address their shortcomings. Michaux bicycles were wooden-framed and cart-wheeled, with pedals attached to the front wheel's axle, a back wheel a little smaller than the front, and a saddle mounted above the frame on a long leaf spring to provide a primitive element of suspension. The 'tyres' were iron bands to protect the wooden rims. They had the twin side effects of amplifying the effect of every bump and stone in the road and of reducing grip on any hard surface (cobbles, say) to a minimum, so that the only escape from road-vibration was to fall off. On a softer surface neither of these was so much of a problem, but there, of course, the wheels dug into ruts and progress would be almost impossible in the first place.

The third man who might, or might not, have invented the bicycle for France was an associate of the Michaux father and son, Pierre Lallement. Lallement claimed that it was really he who came up with the bicycle that was produced by the Michaux company, and that Pierre Michaux had muscled in on the credit for his invention.[15]

Perhaps all of, two of, one of or none of them were really responsible. Maybe they nicked if off each other, maybe they all got their heads together and nicked it from someone else altogether – Lefebvre, MacMillan, or another quiet artisan who invented the greatest machine the world has ever seen without realising what they'd done.

If it really was Pierre Lallement who was responsible, it was an uncharacteristic outbreak of competence. If his sole ambition in life had been to avoid cashing in on his claim, he could hardly have spent the following few years better.

In the mid-1860s the idea of the bicycle began to gather some momentum in fashionable Paris. There was a perpetual thirst for fashion and novelty, and Paris was the only place on earth where the *draisine* had been a subject of anything more than mockery and hostile by-laws. This was the perfect combination, and just the place where a man of destiny would have seen opportunity, with or without the Michaux family.

So Lallement decided it was the perfect moment to emigrate to the United States and seek his fortune there. He arrived in Connecticut in 1866, took out a US patent for the bicycle the same year, and started to manufacture them. The invention was received with all the warmth with which the *draisine* had been greeted 40 years earlier – the machines were ridiculed. Lallement redesigned them, and they were ridiculed some more. If anyone on the entire Eastern Seaboard wanted a bicycle, Pierre Lallement certainly managed to avoid running into him.

He sold his bicycle patent for a fraction of its real worth, and returned to Paris. There, of course, he found a bicycle craze in full swing, and inevitably Michaux, father and son, were in the midst of it, apparently making more money than they knew how to spend. Lallement started his own company to compete with them, calling it the Ancienne Compagnie Vélocipèdienne to try to establish some sort of prior claim via the thoroughly modern medium of a branding exercise.[16]

As Lallement had travelled dejectedly home from America to France, his dreams of bicycling wealth in the New World shattered, news of the bicycle craze gripping fashionable Paris crossed the Atlantic in the opposite direction. It tripped off a similar bicycle mania on the East Coast of the US. It made the patent Lallement had all but given away into a very hot property, and, as we'll see, it found a place at the heart of one of nineteenth-century America's great corporations.

It will probably not be greatly to your surprise to learn that, given his considerable ability to achieve commercial failure amid even the most propitious circumstances, Lallement's Ancient Bicycle Company was not a success. The chances are that he didn't invent the bicycle either, even if it's tempting to decide that he did just so one can adopt a romantic view of the unworldly inventor getting done over by the wolves of commercial reality. Personally, I think the most likely of the contenders is Pierre Michaux. Michaux at least set about manufacturing something relatively rideable – unlike MacMillan and Lefebvre's machines, you could steer a Michaux bicycle properly because there was no treadle linkage to foul the front wheel. (The only way to take a sharp corner on one of the suggested earlier machines would have been to get off, pick it up and point it in the direction you wanted to go next.)

The various evolutionary stages of the bicycle through history tend to get their names retrospectively. While they're the state of the art, they are simply bicycles. The 'penny-farthing' was a bicycle – only when the chain-driven safety appeared did it become the 'ordinary' and later the disparaging 'penny-farthing'.

The bicycle that the Michaux company launched on the world was the most important of them all – it may or may not have been the first bicycle, but it was the bicycle that started the sport, the pastime, the transport revolution that was cycling. That didn't stop posterity giving it the name we have for it now, the 'boneshaker'.

CHAPTER 2

The 1860s: Parisian Perversions and the World's First Bicycle Race

Seen in the flesh, the boneshaker is a very odd thing. And that's to modern eyes that have managed to fully assimilate the ridiculous idea of balancing on two wheels. A penny-farthing manages to show a hint of the modern – it's made of steel, and has an unmissable resonance with a present-day bicycle. But the boneshaker is made from wood and looks medieval. A penny-farthing puts you in mind of iron bridges and steam locomotives, while a boneshaker puts you in mind of ox-carts and ploughs. All that is before you do anything as foolhardy as try to ride one. They are bigger than you think. Much bigger. I'm about average height, and the saddle of one is, on me, nearly shoulder level. The back wheel is almost the same size as the front, so clambering on board from the rear as you do with a penny-farthing is impossible. The only way to mount one if there's no groom to hold it for you is with a ludicrous running vault into the saddle, which happily no one was willing to let me try with a 150-year-old bike.

If anything, it feels even more medieval when you're on board. The machine I rode creaked and groaned like a galleon in a gale, and there was a very disturbing sensation of the various component parts being only rather casually connected to each other. Maybe it was better when it was new – I don't suppose a 150-year-old steam engine would feel terribly showroom-fresh either. As it was, it felt like no more than a rattle of loosely attached machinery. Add to that an iron 'tyre' that skittered and bounced over an asphalt road, an unbalanced riding position with the body bolt upright and the feet much too far in front of the saddle, and the whole experience felt pretty precarious. Given the extravagant altitude involved, it was also very difficult even to stop and get off. At least I knew how to ride a bike, and this thing was still roughly speaking a bike, albeit more in the way of a party trick than a means of transport. What it felt like to a new convert in 1866

I don't know. Anyone who – as people did – took a handful of lessons and then rode one from London to Brighton has my undying respect.

In spite of all that, Pierre Michaux's machines caught on. By 1868, 50 years after the *draisine* took over the streets of Paris, the city was in the midst of another two-wheeled craze. Young men rode boneshakers along the narrow stone parapets by the Seine. Equipped with lanterns, boneshakers were ridden through the night-time parks and boulevards like a swarm of fireflies. Parisian society congregated to watch races, and several indoor riding schools opened. Once you'd mastered the basics, you could move on to tricks, like standing on the saddle, pedalling with one foot, and what we now call the track stand – balancing with the machine stationary.

There were 'gymnastic cycling' displays, and all sorts of plays and entertainments managed to find an excuse to include a boneshaker. A substantial measure of the appeal of this was the opportunity it offered to have a woman ride a bike – Parisians of the 1860s got more sexual gratification from a woman on a bike than you would believe possible. They could even hire a woman to come to their own home and ride a boneshaker around their living room. ('Honestly, officer, this delightful young lady was just showing me how to ride a bicycle.')[1]

A periodical of the day said that in Paris velocipeding was 'as necessary an accomplishment as dancing or riding' – though it went on to mention the 'terror of the aged or short-winded' caused by riders on the streets.[2]

The craze's next stopping off point was New York – as you'll recall, cycling went west in a buzz of excitement at the same time Pierre Lallement was heading east in a sulk, carefully avoiding making his fortune on either side of the Atlantic. New York was Paris all over again. Gymnastic displays, music hall, riding schools, angry old men with beards waving their canes at young blades on Broadway, the whole works. *Scientific American* got a bit hot and flushed with all the excitement and proclaimed that 'The art of walking is obsolete.' Henceforth, it would be nothing but velocipedes.[3] Maybe the editor had had a female French velocipedist round for lunch.

This being America, the showmanship was ramped up a notch. The seven Hanlon Brothers, who'd been running an acrobatics show for several years, created a fancy-dress stunt-riding spectacular called the Hanlon Superba which stoked demand for bicycles. Fredrick Hanlon, on the basis he was arguably the best velocipedist in New York, proclaimed himself 'Champion Velocipedist of the World'. Their shows may have been about danger and thrills, but the Hanlons were also shrewd businessmen. Making the most of the publicity, they became one of the most prominent US manufacturers, and went on to own a substantial share of one of New York's largest riding schools.[4]

The other defining characteristic of American cycling was, of course, patent attorneys. At one point there were reported to be 400 machines in a store at the US patent office awaiting examination, with 80 new applications arriving each week.[5] But the big money was in none of them: it was in Lallemont's original patent. It had been bought for a bargain $2,000 by a bicycle maker called Calvin Whitty. Whitty had all the commercial nous the Frenchman lacked, and immediately notified the other manufacturers that they were infringing his patent, and started collecting a $10 royalty on every machine sold in the US. Given the rate at which bicycles were selling, it was like having a faucet that ran liquid gold.[6]

The craze in Paris was stopped in its tracks by the unexpected outbreak of the Franco-Prussian war in 1870. The craze in New York petered out even sooner – it had gone by the summer of 1869 after not much more than a year of utter mania. Even the Hanlons retired the bicycles from their act, and returned to their more traditional dwarf-throwing flying-trapeze show. (They also went on to invent the safety net, which seems to have come a worryingly long time after the invention of the flying trapeze.)

❙❙   ❙❙   ❙❙

In Britain, things were different. Cycling may have started in France, it may have caught the imagination of the US, but it was Britain where it was nurtured, where it got the care and attention it deserved, and where it grew up into something more than a fad.

It might have been the slightly more staid British Victorian outlook, or possibly a pre-existing interest in three- and four-wheeled human-powered vehicles which had been around long enough to rub the novelty off the boneshaker, but, for whatever reason, cycling in Britain started off rather quietly. To the extent that you could creep up on anyone while clattering along a nineteenth-century road on an iron-tyred bicycle, that's what Britain's early cyclists managed to do.

The man who seems to generally get the credit for introducing the Parisian-style boneshaker to Britain was Rowley Turner. There may have been earlier adopters, but Turner had an outstanding advantage when it came to being remembered: he was the French representative of the Coventry Sewing Machine Company.

A nineteenth-century bicycle and a nineteenth-century sewing machine, from a mechanical and manu-facturing point of view, shared about 95 per cent of the same DNA. Sewing machines had been developed over the first half of the 1800s, with metalwork and bearings that were similar to those that would feature on a bicycle and on roughly the same scale. A workforce that could make a sewing machine could very easily transfer its skills to making a bicycle. As a bonus, in the late 1860s, sewing machines were becoming one of the very earliest items of domestic machinery – and a very fashionable one at that – so a successful sewing machine company also understood the art of sales and marketing. It's not a coincidence that Isaac Singer, while best known for the Singer sewing machine, also devised the world's first hire-purchase arrangements.

While he was in Paris selling sewing machines Turner had been bitten by the bicycle bug to the extent that he'd invested in a riding school and workshop. He also noticed that the manufacturers in Paris were struggling to keep up with demand, and connected this observation to the over-capacity that existed back at the factory in Coventry. In 1868 he brought a Michaux-style boneshaker to London by boat and train, rode it over London Bridge, along Cheapside, and onward to Euston station. He caused a sensation. No one had ever seen such a thing. Turner was an expert rider so the astonishing, impossible machine was shown off to its best advantage. The effect must have been like the arrival of something from outer space. At Euston, even though he was the very first cyclist in the history of the British railway industry, he caused much less consternation among the train staff than a modern-day rider typically produces. Despite not having a reservation for the bike, he caught the train to Coventry, and when he got there, he repeated the PR offensive on his way to the factory.[7]

Rowley Turner's idea was simply to make bicycles to export to Paris. If there turned out to be a market in Britain, I don't suppose anyone would have complained, but that was not the original basis for the operation. He just wanted to cash in on a craze while the going was good. But Turner's imported bicycle lit a fire under one of the founders of the Coventry Sewing Machine Company, and sewing machine engineer James Starley became the first real genius of cycling design. He was the man who turned the bicycle into something more than a grown-up toy.

Starley was a farmer's son from Sussex. He didn't have any engineering training at all – he just couldn't help inventing things. His first innovation had been a rattrap that consisted of a sharpened umbrella rib attached to a bent-back piece of willow, so that when a rat stood on a lever it would be impaled. His brother mockingly offered to eat everything he caught with this ridiculous device. He was woken the following morning by a cry of 'Breakfast!' to find young James standing over his bed waving a large, freshly skewered rodent.

Starley left for London aged 16. While working in Lewisham he invented the 'duck balance' – a mechanism which used the weight of a duck to open a door to access a farmyard from the river, but which prevented the lighter mice and rats from following them. It was so complicated that no contemporary witness managed to describe it in such a way as to leave you with the first idea of how it worked. Starley's brother's account makes it sound more mystifying than the internal workings of an iPhone. It wasn't even really necessary; he invented it for fun.[8]

The first thing Starley did with the French velocipede was install a step so that men (like the portly Starley) who were not built like an acrobat could successfully climb on board. A trivial detail, maybe, but one that also allowed him to make the front wheel of a bicycle bigger without putting the saddle so far off the ground that it was impossible to reach – and, of course, a bigger wheel meant more distance covered for each turn of the pedals.

Starley also reduced the size of the rear wheel, which saved weight, and made the machine even easier to mount. I imagine you can see where he was going with this. The first advert for his bicycles published in Britain appeared in 1869, and was already offering machines with up to a 48-inch front wheel – well on the way to a penny-farthing.[9]

Exports thrived. Each batch of bicycles that left Coventry was better than the one before. And bicycling began to catch on closer to home, especially in Coventry, Liverpool, and, after a slow start, London. In comparison with France or the US, though, there was a slightly different tone to early cycling in Britain. Where the French or American bicycle ride was for amusement and strictly the province of the boulevardier and the *flâneur*, the

British – insert a national stereotype of your own devising here – adopted a more Starley-esque view of bicycles and immediately started to size up the possibilities they offered for going places.

An early adopter called John Mayall acquired a bicycle after seeing Rowley Turner (on another PR offensive) demonstrate one at a gymnasium in Old Street in London. Mayall later wrote of his astonishment as Turner took a short run and leapt in to the saddle, '. . . whirling himself round the room, sitting on a pair of wheels in a line that ought, as we supposed, to fall down immediately he jumped off the ground. He gave us a rapid explanation of the process of keeping the machine from falling whilst in motion by the management of the guiding handles, but we were too much absorbed by wonder to fairly seize and comprehend his explanation.'[10]

Mayall decided that bicycles were for more than riding circuits of the local gym, and set his sights on Brighton, in mid-winter. The first attempt got him as far as Redhill – 25 miles or so. He got the train home. He made it to the seaside at the second time of asking, and *The Times* reported it under the headline 'Extraordinary Velocipede Feat!'. Mayall had actually set off with none other than Rowley Turner – but dropped him (and another friend) at Crawley, and set a pattern for gentlemen on bicycles by scoring that as a victory and refusing to wait. *The Times* reported that Mayall arrived in Brighton in good condition for dinner, and 'the second part of Kuhn's concert at the Grand Hall'.[11]

It still took him more than 14 hours to cover 56 miles. To give that some perspective, the record for a steam motor car (carrying 11 passengers) was under ten hours, and by coach, under four (with quite a few changes of horses). A month after Mayall, two brothers walked it in less than 12 hours, apparently for no purpose more glorious than beating the bicycle. (Other notable records for London to Brighton contained in a list in a 1906 copy of *Cycling* magazine include the 'first' one – 5½ hours on horseback set by George IV – and a fine 12¼ hour effort by one J. Fowler in 1906, who walked it carrying a two-gallon jar on his head, for reasons that the magazine leaves tantalisingly unspecified.)[12]

Mayall's ride might not have been a feat of astonishing athleticism – within a few weeks the cycling record was reduced to just over nine hours – but it attracted quite a lot of attention and did much to set the tone for how cycling developed in the UK. Only two months after Mayall rode to Brighton, three men from Liverpool rode to London in just three days – despite having stones thrown at them between Wolverhampton and Birmingham – and again *The Times* felt it was worth its while to cover the journey.[13]

The very early cyclists in Britain were a varied bunch – there wasn't really a place in the class order for the bicycle, so it boiled down to who could afford one (they weren't especially cheap), who was athletic enough to get onto one and who was brave enough to accept that once they were up there the learning process was going to involve quite a lot of falling off again. The younger middle classes were probably the core of it, men like clerks, engineers, tradesmen and shopkeepers. Queen Victoria's youngest son Prince Leopold owned a bicycle, even if there's not a great deal of evidence that he used it very much – the fact that the bicycle didn't immediately take off among the aristocracy would suggest his bike spent most of its time in the Royal garage. Bikes were still popular enough at Eton for them to be banned. But other public schools were somewhat more open to the possibility of students meandering off into the countryside, or injuring themselves trying to invent the astonishingly dangerous sport of boneshaker point-to-point racing.

In retrospect, those early years had a pleasing chaos about them. The bicycle was clearly an object of great intrinsic interest. It could be so many things: a conjuring trick, a healthy exercise, a means of transport, a piece of modernity to put alongside the railways and the factories. But still, its best use wasn't immediately obvious. In a world of wildly varying road quality, and on bikes with no suspension beyond whatever give there was in the fleshy parts of the rider's behind, seeing the bicycle as a means of swift, cheap, long-distance transport required a certain amount of vision and, literally, a thick skin.

Indeed one of the more plausible explanations for the death of the boneshaker craze in New York was that in the spring of 1869 all the riders who had spent the winter perfecting their riding on the smooth boards of the gyms came outside and discovered that it was a lot less fun to ride them in the city streets. It's hard not to laugh at riders who went outside for the first time and reported totally unexpected vibration from the road, but without 150 years of experience to draw on, how would they have known?

One immediate use for the bicycle was, of course, racing. How could it be otherwise? Given the kind of people who took to riding boneshakers it's hard to imagine that bike racing took very much longer to invent than it took to produce the world's second bicycle. Hard to imagine, that is, but difficult to prove, because the early racers were keener on racing than on record-keeping. There is, at least, a widely accepted answer to the question 'Who won the first bike race?'

Conventional wisdom holds that the first ever bicycle race meeting was held in Paris, on the paths of Parc de Saint-Cloud, on 31 May 1868. The course was over a distance of 1,200 metres. Contemporary reports have the riders in jockeys' silks and high leather boots, and describe a large crowd, containing many women standing on chairs to cheer and laugh at the spectacle in about equal measure. It's not clear whether Parisian women carried chairs around with them as a matter of course, or whether the chairs were provided by the organisers. The first race of the day was won by Englishman James Moore, originally from Bury St Edmunds, who'd been resident in Paris for many years and had the good fortune to live across the road from the Michaux bicycle works.

The problem with this generally accepted version of events is one of inconvenient evidence. An official programme for the day suggests the race Moore won was the second event on the schedule – for velocipedes with wheels of over one metre. The race for 'wheels less than one metre' took place before it and, according to a Parisian newspaper, was won by Charles Bon.[14]

Yet James Moore claimed from very early on to have won the first bicycle race, and it seems to have been something he'd have been unlikely to get away with making up – because there was a whole crowd of fellow competitors, not to mention hanky-waving women on chairs, who would have needed to forget Bon's triumph. Perhaps that very first race was for old *draisines* with smaller wheels? Or maybe the races didn't run in the advertised order? This wasn't a modern, highly organised event – all it would have taken for the running order to be changed would be someone getting there late, or a damaged machine. Or maybe Moore recorded the faster between the two, and they were considered as heats of the same race? The race report noted that the winner of the smaller-wheel race received a silver medal, the bigger-wheel race a gilt medal, suggesting there was a pecking order to the two events. – although this explanation for the anomaly is somewhat undermined by the winner of the afternoon's later 'Grand Race' receiving a gold medal.

Whatever the truth, Moore was subsequently awarded a medal proclaiming him the winner of the first bicycle race, and seems to have been universally accepted as such. No one appears to have tried to set up Bon as the trailblazer. Maybe the lack of committed argument is because Moore was exactly the sort of man you'd like to have winning a new sport's first event, especially since he went on to become one of the sport's first stars.

A year after Paris, Moore definitely and unequivocally won the world's first long-distance race on the open road, the inaugural Paris–Rouen event, run in November 1869. 123 kilometres of nineteenth-century northern European roads in winter was a serious undertaking by any means of transport, but over a hundred riders approached the start line to face the mud, the ruts and the crashes.

The rules specifically banned the use of dogs for towing, or sails for sailing. Other than that, anything went. It was one of those anarchic events that happen early on in the development of a sport, when there are almost no rules because no one has even worked out the problems that the rules will one day have to address. Like the very earliest air-races, it was a chaotic free-for-all.

There were two-wheelers, three-wheelers, four-wheelers and even a couple of brave souls on one wheel.[15] There were at least four women, racing on level terms with the men. It's impossible to be certain about whether this was because the French were much less horrified about the idea of women racing bicycles than every other nation on earth, or because they got the same sort of kinky thrill out of it as they did out of women and bicycles in music hall acts, although I think we can all guess.

There were dozens of non-finishers. Just 34 riders made it to Rouen – including one female rider, an Englishwoman competing under the (I assume deliberately) misleading sobriquet 'Miss America', which points firmly in the direction of women's participation being less than respectable.[16] ('Miss America' seems to have been married to Rowley Turner, of the Coventry Sewing Machine Company, which suggests he'd gone more than a bit native selling British bicycles in Paris.[17])

Moore won comfortably – the ride took him ten hours and 40 minutes, a not-exactly-dizzying 11.5 kph. But on a boneshaker with a smallish gear, on iron tyres over rutted roads and in race-long rain, it was a very fine start to what became the dominant branch of cycle competition.

Also starting the first instalment of what became a firm tradition, while Moore ate his celebratory meal in Rouen a local miscreant stole his bicycle. It was never recovered. This is something of a pity, because if the bike had not been stolen much very earnest debate among cycling historians about whether it incorporated the first ever example of a ball-bearing on a bicycle could have been avoided. However, this is the sort of detail I promised I wasn't going to dwell on, so I'll have to leave the possibility of the first ball-bearing hub just dangling here.

Moore went on to become one of the first bicycle racing stars. Among a lot of other miscellaneous glory, he set a record for the maximum distance covered in an hour (14.5 miles) in 1873, and won the World Championship for the mile, in Wolverhampton in 1874.[18] (Albeit this was an era before there was a properly recognised international governing body, so almost anything could call itself a 'World Championship' if the promoter fancied it and had enough bombast to carry it off. Moore did at least beat most of the big hitters in British racing at the time.) He retired in 1877 at the age of 28 having won most of what was available to him, and became a racehorse trainer.

The Paris–Rouen road race might have been a bit of a rules-free bun fight but at least it made sense to a modern spectator. If we go back, for a moment, to that first meet in Saint-Cloud, there were four races on the programme. The third was a 'slow race'. This is exactly what it sounds like: the now-traditional slow bike race beloved of village fêtes, cycling proficiency tests and risk averse parents everywhere. The *Petit-Journal* described it as 'very amusing', and noted that everyone fell over except for J. Darentry, who won a prize that the report left unspecified.[19] Clearly this wasn't the afternoon's grand race – Darentry's prize was presumably not of any great value. But it was still part of a race meeting for grown-ups.

In the early, uncertain days of competitive cycling they tried everything. Despite the success of the Paris–Rouen event it was clear that road racing was very difficult to do – in anything short of the best conditions it might be almost impossible. That meant that what now seem like novelty events you could run in a gymnasium – slow races, stationary balancing, trick cycling challenges – were hugely popular everywhere that cycling caught on. They were easy to stage, easy to watch, and they fitted with the idea that one of the main objectives of the competitive cyclist was just to show off his ability to stay upright in the first place.

In the UK many of the novelty events had an odd obsession with things borrowed from medieval tournaments. There was jousting. There was tilting at rings. There was javelin throwing. In one especially alarming innovation there was a discipline that consisted of fighting with broadswords while riding a bike, which sounds like something the Ancient Romans would have made Christians do, assuming they'd been able to set aside their famous concern with health and safety regulations. It didn't catch on, for all the same reasons that I imagine have more recently ensured no one has tried to combine trap shooting and trampolining.

Still, things you'd recognise as races did start to get a foothold. The first race in the UK is claimed to have happened just 24 hours after that first race at Saint-Cloud, in a field near the Welsh Harp pub in north London, handily located today just beside the London end of the M1 motorway and adjacent to the Brent Cross Shopping Centre.[20] The area is now covered by the Welsh Harp reservoir. (Some historians have expressed doubts about the event, on the basis that no trace of it can be found in contemporary sources.[21])

Just because no one was quite sure where the competitive side of cycling was going and what form it ought to take didn't mean there was anything tentative about it. The enthusiasm for bicycles was huge, and there was a whole sport to be invented. Or perhaps it was a new branch of show business? Or a combination of the two?

Whichever it was, any bicycle event attracted a crowd. In 1869 *The Field* noted, with magnificent sniffiness, that, 'The announcement of a velocipede race was sure to draw many hundreds of that faithful British public who, day after day, from one year's end to the next, go everywhere to see anything.'[22] Lest you have any doubts about this, in Liverpool in April 1869 a gymnasium offered an evening of 'tilting at rings, throwing the javelin, and demonstrating general proficiency in the various modes of managing the bicycle' that was many times oversubscribed, despite what I'd have thought was the fairly obvious risk to spectators of watching a selection of cyclists graduating in a single evening from 'general proficiency' to throwing a javelin from a moving bicycle.[23]

And where there was a crowd, there was money. Victorian sport loved an amateur, but no one ever suggested it was a philosophy that ought to extend to promoters. The promoter of an early race at the Islington Agricultural Hall, in June 1869, offered a £20 cup as first prize, spent £500 installing grandstands and still made a good profit at a shilling a ticket. Many, perhaps most, of the very early racers in that first year or two were professional riders as well, at least when assessed by the standards of a Victorian gentleman. Bicycles were expensive, and the kind of young man who would race one to the advantage of a promoter selling tickets, or a manufacturer selling bikes, was probably not the kind of young man who could afford to buy one and race it as an amateur. So professional sponsorship in the form of free bikes was common, as was a maker paying one of his mechanics to race his machines.

At Islington the course was simply a lap of the arena, marked out with a tub of flowers a few yards in from each corner, outside which the riders had to pass – but considerable expense had been required to board the arena, which normally hosted nothing other than horse and livestock shows. Nine laps made a race.

This formed, of course, the very beginnings of indoor track racing, and so close to the invention of the whole activity of cycling that, according to the report in *The Field*, many of the competitors could barely ride a bike: 'At least half the velocipedists who competed were mere scramblers on their bicycles, and could not even sit them when going on a straight course . . .'[24]

For the handful of events that ran successfully on the open road the crowds were even bigger. The view was free, and there were even more crashes to enjoy. One race from Chester to Liverpool in April 1869 was such a sensation that 3,000 people crossed on the Mersey ferry to spectate at the finish, never mind those who crowded the verges and hedges along the rest of the route. From 13 starters, the race was won by Henry Eaton of the Liverpool Velocipede Club. He took almost an hour and a half over the 13 miles, slowed by the crowds in the road and a stiff headwind. (It's rather touching to see just how quickly the invention of the bike race was followed by the invention of the excuse.)

But initially the main outdoor racing venues were parks, like Crystal Palace in south London, and the Molineux Gardens in Wolverhampton. A makeshift course could be marked out on grass, or on a running track, or just follow the park's existing paths. There was ample space, it was out of the way of other road users, and a race in a park could be ticketed and combined with other opportunities for spectators to spend money. Sometimes they ran as stand-alone race meetings; at least as often they were part of a bigger event. For instance, the Licensed Victuallers' Asylum ran a 'Grand Gala Fête, Bicycle Race and Cricket Match' at Lord's cricket ground in September 1869, which sounds very agreeable indeed.[25]

Racing started in Ireland at much the same time, but was sometimes a rougher affair, and seems more often to have been on improvised courses. One race on the slopes of Cave Hill in Belfast included a substantial section through waist-high grass, meaning almost all the riders had no option but to dismount and push. A few years later, a course near Coleraine in County Antrim included a freshly ploughed field.

One especially fine early Irish road race occurred near Dungarvan in County Waterford in September 1870. Many thousands turned up to watch, essentially turning the event into a public holiday, and the middle of the road into a grandstand. The way was cleared for the riders by the police and local magistrates riding horses through the crowds. Horses and bicycles and crowds were no better a mix then than now, and the eventual winner of the race was just one of the competitors who came very close to being trampled down by his escort. But perhaps the highlight was when one of the fancied riders, in desperation, threw his machine across his shoulders and took a shortcut on foot across several fields. This was, of course, the invention of cyclocross, but it was successfully hushed up for many years.

Brazen as it was, this tactic doesn't appear to have broken any rules, or if it did no one seems to have been too bothered about it – something that would have been surprising given there was significant betting on the outcome of the event. Maybe the reckoning was that anyone who fancied running across fields and clambering over hedges while carrying a 35-kilogram lump of uncooperative wood and ironmongery was welcome to whatever he could get.

It's also clear that this sort of race was a long way from what you'd think of as a modern bike race – as well as the horses, the riders were accompanied the whole way by soldiers on foot, who had no trouble keeping up.[26] 'Quaint' would be one word, and 'chaos' would be another, to the extent that they don't cancel each other out.

It was a start, though, and it was a very impressive one. There were no shortage of dead-ends (tilting at rings didn't last, nor did the sword-fighting, to no one's great regret), but it was striking how quickly a lot of cycle racing began to sort itself out. Within a couple of years the sport was starting to shape itself into forms that are recognisable 150 years later – indoor racing in the winter, long-distance road races, unruly crowds, greedy race promoters, as well as professionalism and sponsorship arrangements designed to sell bikes. Some of it was stolen from other sports, like running, but a lot of it wasn't – the fixed overhead costs of running were trivial compared to the price of a bike.

And all of this was accomplished with a machine that was, fundamentally, very, very hard to ride, and really not terribly well adapted to the open-road environment that was, even then, quite obviously what a bicycle should be for.

Happily, though, something much better was just about to arrive. The age of the penny-farthing was dawning – and, with it, the beginning of cycling as we really know it today: clubs, Sunday rides, café stops, track racing, road racing, cheering crowds, angry exchanges with coach drivers . . . all were just around the corner.

CHAPTER 3

The Dignity of the Victorian Clubmen

On Sunday mornings people ride bikes. Often they choose to do it together. In ones and twos they arrive at a gathering point somewhere – a particular road junction, a bus stop, a war memorial or a clock tower. It happens more in winter than in summer, so often there are clouds of breath in the air, and frost dusting the ground. This is nothing new. It's been happening since 1870, and it's always been exactly the same. The riders talk quietly while they wait for latecomers, partly because they're trying not to disturb any local residents, partly because at an instinctive level they know that the conversation is not what they really came for.

I've done it myself. Not as often as I'd have liked, because I always seemed to have races to go to, or specific training sessions to complete. But in London and in Cambridge, where I've lived, and in foreign cities like Sydney, Melbourne and New York, I've stood and waited, sometimes in the dark, sometimes in temperatures far below freezing.

Sometimes in an unfamiliar city I've stood there not even sure I was in the right gathering place, only to be hugely relieved when someone else showed up. Even then you're not safe. In Sydney I once went to the wrong junction, where by unhappy coincidence I met a different ride altogether, and instead of heading out for a relaxed 40 miles to a beach-front café with some friends of friends, got myself tangled up with the local psychos for 100 miles of arse-ripping. I couldn't even just let them go, because after the first ten minutes I was lost without hope of redemption.

Generally there's a pre-ordained distance and an approximate route, often to a café somewhere, and a rough target speed so that everyone knows what they're taking on. And you roll out of town together till you hit the country roads, where you can usually ride two abreast, chatting, and enjoying that wonderful level of moderate effort cyclists know so well – it falls between the exertions of walking and running, so it's almost unknown to pedestrians.

Such rides are not really competitive, or at least they're not supposed to be. There might be a bit of pressing on when you get to a hill, but those who get to the top first will usually wait for the others. They're primarily companionable. And never more so than when you get to the café, where, if it's winter, you'll sit in a fug of condensation as you all have a coffee and eat every scrap of food in the establishment like a plague of Lycra locusts.

The club run has been the strongest thread through the history of not just the sport of cycling but the pastime, and it's continued almost unchanged because when you get a group of cyclists together, well, what the hell else are you going to do?

To find the first club run, you shouldn't need to do very much more than find the first club, but in the bubbling froth of excitement at the start of cycling, a lot of clubs came and went with very little ceremony or fanfare. The Liverpool Velocipede Club was extant by April 1869, because that spring it organised some of those slightly daffy bicycle tournaments. There's every chance that it wasn't the first – it's more than possible there was a (short-lived) club in Cambridge in 1868.[1] And that's not to mention the probability of clubs in Paris earlier than that again.

On the other hand, the oldest club in Britain that still exists (and which hasn't at any point disappeared and had to be re-established) is easy to pin down. The

Pickwick Bicycle Club is, to put it mildly, something of a curiosity. Its foundation in 1870 occurred at a meeting in the Downs Hotel in Hackney Downs, east London.

The date coincided with the death of Charles Dickens, and the founder members had formed the impression, backed up by no evidence whatsoever, that Dickens had been a velocipede rider, so they named their club as a tribute. From that point onwards, notes the club's website, 'The Pickwick Bicycle Club has an unbroken history as an active cycling organisation and in the worthwhile task of spreading fellowship and conviviality.' Though it has to be said, in recent years there has not been much actual cycling. In this instance 'recent years' includes this century and the one before it. As to the rest of the club's activities, I was a guest of one of the members at a Christmas lunch a few years ago, and the conviviality was spread so thick that neither I nor anyone else can remember very much past the main course.

Today, the Pickwick Bicycle Club is a male dining club where, bizarrely, each member adopts the sobriquet of a named male character in *The Pickwick Papers*. This is the only name by which they will be addressed in the club. The total membership of the Pickwick is limited to the number of such characters in the book, which despite several microscopic analyses of the text to try to find more – there is a member who will serve out his time known as 'the Red-Nosed Man'; two different 'Martins'; as well as 'George, the father' and 'George, the embarrassed man' – has come to rest at 185. There is a long waiting list to join, which means that most of the members are of a certain age. It wouldn't be wildly misleading to repeat the joke Gyles Brandreth made when he spoke at the lunch I attended: after several Chelsea Pensioners had entered and sat down as guests of the club, he said he'd never previously been at an event where the arrival of such a group had lowered the gathering's average age.

It is still, though, very much a club of cyclists. Its membership includes numerous former champions, journalists and event organisers. And in its early years, the Pickwick did see its way to doing some cycling. Its members were regulars at mass rallies of cyclists that came to be a feature of the scene in the 1870s and 1880s, along with the other early London clubs, like the Ariel, the Middlesex, and the St George's. Outside London clubs established in the same era included those of Birmingham, Brighton, Coventry, Northampton, Sheffield, Wolverhampton, and Oxford and Cambridge universities.

The grandest of the rallies was the annual Hampton Court – by the early 1880s the tightly disciplined parade of cyclists was an astonishing six miles long and included 2,177 riders. It was the sort of exhibition and celebration that the Victorians excelled at. It was about being cyclists, about showing their respectability and their gentlemanly dignity. Crowds – the ones who would go everywhere to see everything, I assume – came to watch, from the roadside, or from their open-topped carriages, as the procession passed. The parade must have been spectacular: by the mid-1870s the boneshaker had been displaced by the magnificent 'high-wheeler', later known as the 'ordinary', and long after that as the penny-farthing. They were a spectacular marvel of Victorian engineering; the era was, in many ways, the finest cycling has known.

That the front wheel of the bicycle had grown and grown is not a mystery – with cranks mounted directly on the axle, one turn of the pedals was always going to be one turn of the wheel, so the only way to get the bigger gear you needed in order to go faster was to make the wheel larger. That was apparent to the earliest boneshaker riders. The problem was that if you scaled up a wooden cart-wheel, it became heavier out of all useful proportion to the size.

The technology behind the penny-farthing was the wheel itself. (I'm calling it a penny-farthing because that's what most of the riders of vintage machines I've met call it. I accept that it might be more historically respectful to call it an 'ordinary', it's just that it seems a little prissy. If prissy was what you were looking for, I apologise.) The wire spokes allowed the weight of the wheel to be dramatically reduced, even as the diameter grew. The process started in Paris, with a maker called Eugène Meyer, and it was the racers who took to it first. Race programmes from

Wolverhampton track in 1870 helpfully classified riders by wheel size, and show a progression from 36- to 38-inch wheels in April to 44- to 46-inch wheels by October.[2] In essence the penny-farthing happened in a season.

If Meyer had invented the wire-spoked wheel, it was the genius of early cycling, James Starley in Coventry, who made it a hit. In 1870 he designed the Ariel bicycle around it, and created the first real penny-farthing. It set new standards – it was lighter than the competition at 50 lb, faster due to the larger wheel, and cost £8, which was not cheap but was by no means expensive for something that good. (Relative to the average wage at the time, it was somewhere around £4,000.) It was maybe an equivalent to the E-type Jaguar of the 1960s.

Penny-farthings were sized by wheel diameter rather than frame size, and very quickly riders came to ride the largest wheel their leg length could manage, usually somewhere between 48 and 54 inches. The bigger the wheel the bigger your gear, so the longer your legs, the faster you could potentially go. The Honourable Ion Keith-Falconer (of whom we shall hear more later) was one of the age's faster riders, and he was 6 foot 3 inches, which allowed him to ride an awe-inspiring blot-out-the-sun 60-inch machine.[3] Compared to a 54-inch wheel, that's an extra 19 inches (48 cm) of road covered with each turn of the pedals – a gain that was a great deal more than marginal.

(Keith-Falconer, while a student at Cambridge, wrote to his sister-in-law of riding an 86-inch bike to the nearby village of Trumpington and back, '. . . to amuse the public . . . there is a little scale of steps up it, up which I am helped and started off, then left to myself. If I fell off it I should probably break an arm or a leg – so I shan't repeat the performance after today.'[4] To deal with the exceptionally big wheel, an 86-inch bicycle was pedalled via a set of rather clunky levers that made it unsuitable for racing. It was impossible to mount or dismount without help, and about as safe and convenient as riding a giraffe. I don't suppose that on its own would have been enough to stop people racing them if they'd been faster.)

The penny-farthing had a ridiculous charm, to the extent that its very distinctive silhouette has become shorthand for the antiquated and eccentric. It was as innovative a product of a rapidly industrialising age as the light bulb or the phonograph, but its place in the popular consciousness is as something much more peculiar, or even misguided. As a friend put it, 'How on earth did no one, as this thing was developing, stop and say, "Hang on – this is stupid?"'

The truth is that the penny-farthing was rather well adapted to its environment. In a time when any cyclist who wanted to ride outside a gymnasium or a park was faced with rough, rutted roads – and when the only tyres were a thin strip of rock-solid rubber – that monster wheel had the priceless ability to roll over almost anything. And not only was it lighter than a wooden wheel, the long wire spokes provided a considerable element of suspension.

I learned to ride one, and was rather impressed, especially in comparison to the boneshaker I'd ridden a few months earlier. In fact, I sort of learned twice. The first time was at an event in London where there were a number of penny-farthing riders. I stopped to say something innocent (probably, 'How on earth did no one, as this thing was developing, stop and say, "Hang on – this is stupid?"') only for one of the riders to insist I have a go. So I got less-than-willingly loaded onto one and pushed out into the traffic around the Barbican one-way system, accompanied by well-meaning shouts of advice that just made me feel like a stewardess trying to land a jumbo jet by following instructions from air traffic control.

The second time, a bit more effective and slightly less terrifying, was in a park in Worcester, with the help of a man called Dave Preece who had successfully ridden his machine from Land's End to John o'Groats, and won the British National Penny-Farthing Championships, all without killing himself.

You mount a penny-farthing using a little step just above the small back wheel. I put my left foot onto the step, raised both arms up in front of me to hold the bars, and scooted the bike along with my right foot. 'It's very simple,' said Dave. It wasn't, really. But all the same, eventually I got brave enough to stand up on the step, and trundle along.

So far so good. Next, I scooted a bit harder, so that when I stood up I had enough momentum, and hence time, to slide my hips forwards and get onto the saddle – this isn't as hard as it sounds, because the step is at just the right height to make it quite a natural movement. I was now sitting in an unfamiliar bolt-upright position, with the bars right over the top of my thighs. Finally, I found the rotating pedals with my feet, albeit after a few bruising clonks about the ankles.

'Well done!' said Dave. The alarming truth, I was just about to discover, was that the point at which you've managed to clamber into the saddle of a penny-farthing is the point at which your problems begin. Problem one: the pedals are bolted straight to the front axle. No namby-pamby rear-wheel chain drive here. Every time you pedal you twist the direction of the wheel, and the bike swerves. To keep your balance, you have to correct this with the bars. Then you pedal again, and twist the wheel again.

For the novice penny-farthing rider, the interaction between pedalling and steering can set up a negative feedback loop. So as soon as I started to put any force into the pedals, I started to weave a sine curve down the path. This grew inexorably in amplitude until everyone in sight was holding their children close because it was becoming clear that I could be coming for absolutely any of them with my enormous, out of control, child-shredding wheel. Dave was probably sauntering in the opposite direction with his hands in his pockets, whistling, but there was clearly no way I was looking over my shoulder to check.

The solution is to pedal very gently, which reduces the unfamiliar torque you're applying to the wheel. This works, until you slow down to the point where you can't stay upright. I'd be quick to point out that penny-farthings are superb for riding very slowly – the high centre of gravity makes it a little like balancing an upright broom-handle on your palm – but you will still run in to trouble eventually.

That's when your difficulties shift up a gear. Getting onto a penny-farthing, and riding a penny-farthing, and regaining control of a penny-farthing are peanuts compared to getting off a penny-farthing. You have to take your feet off the pedals and reach round behind you with a foot and try to find the step. The step is small enough when you are getting on. Trying to find it when you're getting off is like stepping blindly backwards off a roof onto something that wouldn't look entirely out of place sticking out of the front of a bird's nesting-box. You can't look to see where it is, because you'll almost certainly swerve. You can't miss it by much, because if you do you'll probably put your foot into the spokes, which will do considerable damage to the bike and, more to the point, you. (Not that the terrified users of the park in Worcester would have shed many tears over this development.) But if you can manage to put your foot on it, you ease backwards off the saddle, and down to the ground.

The first time I tried to dismount I couldn't find the step at all. I was on a gentle slope – it helps to maintain some momentum without having to pedal too hard – and, as it steepened, I was gaining more and more speed. I noticed that at the bottom of the slope, the path ended with a grassy verge and a small river. So I just jumped off sideways, the way you might on a normal bike. This wasn't a normal bike. I have a distinct memory of being in the air for quite a long time.

I landed on my feet, even if I had to hit the ground both running and trying to catch Dave's lovely bicycle so it didn't fall over. It was a trick that felt like it belonged in a circus. I was impressed to read later in a book from 1874 that what I'd done was exactly how an experienced rider normally dismounted. It would be a nerve-racking – if spectacular – way to arrive places.

Once I'd got the hang of getting on and off, and learned to deal with the unfamiliar pedalling–steering interaction, I got to rather like the bike. A penny-farthing is not quick, but there's something rather magnificent about trundling along up there. It's stately, dignified and actually rather comfortable. The view is excellent, though it needs to be, since there is almost nothing in the world,

CHAPTER 3

animate or otherwise, that you're not at least a little bit frightened by.

It certainly attracts attention. If you take to the open road, no one cuts you up in a car. (Of course they don't: you're an unpredictable lunatic on a penny-farthing.) You'll also notice that your altitude, while odd for a bike, is not so very different from a horse rider's. I tend to assume this familiarity had at least some role to play in the acceptance of the penny-farthing, because otherwise the idea of being that far off the ground, sitting atop something which often appears to have a mind of its own, would have been utterly impossible to sell to anyone who wasn't already an acrobat. (Horses, incidentally, are really, really not impressed by penny-farthings. They react much as they would if one were riding a firework. I don't imagine nineteenth-century horses were any more relaxed about them.)

There are downsides. Even if the gear is theoretically quite small compared to those on a modern bike, penny-farthings are not much cop up a hill. Similarly, you can be reduced to walking by even a moderate headwind. But the big one, and one that was horribly familiar in the bike's heyday, was variously called 'taking a header', 'coming a cropper' or (my personal favourite) the 'imperial crowner'. This is the doomsday scenario where you ride into a hole or a big stone too large for the wheel to roll over, and the bike stops more or less dead. You, with a high centre of gravity located right over the front wheel, keep right on going, straight over the top.

Your legs are trapped under the handlebars, so the only thing you have available to break your fall is most probably your face. The danger was much greater on rough nineteenth-century roads, and no small number of Victorian riders died this way. A significant proportion of the advertisements for second-hand bicycles in contemporary cycling journals offered 'injury' as the reason for the sale, and it's safe to assume they weren't talking about recurrent Achilles tendonitis.[5]

Yet it was also part of cycling – if you read club newsletter accounts of rides at the time it's not all that uncommon for the writer to note this misfortune occurring to one or more members, who simply got up and continued on their way. One of the ways nineteenth-century roads were resurfaced was to place largish blocks of stone across them which would then be broken up by passing coaches and carts – lethal if you were on a bike.

Risk is multiplied if you are riding down a hill on a penny-farthing. If you can't see the road clear all the way to the bottom, and you can't control how fast you're going, you have to get off and walk. Slowing a penny-farthing from any significant speed by braking or back-pedalling is risky, because your inertia will still quite probably throw you over the front wheel anyway, just the scenario you were trying to avoid. In practice that means a decision point at about 15 mph – because any faster than that and you can't get off even if you want to. This advice on hills was a universal top tip in every cycling magazine or book of the period, and good advice it was too.

That's not to say that a lot of riders didn't ignore it. One favoured safety trick ('safety' in an unconventionally broad sense here) used by riders who wanted to take their feet off the pedals and 'freewheel' was to place the legs over the top of the handlebars. The idea was that if you hit a stone and came a cropper you could fly through the air unencumbered by the bars and land, cat-like, on your feet. Of course, once a rider's legs were over the bars, he was completely at the mercy of the terrain and the bike, since attempting to put his feet back on the furiously whirring pedals was going to be something akin to putting them in a blender.

Several manufacturers attempted to give riders the best of both worlds with handlebars that would detach, freeing the trapped legs and making them ready for a safe touchdown. There was a fine advertising illustration for Schröter's Self-Detaching Handlebar that showed a rider in his best tweed riding suit flying resignedly through the air and casually holding a pair of handlebars that were now attached to nothing at all. The effect, I imagine, was less reassuring than the illustrator intended.[6]

That's before you got to the main problem with such bars, which was that they didn't always save their party piece for a serious emergency, but quite often did their best to liven up a perfectly normal situation by detaching at random. A skilled rider might survive such a calamity – it's possible to ride a penny-farthing no-hands, and indeed there used to be 'no-handles' track-races – but more riders would do what you'd expect, and fall off. I do occasionally find myself speculating that there must have been a few more cruel laughs to be had in cycling before product liability laws knocked that sort of thing on the unhelmeted head.

It was the penny-farthing that truly begat the cycling club, and the cycling club that underpinned so much of cycling for the following 140-plus years. Cycling clubs in Britain grew rapidly in number throughout the 1870s – from a handful of the likes of the Pickwick in 1870, to 29 by 1874 then 189 in 1878. By 1882 there were an astonishing 528 (including 199 in the London area alone). On the other hand, the clubs were usually quite small, with an average of maybe only 30 riders.[7] (This is still the case for many modern clubs – I'm aware of several where the entire membership could share a car to an event, and of at least two that have only a single member – an eccentricity that comes of rules requiring club membership to enter certain races.)

The clubs may have been, for the most part, small, but that didn't mean they weren't regimented. There were constitutions, rules and regulations as only the Victorians could do, and most clubs imposed fines on the sort of scofflaws who overtook the club captain on a ride (there was often a race for the office of captain), failed to wear the club uniform and badge when riding, or alternatively *did* wear the club uniform and badge when riding on a Sunday as, in the very early days of the clubs, Sunday rides were not seen as quite proper.

The Christchurch Bicycle Club from Dorset was probably fairly typical. Founded in 1876 by a local bicycle merchant called Ernest Clarke, and three of his friends, it quickly grew to around 25 or 30 members. The local paper reported on its club runs – 22 miles to Lymington, 50 miles to Salisbury and back, with a stop for lunch. Even night-time runs on moonlit evenings were popular. Maybe that's because they tended not to be too strenuous, and because they invariably took a substantial rest at an inn, where the riders drank a very great deal and sang songs. They often included comic songs about the club and its members, which the riders composed themselves. Drinking and singing and drunkenly riding a penny-farthing home over a rutted road in the dark sounds fun, but also sounds like a good way to keep the club's membership numbers under control.

Don't overestimate the quality of the songs, by the way. The chorus of one of Christchurch's that was popular enough to have been a fixture at the club annual dinner went:

Oh, we're jolly good fellows in the CBC,
We're very jolly fellows, so we all agree,
For we all love one another,
And our captain as our brother,
We're so awfully united in the CBC.[8]

Just because the Victorians could make their own entertainment doesn't mean they were all Gilbert and Sullivan.

The Christchurch club had a bugler, as was usual. He relayed the captain's commands on the club run. This might equally have been done by the sort of general consensus that exists on a modern club run, but the Victorians seemed to like something more formal. It gave matters a sense of organisation, maybe an official-feeling status or perhaps just good old-fashioned self-important pomposity.

Christchurch's bugler had his own calls, based on military bugling, for the muster, for the riders to mount, to ride single file, to ride double file, to dismount, and to take refreshments. Other clubs had an even greater variety.[9] Buglers had, by all accounts, a tendency to work up their part. Blasts were regularly sounded to warn local villagers of the club's approach, and the deafening warnings often continued long after the locals had cleared the way. This caused a certain amount of rather modern-feeling resentment: a contemporary cycling guide noted the hostility cyclists might encounter from 'the bucolic intelligence'.[10]

To look back, there is something goonish about a gang of young men in tweed jackets, knee breeches and stockings riding about the countryside on penny-farthings, blowing bugles at the locals. The thing is that the riding was rather special. Since the coming of the railways a few years earlier (Christchurch station opened in 1862), many of the old coaching roads were almost deserted. Even the main roads were not much more than tracks – photographs of the Great North Road (now the A1(M)) taken in the 1880s near Barnet, north of London, show it as not much more than two wheel ruts with grass growing up the middle. A club's run might cover many miles without meeting a single other road user. When they did it would probably be a ponderous farm cart.

To ride the old roads on a bicycle was to set off into a little-known world in a way that doesn't make much sense now. The roads, even the roads close to home, were not really familiar. There were few maps and almost no signposts. Directions and distances from locals – assuming you could find some whom your bugler had not permanently alienated – weren't even all that reliable, since most of them still rarely travelled far from their homes.

While industry had changed the cities beyond recognition, the countryside would have looked familiar to someone from the Middle Ages. To master the bicycle, to take it on an adventure in this almost forgotten world was a wonder. To spend the day, or a couple of days – or even to take a week's tour – with a few friends on the old roads, through the villages and the small towns that the Industrial Revolution hadn't laid a hand on, must have been like riding into a dream world.

The riders of the old ordinary bicycles felt that they'd been part of something special. You don't have to be a helpless nostalgia-junkie to wonder if maybe they were right. Even by the 1890s, when the chain-driven safety bicycle arrived, many of the old penny-farthing riders were already harking back to an unspoiled world that had gone for ever. More than a few of them disliked the safety bike, because it represented a sort of cycling, in a sort of Britain, that wasn't what they had fallen in love with. It's not all that hard to find a bike rider today of a certain age who will, with very little persuading, provide a similar depiction of cycling after the Second World War – of roads left empty by petrol rationing, of sleeping in haystacks, of wayside inns. Change itself is, in a way, unchanging.

The lonely old coach-roads the penny-farthing riders rode were peaceful. They were also neglected. They were rough in places, impossible in others. How passable the roads were was an obsession, and clubs like the

Christchurch planned their runs depending on the state of each road at the time of the year. There were often weeks on end in winter when riding was impossible, and the members would turn to the club room they'd established above a shoe shop, and read the papers, or play cards or billiards. There was a boxing ring, and swords for fencing. They had stained glass installed in the sash windows, with the name of the club picked out. They even created the class of non-riding membership, for those who weren't too bothered about bikes, but just wanted to read the papers in peace and take the occasional swing at each other with a borrowed sword.

The members were young(ish), since a degree of indifference to the inevitable dangers was required. Club cycling was one of the early extreme sports, albeit one where a major attraction was the ability to turn up at an old coaching inn and sing songs.

A degree of affluence was still needed to buy a bike, and it's clear that the club drew its members from the middle to the posh end of the town's social strata, even if its captain was the sort of person who made a living in trade. Christchurch still wasn't posh enough for some, because a second club started up in the small town in 1879, the Mudeford Bicycle Club. Its first advert for potential riders stated that members would need undoubted proof of their respectability, and that specifically 'quill-pushers and counter-jumpers need not apply' – clerks and shop assistants to you and me.[11] For all that, the two clubs seemed to coexist quite happily, and went to each other's events.

Social class was inevitably a big deal in Victorian cycling. In that era it could hardly have been otherwise. Riders advertising for a touring companion (this was a thing people actually did – you said where you wanted to go, how many miles a day you proposed to cover, and saw if any strangers fancied it) were advised always to 'State your social position, so that the associate chosen will be suitable.'[12] In 1884, the Cycle Touring Club (a UK-wide body formed to represent the interests of cyclists) increased its membership fees specifically to squeeze out undesirables.[13]

There was even a surprising degree of internecine hostility between bicyclists and tricyclists, which seems like something Jonathan Swift would have rejected as a bit unlikely. In the era of the ordinary, trikes were quite popular because you didn't have to clamber on top of a five-foot-high wheel to ride one. The timid, the old, those whose dignity would not survive being seen in breeches atop a penny-farthing, all could ride tricycles. Country doctors used trikes to make house calls, especially to get to night-time emergencies when it meant they didn't require a servant to saddle a horse. A clergyman could ride a tricycle and not have to be concerned about ridicule from his congregation.

Even women could ride tricycles without fear of titillating any passing Parisians, though often they used a tandem tricycle of some sort, accompanied by a husband, father or brother. There are photographs of women of the era posing on tricycles, all wearing floor-length skirts, hats, and that particular glum expression that all Victorian women have in photographs. (There's quite a well-known photo of Arthur Conan Doyle and his wife Louisa setting out on a tandem tricycle from their house in South Norwood, London. Arthur looks like a moustache with a hat; Louisa looks like she's being kidnapped. As was quite common at the time, Louisa sat in front, while her husband steered from behind – this weirdness being the only way to obey the twin Victorian precepts that a man must never turn his back on a lady, or let her be in charge of anything.)

The feeling among many of the tricyclists was that the association with the rather faster, more daring, and frankly rather racy penny-farthing riders was something of an assault on their respectability. There was a move to form a breakaway faction from the Cyclists' Touring Club because, according to one circular that was sent to the CTC's tricycling menbers, 'Bicyclists . . . are a disgrace to the pastime, while tricycling includes Princes, Princesses, Dukes, Earls, etc . . . It is plain that the tricyclists are altogether a better class than bicyclists and require better accommodation on tours, etc.'[14]

Queen Victoria even owned a tricycle – she saw a Salvo being ridden on the Isle of Wight in 1881, and commanded the doubtless rather surprised young woman riding it into her presence to explain what on earth it was. The young woman, as luck would have it, was the daughter of the local tricycle merchant. (At least I assume it was luck – it's not impossible that she had been riding it up and down past Osbourne House for weeks.) The Queen ordered two. As was the case with most tricycles, they were large machines, with the rider sitting on a bench between the penny-farthing-sized rear wheels and steering with a small wheel at the front. The Queen's tricycles were delivered in person by their designer, who was, inevitably, the Coventry genius James Starley, and in a minor PR triumph the model was renamed the 'Royal Salvo'. It seems very unlikely the Queen ever rode either of them.

That is a pity, since I'm sure she'd have enjoyed one of Starley's last bits of brilliance, the differential gear. In 1877 Starley had built a two-rider side-by-side tricycle. The riders drove one wheel each. Climbing a hill on it with his son had revealed the flaw – when his much stronger son applied a bit of heft to the cranks, the machine swerved all over the road. It proved impossible to go in a straight line, and they had to get off and push. Halfway up the hill, Starley said, 'I've got it.'[15]

Next morning at 6 a.m. he was at a brass foundry. By 8 he was on the London train, and not long after that he was patenting his idea. What he'd come up with was a differential, a mechanism that distributed the power equally between the wheels, and also let the outside wheel on a corner rotate faster than the inside one. It was a seriously clever bit of engineering from the farm boy from Sussex. (It also made the first cars possible – something which many cyclists would, in time, come to be less enthusiastic about.)[16]

Queen Victoria was not the only person surprised by the sight of a tricycle or a bicycle. They presented the same novelty as the steam locomotive had done a few decades earlier, and as the car or the aeroplane was going to have a little later on. In Ireland, for example, the large village of Killyleagh in County Down was brought to a standstill in 1875 when two cycle tourists took up the suggestion of a race made by the owner of a carriage. Killyleagh was packed with tourists there to watch the annual sailing regatta, practically all of whom abandoned the shore front to cheer as the cyclists beat the carriage. It was much the same a year later in Millstreet in County Cork, where a tourist reported a crowd of several hundred running after him, cheering with delight. Some of them continued to pursue him for over a mile.[17]

On the other hand, a tourist from Dublin was surprised to meet a group of elderly women near Waterford, who hosed him down with '. . . no very choice adjectives in their denunciation of bicycles in general and myself in particular.' The explanation came from a man he met further down the road. The same group of women had been taking butter, milk and eggs to the local market one evening a few days earlier when they had seen mysterious lights in the dark of the road ahead, hovering and shimmering, and coming towards them. It was clear to them that the lights were announcing the arrival of the devil himself. In terror, they threw away the butter, the milk and the eggs, and dived into a stream to escape. When nothing more apocalyptic than the local cycling club arrived, lamps swinging, the drenched women set about them, and the riders fled for their lives.[18]

It is odd now to look back at the bicycle in its first flush of youth, when it was something so outlandish it could cause mania or panic with equal ease. Yet the excitement that surrounded it then, especially in the eyes of the clubmen, does feel familiar. There is the same freedom to it, the same combination of companionship, a purpose, maybe even a little competition. What those early riders loved was recognisably the same thing that happens on Sunday mornings all over the world to this day.

CHAPTER 4

1870–1900: American Cycling and the Genius of Colonel Albert Pope

American cyclists of the 1870s had much in common with their counterparts in Britain. The same kind of young men rode the same sort of high-wheeler bicycles over the same sort of old, abandoned roads, and they did it for the same reasons. The main focus was in the eastern US, cities like Boston, New York and Philadelphia, where the stuttering boneshaker craze had run into the deep mud of the unpaved streets a few years earlier.

There was, however, a significant difference. One of British cycling's defining characteristics was that its evolution was somewhere between democracy and a very well-mannered variety of anarchy. Cycling was made by the riders, the makers and the clubs. It just happened, with relatively little in the way of a guiding intelligence. In the US, on the other hand, they had Colonel Albert Pope.

It's in the nature of things to over-decorate any major figures in the history of anything. But while it would be an exaggeration to say that American cycling in the nineteenth century wouldn't have happened without Albert Pope, it would certainly be fair to say that it certainly wouldn't have happened the way it did. You honestly can't take ten paces in any direction in the history of US cycling in the late part of the century without crashing headlong into him, and his influence spread far beyond North America.

The young Albert Pope had grown up in a wealthy founding-settler family in Boston, but his father lost his very considerable real-estate fortune in the 1850s. At the age of 16 Pope was forced to go to work, rather than go to an Ivy League university and then take over the family business, as he had assumed was his destiny. He was apparently very upset by this. If you were an armchair psychologist you might speculate that this early disappointment was to set him on the course of making money, and making it in the sorts of quantities that would cushion him against anything else the world might throw at him. You'd certainly have quite a lot of evidence on your side.

Before he could start making money, though, the Civil War intervened. He joined the 35th Massachusetts Volunteer Infantry, and emerged from it at the end of the war with the rank of lieutenant colonel. He called himself 'Colonel' for the rest of his life. It suited him. His first business was in the niche trade of making of decorations for slippers (for which, if we're honest, 'Colonel' might have been a bit much). His life changed at the Philadelphia Centennial Exposition in 1876 when he saw his first bicycle. It was love at first sight. He began by importing eight bicycles from England. Then he rode one of them to a local sewing-machine company and, using it as a prop, persuaded them to build 50 copies of it.[1] It was the foundation of an empire.

But those first bicycles were a monumental pain to produce. They were made the way most bikes of the era were produced, which is to say they were individually hand-built. The design needed multiple different dies (the moulds used in forging the frame), the most important of which broke very early on and needed to be rebuilt. Then no suitable iron could be found for wheel rims, so lengths of v-shaped angle-iron had to be individually shaped to fit.[2] In spite of all that, the bikes still came in costing $95 rather than the $112.50 for an imported one.[3] As a bike maker, Pope was up and running. He called his brand Colombia, and it went on to completely dominate US cycling for the rest of the century. As you'll have noticed, the slipper decoration industry never really recovered, but that loss was cycling's gain.

The manufacture of bikes was just one spoke in Pope's wheel. Another was the hiring of rafts of patent lawyers. At his head office, the patent lawyers' office was right next door to Pope's – they were key to his strategy. Patents like the one originally filed by Pierre Lallement, who was last heard of repeatedly zigzagging back and forth across the Atlantic like a man hell-bent on avoiding making his fortune. After Lallemont had abandoned the US the first time, the patent he'd sold to Calvin Whitty made its way into the hands of Colonel Pope. It formed part of a large collection of patents Pope bought for anything remotely bicycle-related, until he'd reached the happy position where it was almost impossible for anyone else in America to make anything even vaguely bicycle-shaped without infringing at least one of them.[4] He then used all those lawyers to ensure that no one could make or import a bicycle without paying Pope a $10 royalty. Whitty had also charged a similar royalty, but Pope and his lawyers were better at enforcing it as the bicycle industry in the US grew.

(Pope and a group of other manufacturers later tried a version of the same trick with an early motor-car patent, and used a sophisticated bit of lawyering to try to destroy the nascent car business of a young Henry Ford. They had, however, bitten off rather more than they could chew with that Ford. He took them to court and won, then steamrollered them in the marketplace.)

When Pope visited England with a handful of his staff in 1878 on a research trip, most of the factories he visited were surprisingly happy to show him round, let him measure whatever he wanted to and answer questions on their manufacturing processes. Pope, on the other hand, was less of a gentleman about it. On an occasion where the management politely declined the opportunity to show a rival round their factory floor and hand over all their trade secrets, Pope and his team returned a little later disguised as workers, and walked straight in.[5] The espionage trip was clearly worth his while, since one of his engineers made similar trips regularly for many years afterwards to reach out a friendly hand across the Atlantic, to look for new developments and to steal them in their entirety.

Still, Pope wasn't all bastard. Even that $10 royalty was carefully calculated to do not much more than give him a home advantage – he didn't want to destroy everyone else's business, just make sure that they didn't threaten his. It had originally been $25, and he cut it to $10 because he knew it was very much in his interests that young men were able to afford bicycles, even if, in some cases, they weren't his. More cyclists would mean better provision for cycling, which would attract more cyclists and in turn create more demand.

What Pope created was a very modern manufacturing company. Henry Ford gets a lot of the credit for the idea of a production line. But in many respects something at least as important, and much more basic, was the idea of interchangeable parts. That there was ever any other way of making things seems absurd now, but, in the early days, bicycles were produced the same way carts and farm implements had been made for decades – one at a time, from beginning to end, often by an individual craftsman. Pope's Colombia bicycles had all of their parts manufactured to micrometer-measured tolerances that meant they were effectively identical. Once all your parts are identical and interchangeable, it's suddenly possible to produce them in large quantities, and then just assemble bikes out of the result. You can replace men with machines, to create a very modern style of factory. You can make them cheaper for the same quality. And you can repair and service them much more easily – 'All interchangeable parts!' was even a Colombia advertising slogan.

It wasn't a totally new idea, however. Armaments and sewing machines were already made that way – another reason why sewing machine companies adapted so readily to making bikes. But Pope took it further than most others. By the end of the 1880s, when the penny-farthing began to give way to the chain-driven safety bike, the same parts were being used across several different models. The quality control and inspection regime was extensive – at its height the company had 24 inspectors looking at up to 500 elements of each individual bicycle.

And there was marketing. In fact to say there was marketing is to understate the sheer quantity and inventiveness of Pope's bike-selling behemoth. There was no known method of selling that he didn't deploy with precision, and quite a few that he invented from scratch. One historian has suggested that it wasn't so much the Pope Manufacturing Company we're dealing with here as the Pope Marketing Company. It happened to sell bicycles, but it could have sold anything at all.[6]

There was advertising, naturally. It frequently referred to records set on Colombia bicycles. And it not infrequently referred to records set on other brands as well, with a degree of ambiguity that would be frowned upon these days. There were meticulously produced brochures, published to coincide with just that point in the spring when a young man's fancy would turn to thoughts of a new bicycle. Pope enjoyed the sort of stunts to which P. T. Barnum would have tipped a respectful hat. Following the invention of the pneumatic tyre, for instance, Pope announced that at the company's Boston head office he was making available, free of charge to all cyclists, 'The finest quality of air, compressed by electricity and stored in a brass tank.' He also very publicly offered a $50 reward to anyone returning a stolen

Colombia to its owner, if the thief was convicted. 'It's grand larceny to steal a bicycle: it's arrest and conviction to steal a Colombia,' declared the Colonel.

The thing that is easy to miss amid the hoopla is that Pope was also a cycling advocate. He loved it, he wanted everyone to do it, and there's every suggestion that he'd have felt that way about the activity even if he'd stayed in the sunset industry of slipper decoration. He was a leading light in setting up the Massachusetts Bicycle Club, and had one of his company lawyers draw up an example constitution for other clubs to use as a starting point. He imported cycling magazines from Europe, and distributed them for nothing. He provided security of $60,000 to start up the *Wheelman* magazine in the US – an act of altruism that it has to be said did no harm whatsoever to its subsequent review coverage of his bicycles. He subsidised a road-building course at Massachusetts Institute of Technology. He even paid to have a part of Columbus Avenue in Boston resurfaced with the smoothest possible macadam, to show just how good cycling would be if every road in every city was just like that one.[7] In a world of mud and ruts, riders would travel for miles just to ride on it.

From a long-term point of view Pope also fought for cyclists' rights through the courts. City ordinances banning cycling were not uncommon – the tension between cyclists, coach drivers and pedestrians is nothing new. When the city of New York banned bikes from Central Park, three riders were dispatched to deliberately break the law, with Pope poised to back their defence. The litigation ran an expensive course through the appeals courts for years. While ultimately the case was lost, the eventual consequence was legislation giving cyclists the same status as carriages, on all roads, including Central Park.[8] For Pope, it was important to keep applying enough pressure that freedom for bicycles to go anywhere became a default setting.

What was good for cycling was good for Colonel Pope. No good deed was quite complete until at least a small promotional claim had been added to it. 'Following any good work, there was always an advert closely shadowing the act,' as a contemporary put it.[9] If you'd tried to explain to him the saintly pleasure to be had from doing good works in secret, he'd have thought you were an idiot. Pope was a man who thrived on the same confident American free-market optimism as Andrew Carnegie or John D. Rockefeller.

Pope's promotion of himself, cycling, and Colombia bicycles was capable of advancing on several fronts simultaneously. He gave frequent lectures on the commercial advantages for everyone in improving the quality of the nation's roads. This was as popular a message then as it would be now. It meant there was regular favourable press coverage, and he was careful to make sure that it had to mention Colombia bicycles, which associated cycling and his brand with something almost everyone approved of. He diligently, personally, collected every press cutting and filed it away.

Pope was perhaps at his inventive best a little after the penny-farthing era, as safety bicycles came into their own and women took up cycling. In the UK there was more controversy than you would have believed possible about what women should wear to ride bikes. It's a subject we will return to, but the argument was between the only respectable garment – the floor-length skirt – and the much more practical option of some sort of trousers or divided skirt. The only reason it didn't result in a proper civil war in the UK was that there were too many sides and none of them agreed with each other.

Pope's wondrously ingenious solution in the US involved the society ladies of New York City. They did charitable works during Lent, among the most popular of which was their annual doll show at the Waldorf hotel. (I'm shaky on exactly how this was a charitable work, but never mind.) Pope simply offered a prize of $100 for the best doll dressed in a women's cycling costume. This was simply beautiful. He associated himself, in a charitable setting, with exactly the sort of women he wanted to see riding bicycles, women whose interest in cycling would encourage acceptance of the idea of riding for women. He got them to design a costume that they approved of. He got them to promote it for him among New York's high society, and he got, in turn, to promote it right back at them. All for just $100.[10]

In nineteenth-century US cycling, Colonel Albert Pope was everywhere and all at once. He was a magisterial figure. His brand was dominant. All of this was in the era before the cyclists' cultural cringe took hold – there was nothing apologetic about the bicycle, nothing second-class, not in the eyes of those who rode them, nor in the eyes of those who did not. A bike was silly, maybe – dangerous, certainly – but it was definitely a status symbol, in a land that came to love the status symbol more than any other. Pope was the Napoleon of Bicycles.

Yet it all faded away. In the end the motor car did for Pope, as it did for so many others. It changed the dynamics of who rode bikes in the US, and why. Bicycles changed from being a luxury, semi-custom product, to being a more ordinary consumer durable, and Pope managed to get himself boxed in in the late 1890s by collapsing prices. Worse, in an attempt to dig himself out, by the turn of the twentieth century Pope had invested heavily in making cars, and got it all wrong – he just didn't have the feel or the flair. He was a cyclist, not a motorist, and it showed. His companies were, by that time, a huge, almost unmanageable affair – even Colombia's supposed head office was split three ways between Boston, New York City and Hartford, Connecticut. It had 45 factories across four states, and Pope had failed to put in place the sort of management that would lead to a successor. As he grew older, the business struggled, and inexorably declined. Pope himself died in 1909 at the age of 66, and it's sad to report that his empire was pretty much gone by 1913.

His influence, however, had not faded. It still hasn't, not completely. He made cycling big, and he made it modern. His companies were the model that everyone else had to follow if they wanted to stay in business, and while there was a ruthlessness to that, and even some of the early aspects of globalisation, it did a lot to make bicycles cheap enough for ordinary people to afford them. While, on the European side of the Atlantic, there was a continual anxiety about the oiks getting bikes and lowering the tone, in North America Pope wanted everyone who could ride a bike to do so. If that made him rich, that seemed to be a side effect he was prepared to accept. And I mean that only half-jokingly.

CHAPTER 5

1874: The Honourable Ion Keith-Falconer

I took up cycling when I was a student at Cambridge University. Long gone were the days when the university cycling club had a clubroom – that disappeared in 1906 when the club defaulted on the rent, for the understandable reason that it had no members. The club's social life, when I was there in the 1990s, was in a succession of pubs, which used to rapidly get tired of us since we sat there all night comparing heart-rate monitor data, front-wheel design and, critically, drinking next to nothing.

We were keener on riding, anyway. The club's runs used to gather at the end of a quiet street called Brookside, just a little south of the city centre. I have no idea why

it was that particular spot. It was on the right side of
town to head out in the direction of the non-fen end of
Cambridgeshire, which was where the rides tended to
go, away from the dispiriting fenland winds and towards
whatever handful of small inclines the region had to offer.
('Hills' would be overstating it – the most significant
climb on the southern side of the city was a motorway
bridge. It was a pretty awesome motorway bridge, but it
was still hard to impress anyone with it unless they were
from Lincolnshire.) But there were a dozen places we
could have assembled ready to head out in that direction,
several of them noticeably more convenient. If we'd done
nothing more than go round the corner, there was a bench
that early arrivals could have sat on while they waited for
the rest of the club to turn up.

Like so much else in cycling, and so much else in
Cambridge, Brookside was just a tradition, and I've no
idea how far it dated back or how it started. The club still
meets there now, and it will quite probably continue to
meet there for the next hundred years, without anyone
being any the wiser.

Much though I'd like it to have been the case, I
can't persuade myself that it was a way of paying our
respects to the Honourable Ion Keith-Falconer. In the
1870s he was probably the fastest rider in the world, and
he and his penny-farthings once lived on a house on
Brookside, just a few yards from where we used to meet.

I occasionally used to wonder what he'd have made of us. I imagined he'd have thought our puny little bicycles looked ridiculous, and our terrible multicoloured clothes would have appalled him. But I was also fairly sure that Keith-Falconer would have been too much of a gentleman to mention it, because, in an era of the gentleman amateur, there was no one more gentlemanly and (in the best possible sense) no one more amateur.

Keith-Falconer had advantages. Foremost among them, he was, for the age, a very tall man: 6 foot 3 inches of strapping Highland aristocratic stock. He won his first ever race shortly after arriving at Cambridge University as a mathematics student in 1874: a ten-mile event that he rode in 34 minutes. That was the fastest time ever recorded for the distance by amateur or professional. In a letter to his sister in law he wrote that he was 'not at all exhausted'.[1] I can't help feeling that had I been one of his vanquished opponents that might have been a bit hard to take. And it was only the beginning.

Keith-Falconer went on to win the British Amateur Championships in 1876, riding a penny-farthing over four miles in a new record time of 13 minutes 6 seconds at Lillie Bridge athletic grounds. A rider long dead, racing over an obsolete distance, on a track that was abandoned in the 1890s. It's hard to make it more than a statistic, so I thought it might make things clearer if I at least went to see where it was. A coincidence made finding it easy.

On the wall of my office I have a map of west London from 1875, bought because the location of my old flat in Battersea just sneaked into the bottom left-hand corner, directly under the 'u' of the word 'slums'. On the other side of the river there are market gardens in Kensington, and fields around Earl's Court. The river isn't embanked, and the Battersea Bridge marked is an old wooden structure. But near the centre of the map, beside the Brompton Cemetery, it says 'Lillie Bridge Athletic Grounds'.

It was the site of the first National Championships, in 1871, and a major sports ground in its day. The track was cinder, three laps to the mile, and sort of egg-shaped. One of the bends was noted for crashes, and known as 'Hospital Corner', not ironically, but because it was literally beside a hospital. ('Many a man who has gone flying past his opponent in front of the grandstand has come a complicated cropper at Hospital Corner,' said a contemporary book. I like very much the phrase 'a complicated cropper'.[2]) There was a wooden pavilion, which was burned to the ground in 1889 in the riots that followed a running race which was abandoned after the two competitors involved realised that, whichever of them won, they were both going to be beaten to death by the bookmakers and an angry crowd.

These days it's one of those bits of land in London that's been drifting from job to job for decades, waiting to fulfil its true calling of redevelopment into luxury flats. After retiring from being an athletic ground, Lillie Bridge spent most of its more recent career as a shabby car park for the Earl's Court Exhibition Centre. Given its anonymity, I don't know why going to look at a car park helped, but I found that when I stood in the middle of it, I didn't find it all that hard to imagine how the grounds looked in their heyday, with tents and banners and cheering spectators and maybe a brass band. I realised it wouldn't have been so different from the Good Friday track meeting that happened every year until very recently at Herne Hill, a few miles away in south London (where I once finished a soundly beaten second in a pursuit competition to a 21-year-old called Bradley Wiggins in the early noughties).

Keith-Falconer's winning ride in the four-mile race took place at an average of less than 20 mph, and most halfway fit riders today would manage to keep up. But at the time it must have looked magnificent, this enormous man, atop his enormous wheel, laying waste to the opposition as thousands cheered him on.

He broke the record for riding from Land's End to John o'Groats in 1882. He wrote an account of it for the *London Bicycle Club Gazette*. It's a remarkably cheerful record of riding alone along rutted country roads on dark, rainy nights, and of shouting at windows at midnight to try to rouse grumpy innkeepers. Between Doncaster and Wetherby a road that had been ploughed up by a traction engine meant he had to walk for over 30 miles: 'I tried to make myself believe I was on a walking tour, and had taken the machine with me to come in handy now and then. About 11.30 p.m. I tramped into Wetherby. Two friendly policemen aided me in making sufficient noise to awaken the landlord of the inn.' Two days later, between Alnwick and Berwick, a headwind meant he had to walk another 30 miles. He reached Wick in northern Scotland at midnight on day 13, 19 miles short of his destination. After an hour and a half in the Station Hotel, 'I started again, to the blank astonishment of landlord, boots, and waiters. The utter solitude, stillness and dreariness of the remaining 19 miles made a most remarkable impression on me. Not one tree, bush or hedge did I see the whole way, only dark brown moor and a road straight as a rule. At twenty minutes past three I stood stiff, sore, hungry and happy before John o'Groat's House Hotel. I had no difficulty in rousing the landlord, and was soon asleep.' He adds simply, 'Thus ended an interesting and amusing ride.'[3]

It was still not his greatest achievement. That had actually come a few years earlier, in 1878, and was a lot less drawn-out. In a specially sanctioned head-to-head, Keith-Falconer had raced John Keen over five miles at the University Ground in Cambridge. Keen was the professional champion of the world. He had reigned supreme in England. He travelled to America, where he dispatched all that was thrown at him there as well. He won races, he broke records, his name was sufficient to attract crowds of up to 12,000 to race meetings. He was generally regarded as the fastest professional rider in the world.

The student Keith-Falconer beat him by five yards. And that after a spectacular bit of absent-mindedness, whereby Keith-Falconer had completely forgotten about the upcoming race, and did no training for it at all. He was reminded only the week before, when a friend asked him how his preparations were going. In a letter to Isaac Pitman (the same Isaac Pitman who devised Pitman shorthand), Keith-Falconer said, 'The first thing was to knock off smoking, which I did. Next, to rise early in the morning and breathe the fresh air before breakfast. Next to go to bed not later than ten. Finally to take plenty of gentle exercise in the open air.' In the match, his time for the five miles was, of course, a new record, amateur and professional.[4] He came to the conclusion that smoking was bad for you.

To prove the win wasn't a fluke, the following year Keith-Falconer beat Keen again, this time by three inches over two miles.[5] He had an extraordinary talent. Yet Keith-Falconer would have been absolutely aghast if he had thought that 150 years later we would be talking about his bicycling. It was, for him, no more than a necessary distraction from studying and working – something to which he was even more committed after he switched his studies from mathematics to theology during his first year. He claimed he only ever rode a bike to make him better able to concentrate on his books. He raced, he said, simply because publicly committing to a race was the only way to make himself train properly. Among other miscellaneous achievements, he became Cambridge University's professor of Arabic, and wrote the *Encyclopaedia Britannica* entry on shorthand.

His life was one of spectacular overachievement – but it was also tragically short. Keith-Falconer's calling was always to missionary work. He died of malaria while in Aden building an orphanage in 1887. He had only been in Aden for a few months, and was aged just 32.

I find the Honourable Ion Keith-Falconer a figure of some fascination because he's almost the only really notable example of the aristocratic gentleman amateur in cycling. He was from a titled Highland family – sufficiently isolated that he often travelled to and from Cambridge by sea. The contrast between amateur and professional in the era was stark, and it influenced cycling (and almost all other sports) for decades. It seems strange from a modern standpoint to think that saying someone was a professional was essentially a Bullingdon Club insult. Professionalism was demanding money for something that one should be doing for love.

It was pimping your legs so your family could eat, and it was the last unholy refuge of those whose unfortunate circumstances meant they actually needed to earn a living.

The National Cyclists' Union's definition of a professional was: 'One who has ridden a bicycle in public for money, or who has engaged, taught, or assisted in bicycling or any other athletic exercise for money, and that a bicyclist who shall have competed with a professional bicyclist for a prize knowingly and without protest . . . shall be considered a professional bicyclist.' This definition was savagely criticised for its liberal approach, especially in that it made no reference to social class.

That's because class was everything. According to *The Times*, 'Artisans and mechanics' muscular practice is held to give them an unfair advantage [in bike racing]. Suchlike troublesome personages can have no place found for them. [If they are excluded] the prizes are more certain to fall into the right hands.'[6]

Of course, the broad definition of professionalism extended to those whose job was not racing bicycles, but just building them, repairing them or selling them. That's one of the reasons that so much of the racing history of cycling has been tied up with professionalism – from the start there was money to be made, because unlike, say, running, boxing, the triple jump or even sports like rowing, at the heart of cycling there was a piece of expensive equipment that people might be persuaded to buy. It was only natural that if you'd started to make bicycles, you'd want to ride them, to race them, and to set records on them. It was just marketing.

Professional bike riders in the 1870s and 1880s were not, in general, held in high esteem by the buyers of the products they advertised. One respected early cycling publication described the professional cyclist as 'A very vulgar creature, whose idea of recreation and relaxation is indulgence in unlimited liquor, and whose habitation is among the lowest classes.'[7] It was accepted wisdom that a professional rider would only train when forced to do so. Otherwise he'd stay in his hovel and drink himself into a stupor. So a professional needed a trainer to coerce him into action, and the more contempt the trainer could summon for his athlete, the better.

Generally a professional had a patron (maybe a manufacturer) who would, together with the trainer, deploy him like a fighting dog. Keith-Falconer's opponent John Keen didn't just ride the normal run of professional races, he was also dispatched to publicity-seeking challenges that were very close to freak shows. For instance, in 1873 he raced against a trotting pony over 20 miles round a track. He won, the pony retiring well beaten at 16 miles.[8] (The same pony had previously beaten two other professional cyclists in the same challenge, and had something of a fan following of its own in the strange world of Victorian cycling.)

Part of the impetus for the odder races was betting. Professional racing – like about 90 per cent of everything that happened in the late nineteenth century – was a magnet for betting, both legal and illegal. The betting changed the racing. Everyone wanted to see the big names ride, but they also wanted to have close racing because it wasn't really in anyone's interests for a whole string of hot favourites to win time and again. So in an attempt to keep things interesting, a very significant number of professional races (and some amateur) were handicap events, with the riders starting from different points on the track. The reports all made careful note of starting positions along with the finishing positions, enabling the experienced judge of bike-flesh to do the full *Racing Post* routine at a track meeting.

The regularity of the handicap set-up also tells you something else about the racing, which is that the tactics were not primarily about drafting behind other riders, which is what governs almost all modern racing. It was partly that the riding was slower, so drafting made less difference, and partly that bicycle racers were still programmed into behaving rather like runners – the aerodynamic factors that govern modern racing were somewhere between a mystery and an irrelevance to most participants. If the racing had revolved around riders drafting and working together, then as soon as any two riders managed to get into contact with each other, or if they started together, they'd have had a joint advantage over everyone else, and handicapping would have become considerably more complicated to calculate.

That's not to say that a sprint finish was unknown. A close finish was, after all, the whole aim of the handicapper. I love the idea of a sprint finish on penny-farthings. The coordination and the courage must have been quite something, never mind the leg speed. Remember that penny-farthings have small gears. A 54-inch bike has a gear around a modern 39x19. So 20 mph – the sort of speed you needed to set a distance record if you were John Keen – was a cadence of 130 rpm. Compare that to a more modern endurance cadence of around 100 rpm. Sprinting, it could get to well over 150 rpm, which is not so far away from the cadence of a modern track sprinter, except that the penny-farthing riders were doing it hunched over the bars and banging elbows eight feet off the ground.

What makes the reports of sprint finishes rather hard to take seriously is the Victorian terminology. I don't, I hope, have an especially dirty mind, but I still struggle to get through sentences like, 'His magnificent spurting down the full length of the home straight brought the crowd to its feet,' without sniggering. ('He spurted past Johnson, who was himself spurting as hard as he was able.' 'After the fifty-miles battle, Corton had nothing left with which to spurt.' And so on. Although I do rather like it. If nothing else, the substitution might liven up some modern Grand Tour stages that dribble their way inexorably and interminably towards a mass bunch-spurt.)

Money also meant that track racing was where the action was. There were events on the road, and wagers on the road, and place-to-place records were regularly used to sell bikes and equipment, but if you wanted to make money promoting a race, you had to put it where you could build a fence round it and charge admission, because it was going to be a very long time before you were going to make anything from the TV rights.

There were tracks everywhere. By the late 1880s there were 17 in southern England alone. In the rest of Britain and Ireland they were almost as thick on the ground, including an 8,000-spectator track in Waterford. Sometimes tracks were round, sometimes oval, sometimes egg-shaped, depending on the available land, and normally worked out at three or four laps to the mile. Generally they were banked at the curves, and covered in cinder mixed with coal, gravel, oolite (naturally occurring tiny, round stones) or maybe clay depending on drainage, usage and the weather . . . none of which sounds like the sort of thing you'd want to land on at 20 mph and from some height. Some tracks were in the centre of town, some not – the Cambridge track that saw so many of Keith-Falconer's triumphs was four miles outside the city in a field that no one seems to have bothered to make a note of for posterity. In London tracks were ridden clockwise, the opposite to almost everywhere else, for no reason that history has ever made clear.[9]

The tracks weren't community facilities, they were the work of entrepreneurs who built them with dreams of nothing more noble than profit. As an example you could do worse than the Wood Green track in north London. It was built in the 1890s by Albert Gamage, founder of a very successful department store at Holborn Circus in London. (It closed as recently as 1972. While it's unlikely to be something you ever need to know, I can tell you that my research revealed that Rudyard Kipling bought a goldfish there in 1922.[10])

His department store thriving, the next step for Gamage was to build his own track, which would make money in its own right, create demand for his goods and publicise his business. He found a site close to Alexandra Palace, cleared it, and for £18,000 built a stadium to the design of (rather improbably) a cycling journalist called

H. J. Swindley. This was a serious sum of money, and not the sort of thing a wise man would usually put in the hands of a cycling journalist, but it paid off. What Gamage got was the fastest bicycle track in London, iron-framed grandstands, a capacity of 10,000, a licensed bar, and even a bandstand.

There were events weekly all summer, for professional and amateur racers. There was always a capacity crowd for pro racing at the Bank Holiday meetings, with trade stands, a military band playing the latest music hall hits, bookies shouting their odds, and a crowd – well lubricated at Gamage's bars – shouting encouragement at the riders.

It was thoroughly modern – the only thing to distinguish it from a present commercial track meeting was the vastly superior music. When Gamage rather daringly experimented with mixed-sex tandem racing, the band was able to play the music hall hit 'Daisy Bell' (that's the 'Bicycle built for two' song) during the event, and the capacity crowd all sang along. I accept that you might struggle to get this going at a modern meeting, but cycling is all the poorer for it.[11]

Everything about bicycle riding was maturing very fast: there was racing, both professional and amateur; there were clubs; there were magazines; there were books that attempted to explain how to balance a bicycle. Above all there were thousands of cyclists, people whose identities were already bound up with iron and rubber. But already everything they knew was on the brink of another revolution, if you'll pardon the pun. Things were about to undergo the biggest change since the *draisine* became the boneshaker.

CHAPTER 6

Safety Bicycles and Extreme Danger: Mile-a-Minute Murphy and the Lion's Den

This is not the story of bike technology. That's not to say it's not an interesting subject. I like old bikes with rod-operated brakes. I derive great pleasure from a detailed study of the history of variable gears. With the perspective of hindsight, I like reading old magazine articles predicting dismal failure for carbon-fibre wheels, aluminium frames and pointy time-trial helmets. I like imagining the frustration the Italian racer Tullio Campagnolo must have felt as he tried to undo the wingnuts on his punctured wheel with frozen fingers, the triumph as he suddenly thought of the cam-action that would produce the world's first quick-release skewer. I adore the sort of book that tells the story of the subsequent Campagnolo component empire, complete with pictures of wingnuts, the first skewer, and the Campag Record rear derailleur, preferably the anniversary edition in its presentation box.

I also accept that, interesting though all that might be, there have only been five real innovations in the whole history of cycling. The first was the *draisine*. The second was the bicycle. The third and fourth came together in the 1880s, and they were the chain drive and the pneumatic tyre. (That's about where we are in the story right now.) The fifth was variable gears, although it was a technology that developed very gradually through quite a lot of the twentieth century. But, to be simplistic about it, 80 per cent of the modern bike had been more or less perfected by the time Queen Victoria died.

Here in the story of cyclists, however, sometimes talking about technology is unavoidable. The chain drive was what begat the safety bicycle, and the safety bicycle is what we're practically all riding today. As a piece of technology, the chain mattered very much indeed, because it changed cycling from top to bottom like nothing else before or since. Chains altered who rode, how they rode, where they rode and what they rode for. It had knock-on effects on roads, women's suffrage, politics and the British class system. Swapping direct drive for chain drive was like the moment in photography when film replaced glass plates – suddenly it was a hobby that was no longer restricted to dedicated enthusiasts; instead anyone could have a go.

Chain drives had been around for a while – James Starley used them on his tricycles. They moved to bicycles, where they were used to create a step-up gear on a penny-farthing, then to produce a sort of semi-safety variety of bike, essentially a penny-farthing with a smaller front wheel.

One or two innovators had actually produced rear-wheel chain-drives in the 1870s. In general, they got the transmission right, and got the rest of it wrong. In 1879 Henry Lawson – who would one day found the Daimler car company – produced what would have been essentially a modern bicycle had he not equipped his rear-wheel-driven bike with a front wheel almost the same size as a penny-farthing's, thereby remaining oblivious to almost all the idea's potential advantages.[1]

James Starley had been the genius behind a workable penny-farthing; it was his nephew John Kemp Starley who produced the first properly modern bike, in 1885. He called it the 'Rover Safety'. It was a modern bike. It looks like a modern bike and it rides like a modern bike. It has more or less equally sized wheels, a saddle and bars at a sensible height off the ground, and a chain driving a rear wheel.

At a stroke the flying-over-the-handlebars cropper had gone; clambering up a step to a precarious saddle five feet off the ground was a thing of the past; getting off no longer involved any elements of free-fall parachuting, now you could take your feet off the pedals and just put them on the ground. After 70 years of muffing about with two-wheeled near-misses – dangerous and inconvenient machines that riders persevered with out of dedication rather than good sense – they'd finally landed it. It was one of those moments – the first cycling had really known and the last it ever needed – where suddenly everything snapped into focus.

We are basically finished with technology at this point. If we're honest, the only improvements that have been made to the bicycle since have been marginal. If an average amateur rider on a twenty-first-century carbon bike took on, for example, Chris Froome on one of the early safety bikes over any course at all, Froome would still win. The same battle re-enacted with the safety bike and a penny-farthing would be a different story.

Of course, no one saw it like that at the time. The safety bike was called 'dwarfish'. It was fit only for the terminally timid, the old and the infirm. 'Manly men would always prefer the ordinary.'[2] Even when the safety bike started to get some momentum, the establishment was still attached to the penny-farthing: 'The riders of the dwarf machines are certain, in the course of time, to outnumber the riders of the ordinary, who will, however, always form the aristocracy.'[3]

To convince the doubters, Starley did what any innovator trying to prove a point in the world of cycling used to do. He organised a race. It was a simple one: 100 miles, from Norman Cross near Peterborough to Twyford in Berkshire, for riders of Rover bicycles only. The winner was to receive a £50 gold watch, the second man a Rover bicycle and the third a £5 watch. The winner came home in seven hours and five minutes, to comfortably beat the 100-mile record, and the safety bicycle was on its way.[4]

If you were being picky, the only real downside to the safety bicycle was the harsh ride. The small wheels suffered over rutted roads. From my own penny-farthing riding, this is not hard to appreciate. The safety bike was quite clearly safer, certainly faster – it went on to prove as much on the track as well as the more demanding road – but the Victorian arse was no hardier than a modern arse, and there was no getting away from the fact that it wasn't very comfortable to sit on.

Within a few months the solution came from a Scottish veterinary surgeon in Belfast, working in a practice that a great uncle of mine was one day going to buy, and which wasn't so very far from where I went to school. He was John Boyd Dunlop – there's a good chance he's the most famous innovator in cycling history.

What he came up with in 1887 was the pneumatic tyre. Well, technically, he re-came up with it, because another Scottish inventor had patented the idea in the 1840s, at a time when there was no practical use for such a thing. Dunlop's inspiration came from trying to make his nine-year-old son Johnny go faster on his tricycle, which seems, if I may say so, a slightly eccentric obsession for a nineteenth-century vet. He made primitive pneumatic tyres for the trike with rubber sheeting, and was delighted at young Johnny's greatly increased velocity.[5] Mrs Dunlop's feelings on the matter are unrecorded.

Just like John Kemp Starley, Dunlop used racing to promote the tyres. He equipped a local rider, William Hume of the Belfast Cruisers CC, with a set for his safety bicycle. Up to this point Hume's career had been competent, but hadn't attracted a huge amount of attention. That changed abruptly when he used Dunlop's tyres to soundly thrash all comers at a local meeting at the Queen's College track in Ormeau Park. An illustration of the time shows him cruising over the finishing line, looking across the track to some far-off figures labouring after him half a lap behind. It clearly made quite an impression. Hume then went to Liverpool for a race meeting there, where he simply humiliated the opposition. When his pneumatic-equipped bicycle was exhibited in a Liverpool shop the police had to disperse the crowd that gathered to look at it.[6]

The next step in the Dunlop PR offensive was to create the 'Irish Brigade' – a whole team of pneumatic-equipped Irish riders. They went to England in 1890 with their pneumatic safety bikes to finish the job Hume had started, to beat up as many unsuspecting racers as they could find. Wherever they went, the reaction of other racers and spectators to the big inflatable tyres, and the bulky contrast they presented with the skinny solid rubber tyres that were the norm, was full-on thigh-slapping hilarity. Poems and songs (I'm not kidding) were composed about how stupid they looked.

The truth is that they did look very odd indeed. They were about three inches in diameter, smooth, and really unlike anything seen on a current bike. 'Pudding wheels' was one of the better-aimed insults. A pair of lifebelts is another comparison that springs to mind. People would still laugh at them today, and that's looking at them from the perspective of an age where practically the only wheels you ever see that *don't* have an inflatable tube round them are on office chairs and vacuum cleaners, or are the London Eye.

The physics of the pneumatic tyre was not remotely discouraged by the gales of laughter, however, and the Irish Brigade swept all before it. The penny-farthing was dead before they got on the boat home. [7]

Either of the innovations – the safety bike or the pneumatic tyre – would have revolutionised cycling.

Together they were a complete reinvention. They changed both the sport and the pastime – indeed it would probably be fair to say that they created the pastime from scratch, since before their arrival there was practically no form of cycling that wasn't distinctly athletic. But that was to come a very little later. The first impact was in racing.

Victorian cycle sport in the 1890s had two obsessions: speed and endurance. Not speed-and-endurance, but the two separate things. On the one hand, track races got faster and faster, and increasingly based on pacing, because pacing was how you got the fastest possible speeds. And on the other hand, interest in extremely long races kept growing. The combination of the safety bike and the pneumatic tyre changed both of these.

For the short fast events, the higher speeds and the better manoeuvrability meant that the benefits of riding behind a pacer increased, so the importance of finding the right pacer increased to match. A modern-day paced race uses motor bikes for this. In the 1890s, all you had to work with was other bike riders. The problem was obviously that if you could find someone fast enough to pace the fastest riders, then they'd actually be the fastest rider themselves, and you'd need to find someone to pace them.

The logic was of the simple variety: two riders on a tandem were faster than a solo, because that was double the horsepower for less than double the weight and much less than double the aerodynamic drag. And if a bike built to carry two riders was faster, then one built for three would be faster again. But even that wouldn't be as fast as one built for, let's say, five. Five riders was what they stuck with. They did play around with six and even seven, but there came a point where the structural integrity of a bike the length of a lorry and with three-quarters of a ton of weight on top starts to become an issue, especially when the weight on top starts to sprint as hard as it can.

Even with five-rider pacing machines – 'quints'– the limiting factor was still the pacers rather than the paced. So the pacing for a single rider for a single race often involved several quints taking turns, and many, many men. As a spectacle a lot of Victorian cycling probably looked rather less than gripping. But something I very much wish I'd seen was a rider attempting a one-mile record, while six quints swapped in and out in front of him: a high-speed, high-risk performance that would make a modern Madison track race look like something you'd do for a gentle spin on a Sunday afternoon. The noise, the sweat, the dust kicked up from the cinder track, and the brutal efforts of so many men would have been perhaps as magnificent a sight as bicycle racing has ever offered. It would be like the speed of cycling combined with the raw grunt of rugby. In the 1890s the only thing in the world that could go any more quickly was a train, and to see something go so fast off muscle power alone must have been exhilarating.

Pacing was such an established part of racing that a lot of the time the reports didn't even mention it. It's not unusual to read a report of, say, a 25-mile race that provides a gripping account of the two riders' neck and neck tussle through five miles, ten miles, 15 miles, with all the ebb and flow you might expect, then suddenly says something like 'with 12 laps to go, Smithers' pacers crashed, and Johnstone took a lead he would not relinquish', and you realise it was not the sort of race you had been picturing.

(The failure to reliably distinguish between paced and unpaced events has some knock-on effects even now. The unpaced hour record has become the most important record in the sport, and all the officially recognised distances, starting with Henri Desgrange in 1893, are indeed unpaced. But the idea of an hour record pre-dated that and there are several commonly accepted distances that were set with pacers or in mass-start races. To pick one at random, the often-quoted hour of Herbert Cortis, set in Cambridge in 1882 at 32.453 kilometres, was established in a mass-start race that included Ion Keith-Falconer. Untangling which were paced and which were unpaced races would present an interesting challenge for someone with inexhaustible patience and a high-tolerance of book-mould.)

The pacers were critical. At the top professional level they were not casually recruited, nor were they monogamous to one star rider. They formed teams for hire. Very big teams for hire – when Thomas Linton of Britain travelled to New York in 1898 for a professional showdown with French champion Edouard Taylor, each rider had 32 men in their pacing team.[8] There were three or four mechanics each, plus several coaches – essentially around 80 men hand-picked so that two other men could have a bike race. The fact that they were all getting paid to be there demonstrates just how much money there was in professional track cycling.

The coaching of the pacing teams was a high-pressure job. If you've seen *Chariots of Fire*, you will remember Sam Mussabini. He was Harold Abrahams' coach for the 1924 Olympics, the one who, because he was a professional coach in the age of the amateur, wasn't even allowed into the Olympic stadium. By 1924 he'd already been a coach for decades, and before he specialised in athletics, he coached in the glamorous, moneyed world of track cycling. He looked after the first British professional National champion, Bert Harris. But perhaps his greatest achievement was with the Dunlop pacing team, a carefully selected, crack outfit sponsored by the tyre company, which contained several riders who were to go on to considerable individual success. A photograph of the team taken at Crystal Palace in the mid-1890s features over 40 pacers posing with at least nine different triplets, quads and quints. Mussabini was responsible for resurrecting the squad after a series of humiliating defeats for their riders by the rival Gladiators pacing team. Under his leadership the Dunlop became unequivocally the best pacing team in the world.

In the end, though, neither the Dunlop, nor the Gladiators nor any of the other teams survived the introduction of motor bikes for pacing. Initially intended to save money – one man could do the work of 40 – they also diminished the spectacle to the point where no one was prepared to pay to see it. Unpaced racing took over as the norm, and the pacing teams vanished for ever.

Motor pacing never really thrived, but it did survive as a minority interest. There's still a National Championships, and there are still some paced records. Generally these use small moped-like dernys, but occasionally they wheel out some socking enormous motor bikes, the kind of heavy artillery that were known as 'the big motors' at the Herne Hill Good Friday meeting – 650cc Triumph TR65 Thunderbirds, with the black-leathered riders using extended handlebars so they could stand upright above the back axle and give the maximum shelter to their riders. Collectively they made a noise like someone re-enacting the Battle of Britain in their living room, and looked like something that would have put the Hells Angels in fear for their lives. No matter how hard you

CHAPTER 6

tried not to, you found yourself humming 'The Ride of the Valkyries' for days afterwards, and reflecting on what the Dunlop team must have looked like in full cry if the nineteenth-century crowds considered the motors to be so dull in comparison.

Paced racing led to other lunacy. Its logical conclusion was to ask the very simple question of just how fast it was possible to ride a bike with suitable pacing help. In New York, there was a cyclist with exactly that question on his mind: Charles Murphy. He was a successful professional rider on the American circuit. Among other things, he'd been a member of a pacing team involved in some of the highest profile races the US had seen, so he understood well the art of paced racing. Having ridden at a virtual 100 mph on a pair of static rollers in training, he'd formed the slightly daffy notion that if he had suitable pacing, even in the real world, he could go as fast as he liked. He said that there was no railway locomotive that could outrun him.

At this point Murphy had the good fortune to meet an executive from the Long Island Railroad in a restaurant. Murphy persuaded him that there was the potential here to provide excellent publicity for the railway. If a wooden surface was laid between the tracks, Murphy maintained that he could draft behind a train and that sustaining 60 mph – riding a full mile a minute – would be relatively simple. He would be famous, the railway would be famous, and everyone would be happy. The railway agreed to this. If the extraordinarily high probability of the whole escapade ending in Murphy being killed in a very memorable fashion occurred to anyone, it seems not to have put them off.

On 21 June 1899, Murphy and a team from the railroad assembled at a two-mile stretch of track that had been boarded over according to Murphy's specification. The rear of the train carriage had had the sides and roof extended backwards over the rails to create a recess and provide better shelter. Murphy got on his bike, a crowd of railway and cycling officials gathered on the observation platform on the back of the carriage, and the engine driver opened the taps.

The first attempt took 1 minute and 8 seconds to cover the mile, and the problem was not Murphy, but the train. The next six runs were barely any better, so they introduced a bigger locomotive. Its weight began to warp the wooden roadway, meaning Murphy was riding on a track which was forming waves below him, making it hard to control the bike. With death or serious injury the inevitable consequence of straying off the boards and onto the sleepers, its four-foot width must have seemed terrifyingly narrow.

Murphy finally managed it. He decided to hold onto the train until it had accelerated and then, with a crowd of suited men on the train's rear observation platform cheering, and encouragement being screamed through a megaphone just inches from his head, he rode the mile in 57.8 seconds. There is a photograph of him doing it, tucked in behind the carriage, with the crowd on the platform above, and passengers in the carriage hanging out of the windows to try to get a glimpse of him – a glimpse they'd only get if things went very wrong. Which was presumably exactly what they were hoping for.

Athletes of the era were no more modest in describing their achievements than their modern counterparts. Murphy said afterwards that he had been pelted with burning rubber from under the train: 'I was riding in a maelstrom of swirling dust, hot cinders, paper and other particles of matter. The whipsaw feeling through a veritable storm of fire became harder every second.' He dropped a few feet behind the train, into the buffeting winds of the slipstream. But he clawed his way back, through the flying dust and the hot cinders from the locomotive. If the accounts of his gearing are to be believed, he was pedalling at around 200 rpm.

The train, and Murphy on its heels, flashed past the finishing line. At this point the train driver, perhaps not really thinking things through, hit the brakes. The triumphant Murphy crashed rather ignominiously into the back of it. He was lucky that two men grabbed him and hauled him onto the observation platform. Semi-conscious, he was carried into the train. When his jersey was pulled off so a doctor could examine him, his skin was torn from his flesh where the cinders had burnt through his jersey. The athletics official who served as referee at the event swore he would never again become involved in such a stunt, '. . . even if it made cycling famous for a century.'[9]

Murphy recovered quickly, and became universally known as 'Mile-a-Minute Murphy'. He eventually joined the New York Police Department, where his speed on a bike was more than a little useful, and where he later claimed to have been the first policeman in the world to fly an aeroplane. For someone with such a bent for the wildly dangerous, he lived to the slightly surprising age of 79, dying in Queens in New York in 1950.

Murphy's was far from the only stunt going on in cycling in the 1890s. Circus-type tomfoolery was as popular then as it had been in the 1870s. There was high-wire riding, slack-wire riding and riding through fire. Riders perfected looping-the-loop on a track that resembled nothing so much as one of those flexible-plastic tracks that you can fire a toy car down with a catapult. When they'd worked out how to do that without killing themselves – being cyclists they did it by trial and error rather than by doing the maths – they did it through fire, or they did it in pairs going in opposite directions.

It was as if, having invented the safety bicycle, everyone was hell-bent on risk-compensating themselves to death. Take 'the Funnel' for example. The funnel was a sort of wall of death, but it was ice-cream-cone shaped, with the bottom cut off. You rode in from the top, and rode round and round for as long as you felt it would take to justify whatever you were charging people to watch, and you rode up and out again.

To make it more interesting, the cone was usually suspended some distance in the air, with the bottom open. If you think about that set-up for a moment, you'll realise it was only a matter of time before someone would feel that the obvious thing to put underneath the funnel was an enclosure full of lions. There have been times in a bike race when I have invoked all the gods of cycling and implored their aid in preventing me getting a puncture. That would clearly be nothing compared to how little you'd want to hear the bang of one of those new-fangled pneumatics exploding while riding round a funnel above some lions. The illustrations of the act show the lions in a state of salivating excitement that stops only just short of holding a knife and fork and wearing a napkin. And with good reason: the historian Rüdiger Rabenstein noted dryly that, 'On at least one occasion, the lions were the beneficiaries of this act.'[10]

Yet there was more to early bike racing than the thunder and lightning of a pacing team in full cry, or the full-on sprinting of a man trying to avoid being eaten by a lion. There was also a parallel obsession with endurance.

Endurance was already a common theme in athletics. Extreme feats of stamina were hugely popular in the nineteenth century. They often involved a wager, and the search for a hard-to-call wager often led to men attempting things of considerable eccentricity. If you could go back to 1809, you could go to Newmarket Heath and watch Captain Robert Barclay attempting to win a wager of 1,000 guineas by walking one mile each hour for a thousand consecutive hours. That's 42 days. He won the bet, walking his last few miles in front of a crowd of thousands.[11]

The curiosity in just what the human body could do was no less when bicycles appeared. Twenty-four-hour races had happened as a matter of course, following the precedent set by athletics. So when, in 1877, a six-day-long foot-race was organised on a track inside the Islington Agricultural Hall[12] it was inevitable that someone would organise something similar for cyclists. Why six days? Simply because that was as long as you could run such an event for without gambling on a Sunday. If it hadn't been for the Sabbath, God alone knows what they'd have attempted.

Islington's first six-day bike race in 1878 was the wager of one rider, David Stanton, that he could ride a thousand miles in six days. He achieved this in not much more than three days. The next year the same venue saw the Long Distance Championship of the World, on an unbanked 150-metre track that was elevated above the floor so that the crowd could mill around below the riders, and so that the occasional exhausted competitor could liven things up by riding off the track and landing, complete with penny-farthing, among the spectators. The leading riders could average up to 240 miles a day, snatching a few hours' sleep here and there, and dashing out to local cafés for a quick meal when they dared.[13]

All the same, the Islington events didn't really attract the huge crowds who had come to see the equivalent walking races. Six-day cycling didn't fully take off until after the invention of the safety bike, when the format was exported to New York. In the 1890s, the six-day racing at Madison Square Garden was the sensation of the city. It happened on a banked wooden track, essentially indistinguishable from a modern indoor track. But that wasn't the important difference. Crucially, the organisers in New York had grasped that a group of men riding lap after lap after lap for six days was probably less gripping to witness in real time than someone simply telling you the results after it was all over. They injected pace and excitement in a way that the British had never managed, by working backwards from what was entertaining for the crowd, rather than relying on simply working forwards from what was a 'proper' race. It was emblematic of the New World versus the Old.

The US six-days had shorter races as a sort of overture on the first evening to kick the whole event off, and they ran sprint events throughout the six days, contested by riders from outside the main event on the upper part of the track, while the endurance riders continued to ride round the bottom. They had celebrity guest appearances, circus acts ('Bring on the Funnel! Bring on the lions!') and famous actresses on hand to garland the victors. In other words, what they created was not so very far away from what we'd recognise as a modern six-day race.[14] There was betting, clouds of cigar smoke and non-stop drink from the bar. There was constant music from the bandstand, although you'd have been lucky to hear much of it because often the fans of individual riders would bring whole other bands into the crowd and show their support by trying to drown each other out.

Beneath the razzamatazz the race was still a horrendous test of riding. It went on for 24 hours a day – though it's unlikely any riders ever got through without sleeping at all. In the small hours of the morning, the pace dropped, but it never stopped. Hallucinations were common – riders became convinced they were being pelted with stones, that their bicycles weren't moving when they were, or they just got off and stood open-mouthed, transfixed and unresponsive.

It wasn't the sort of brouhaha that respectable New York liked to see in its midst. Opinion turned against the event. The *New York Herald Times* said, 'An athletic contest in which the participants go queer in their heads and strain their powers until their faces become hideous with the tortures that rack them is not sport, it is brutality.' The *Herald Tribune* said the event had disgraced New York.[15] Cartoons showed skeletal riders being taunted with bags of paltry prize money by the figure of death. And so legislation was passed to limit the riders to 12 hours of riding a day.

The result of this was not, as the legislature had hoped, the end of the show. Some forgotten genius realised there was a way round this that would make the show better rather than worse, which was to run the six-day as a relay race for teams of two, riding for 12 hours a day each. Brilliantly, he realised that the riders could change over, not once a day, nor once an hour, but as often as they liked. One of them could race, and one of them could circulate at a more casual pace round the top of the track, waiting to be thrown into the action like a tag-team wrestler. And so Madison Square Garden gave its name to the Madison track race, still the frenetic core of a six-day event today, and invariably the grand finale for the Track World Championships.[16]

Cycling grew up in to a real sport very quickly. The Madison Square Garden six-days, the huge track meetings in Britain and Ireland, and similar events in the rest of Europe were all so closely related to modern track racing as to be different only in the details. Track cycling had become a very significant spectator sport – in the late nineteenth century in Britain it was right up there with football – and its ascent was rapid: all achieved in not much more than ten or 15 years. By the time the modern Olympics started up in 1896, only a few scant years since the invention of the safety bicycle, the organisers of the track programme held a match-sprint competition, ten-kilometre and 100-kilometre scratch-race events, and a one-lap time trial that was different from the modern kilometre time trial only in distance.

The Games in Greece were also host to the sole 12-hour track race in Olympic history, the staging of which clearly owed a debt to the sort of mentality that considered a six-day non-stop race a good idea. It hasn't been repeated, perhaps for fear of overstimulating the audience. It was won by the Austrian Adolf Schmal who rode 295.3 kilometres. He beat the British rider Frank Keeping by stealing a lap off him early on, then just sitting behind him for the remaining eleven and three-quarter hours. The other four starters gave up, probably out of boredom, as the event droned on. It was not the highlight of the Olympic meeting. Probably the most interesting thing about it was that Frank Keeping was a butler to the British Ambassador in Athens, competing on his day off.[17]

At the 1896 Olympics track racing dominated the cycling programme. The only road event was an 87-kilometre race from Athens to Marathon and back, where the roads were so bad that even the winner fell off three times. It was certainly not the blue-riband event it is now. In fact, generally speaking, racing on the road in Britain and elsewhere was very much an afterthought, because the glamour was all at the track. Even if bicycles had improved since the early near-impossible boneshaker races, roads were still poor and dangerous, and it was all but impossible to turn a profit running a road race because an organiser couldn't charge spectators an entry fee.

More importantly, in Britain the authorities were very hostile to the whole idea. The police didn't approve, and the recently formed National Cyclists' Union weren't keen either. Road racing, quite literally, scared the horses, and brought the new pastime of bicycling into disrepute. The concern was that touring riders and clubmen would pay a heavy price in terms of bad PR, because all cyclists would end up getting the blame for any aggression or rule-breaking by the racers.

The police would lie in wait for races, and detain the riders, or halt an event on the basis it constituted a public nuisance. In one case in 1883, which I imagine the *Daily Mail* might still use against us, the police stopped the leader of a tricycle race near Godstone in Surrey, and took his name and address. He provided these, but then jumped back on his tricycle and rode off at full speed. The two policemen gave chase in their official police pony and trap, but were unable to catch him. They were, apparently, 'much disgusted'.[18] On the road side of racing, things had hardly moved on for the British since James Moore had his bike nicked after the Paris–Rouen race of 1869.

But to really see what the consequences of all this were for the whole history of road racing in the UK and in Ireland, we need to understand what was going on with all of the non-racing bits of cycling at the time; because the popularity of cycling as a hobby has still not known a time to equal it.

CHAPTER 7

The 1890s: The Great Society Cycling Craze

The changes that the safety bike and the pneumatic tyre made to racing at the end of the nineteenth century were revolutionary. Or at least they were from the point of view of a racer, in that they made racing dramatically faster. A non-racer would possibly have argued that, in reality, all such developments did was allow the same people to do the same things in a bit less time. There might be some truth in this – then, as now, racing fellows tended to get a couple of miles an hour one way or the other a little bit out of proportion. But that is, after all, the whole point of the thing.

The other reason a non-racer might be reluctant to call the changes to racing a 'revolution' is that the changes the technology made to the sport were trivial compared to the difference they made to the pastime. If what had been witnessed in racing could be termed a revolution, we'd be left speechless in any attempt to describe what happened to the rest of the cycling landscape. It was a revolution within an upheaval wrapped in a transformation.

The bicycle was now faster, that much we knew. It was more comfortable. It was more efficient. It was no longer especially dangerous – gone were the extreme sports elements of cycling that had been part of its previous character. There was, of course, a hard core that didn't like that. After all, when I tried riding a penny-farthing, the stupidity was most of the appeal. But there were many more that were ready to take up cycling the minute the activity stopped being the Victorian equivalent of base-jumping. It wasn't just that bicycles were less dangerous; they also became, almost overnight, respectable. The safety bike meant that sober, professional types could now ride – doctors, vicars, landed gentry. And women.

That was the greatest change of all: women could now ride bikes. The first dropped-tube women's bikes in Britain were the work of John Kemp Starley in 1889 – although they'd appeared a couple of years earlier in the US.[1] Up until the safety bike, women's skirts were an almost insurmountable obstacle to riding. Before then, respectable women's cycling had been limited to lumbering about on ponderous tricycles. The only serious attempt at an alternative was when James Starley designed an extraordinary side-saddle penny-farthing in the 1870s, with both pedals on a crankshaft to one side of the front wheel.[2] It was practically impossible to mount, difficult to ride, dangerous to get off, and had all the traditional hazards and terrors of a penny-farthing while you were up there. It didn't catch on.

The new technology prompted not so much an upswing of enthusiasm as a craze. It was like a full-on playground mania, but played out among the British upper classes, and capitalised upon by anyone who knew how to weld a few steel tubes together and put wheels on the result. It seemed like everyone wanted a bike; everyone wanted to learn to ride. To run with the in-crowd, you needed a bike.

This version of cycling was not the pastime of the people. The Victorian craze was unremittingly posh. Quite where and how it started seems lost to time. Certainly the story of Queen Victoria and her Royal Salvo tricycles would have given cycling the sort of seal of approval that high society cared about. Edward Elgar rode a bike – a magazine caption of the period described him as 'the noted cyclist and composer', which might not be the order in which posterity remembers him, but caught the mood of the time. George Bernard Shaw rode a bike. Arthur Conan Doyle rode a bike. The Prince of

Wales rode a bike. It was said that by the mid-1890s every member of the House of Lords was a cyclist, and there hasn't been a time since when a claim as audacious as that could be made.[3]

It would be fair to say that the type of cycling high society went crazy over was not a very normal variety, compared to what had gone before, and even to what came after. It was a few years of the most splendid aristocratic lunacy. Their object was not to race, or to tour, or to really get anywhere at all, but simply to ride, for its own sake. If, on a summer morning in 1895, you had taken yourself off to London's Battersea Park, you would have found the place full of cyclists, many of them women, and most of them gentry or, at the very least, committed social climbers.

Happily, Jerome K. Jerome was there to see it: 'Bicycling became the rage. In Battersea Park, any morning between 11 and one, all the best blood in England could be seen, solemnly pedalling up and down the half-mile drive that runs between the river and the refreshment kiosk. But these were the experts. In shady bypaths, elderly countesses, perspiring peers, still at the wobbly stage, battled bravely with the laws of equilibrium; occasionally defeated, they would fling their arms around the necks of hefty young hooligans who were reaping a rich harvest as cycling instructors: "Proficiency guaranteed in twelve lessons." Cabinet ministers, daughters of a hundred earls, might be recognised by the initiated, seated on the gravel, smiling feebly and rubbing their heads.'[4]

The 'instructors' were exactly the same sort of young man who, a century and a quarter later, would teach rock climbing or kite-boarding. Just as in the 1870s, there were indoor schools for those too timid to learn outside. In New York there was even an indoor school where learners were wheeled around a gymnasium automatically by a sort of meat-hook arrangement suspended from the ceiling.

The riders didn't cycle to the park. Riding in the London traffic was considered neither safe nor respectable. Generally, the bike was placed in a monogrammed bicycle bag, loaded into a carriage by a footman, and driven there along with its owner. If you were properly posh you and your bicycle travelled in separate carriages. The grand houses of Belgravia acquired men and boys to groom bicycles. W. S. Gilbert (of Gilbert and Sullivan) had seven bicycles and a man to look after them.[5] If he was remarkable, it was probably for his self-restraint. All over the country the stables of stately houses were converted – one contained more than forty bikes, with tandems, roadsters, racers, polo bikes, tricycles, 'sociable' tandems that you rode sitting side-by-side, anything and everything. Visitors treated to a tour were left slack-jawed in admiration.[6]

The craze seemed to know no bounds. There was nothing that couldn't have a bicycle shoehorned into it: shooting parties, hunts, paper chases, concerts. Invitations to grand parties came with 'bring your bicycle' written at the bottom. The social season's balls often included cycling, frequently in the ballroom in full court dress.

At a Royal Irish Constabulary annual gymkhana, never mind the horses, the interest was all in the events for ladies on bicycles, which included a slalom around bottles, rolling a hoop while riding, a potato and spoon race and, for some reason that escapes all modern comprehension, opening and closing a parasol while riding, which I can imagine would have reduced a certain sort of 1870s Parisian gentleman to a paroxysm of delight. The grand finale saw eight riders on heavily decorated bicycles perform a maypole dance. Surprisingly, no riders were strangled with ribbons, and none of them ended up as a multicoloured mummy.[7]

Cycling attracted the attention of every variety of sporting inventor, all keen not to let their total inexperience in the field get in the way of improving the sport. Walter Wingfield, for example, was the man who invented lawn tennis. (Although his genius might be called into question when you hear he wanted to call it 'σφαιριστικη' or 'sphairistikê' – semi-literate Greek for 'to do with a ball game' – and took some persuading to call it anything else.) He also took an interest in cycling, and devised a version of bicycle polo where a golf club was used to hit a tennis ball through a set of croquet hoops. He probably felt confident of the success of this, since he'd combined equipment from four of the most popular upper-class sporting pastimes to create a version of a fifth.[8] Despite his connections and determined efforts to promote it, the game was not a roaring success on the basis that it was difficult to play and not very interesting even if you succeeded.

The high-society craze was the strangest – and perhaps funniest – couple of years in the history of cycling. There was the matter of who was doing it. There were the extraordinary ways they did it. There was the mystery of why they were doing it at all. But still, entertaining though it might be, there comes a point in writing about the craze when you worry you're just listing instances of the same sort of oddness.

To actually understand what was going on, you really have to look at cycling from the point of view of the upper classes. They weren't going to use bicycles for transport – they had carriages for that. One of the chief attractions of cycling was that both sexes could go for a ride together, so they weren't going to take up racing. For practically all the upper-class riders, cycling was a skill only recently acquired. So they did with their bicycles more or less what children do with them today – they rode to show off the fact that they could. It would be easier to mock the musical rides that were such a feature of all sorts of events – Walter Wingfield even produced a manual of musical ride manoeuvres with names like the 'serpentine down the centre' and the 'go large' – if I hadn't coerced some friends of mine into helping me mount something identical when we were about seven years old. That may, of course, say more about seven-year-old me than it does about Victorian high society, but I think it makes a sort of sense.

Maybe Friday afternoons in the Albert Hall were where I really belonged. There, at the height of the 1890s boom years, Miss Stuart Snell trained ladies on musical riding. They rode bikes bedecked with flowers (the bikes were imported from the US and made by Colonel Pope's outfit, incidentally), and were accompanied by a group of eastern European musicians known as The Hungarian Band. They rode figures, performed dances like the Lancers, and 'threw soft balls while riding'. They were a star turn at a Royal wedding. The Prince of Wales was, reportedly, a particular fan of the ladies' work. But I suppose, given his reputation for dissipation, he would have been.[9]

Across the Channel in France it was much the same, although the social mix was a bit broader. There was something a bit more sensual about French cycling, something less formal. Sarah Bernhardt was a noted cyclist, one whose every ride was reported on by the sort of paparazzi that operated with a pencil and paper. For all the informality, Parisians had something that London lacked: in the Bois de Boulogne there was a man who made his living pushing people's bicycles up a hill in the park. And in bad weather the indoor facilities were better than in London. There was even a cycling hall off the Champs-Élysées that had three-quarters of a mile of track arranged in a spiral round the perimeter of the hall like a very shallow helter-skelter. You rode up, you rode down, you enjoyed some refreshments, and you took your carriage home.[10]

The craze blazed around Europe and beyond. 'If royal and imperial example count for anything,' said aristocratic authors Viscount Bury and G. Lacy Hillier, 'the practice will soon be universal, for there is not a crowned head in Europe who has not a stud of these useful iron steeds. Whether the grandees of Middle Europe personally career about the *allées* of their castles I do not know, but we may at least, from custom and precedent, infer the existence in dignified leisure of many a Kaiserliche-Königlich Hochoberhoffvelocipedenkurator.'[11]

The same book noted that the Khedive of Egypt had a tricycle decorated with so much silver that it was almost impossible to make out the black enamel it was supposedly adorning. 'It will doubtless come in handy should His Highness take it into his head to ride across the Bayuda Desert,' it said. In India there was a maharajah who had formed a cycling club together with the local British Resident, and had a photograph taken of a club run setting out from his palace, jewelled turbans and all.[12]

However, back in the British Isles, problems were beginning to make themselves known. Life was no bed of roses for a society cyclist. There were class tensions, namely that, given the open-air, open-road (or, at any rate, open-park-path) nature of things, any counter-jumper who could scrape together the necessary brass could buy a bicycle and mix with the 'quality'.

In Ireland cycling was, if anything, even snobbier than it was in England, partly because it was rather more expensive. Even before the craze got up full-steam, the *Irish Cyclist* magazine noted that rather too large a proportion of the riders in Phoenix Park was composed of 'the great unwashed, for the most part, we presume, riders of hired machines'. The editor of the same paper was horrified to hear that a poll on the relative virtues of the *Irish Cyclist* and another Irish cycling paper had been conducted in a common public house. He was moved to write a heavily sarcastic editorial about it: 'How nice to have the merits of the paper discussed by Johnny the shoeblack, on his hired crock, or the messenger boy from the grocer's up the road.'[13] What he must have made of the club in Skibbereen that acquired its bicycles by salvaging them from a shipwreck doesn't really bear thinking about.[14]

Just as cycling reached a high-water mark, the craze collapsed as quickly as it had appeared. In London in 1896, after quite a lot of sustained campaigning, the previously off-limits Hyde Park was opened to cyclists, and took over from Battersea as the mecca. Initially it was a huge success – by June that year the number of cyclists riding there of a sunny morning reached several thousand. But by August, they'd almost all gone. The ladies with floral bikes, and the men in top hats, abandoned their bicycles in droves. By the following season it was clear that fashionable London had moved on. It was over.

There were two issues behind the dramatic change in cycling. The first problem was mundane: the weather. The summer of 1896 was unusually hot. Suddenly riding a bike became just a trifle hotter and sweatier, and a little less appealing than, say, just sitting about being rich. Cycling might all have taken off again the following year, though. What finally did for the society craze was economics, namely the falling prices of bicycles. One problem was that bike manufacturers in the 1890s were like the American car industry in the 1950s – every season brought new colours, new decoration, essential innovations (the chain swapped from the right-hand side of the machine to the left and back again). The result was that there were a lot of second-hand machines around, which were in excellent order and available at a significant saving. So naturally the middle classes copied their betters and took to cycling as well – 'cads on castors' as the aristocrats took to calling them.

That problem joined forces with another issue to create a proper financial meltdown. Much as had happened with the railways a few decades earlier – and as would do so a century later for internet start-ups – there was a mania for investing in bicycle companies. At one point there were four companies a week issuing prospectuses for public investment. New capacity was built, factories were created, bicycles were added to the stockpile ready for the summer rush. All of this came on stream just in time for the downturn.

To make matters worse most of the companies, even some relatively small ones, had been publicly floated. (There was a real enthusiasm for this – practically all the companies involved could have raised the money with a much safer bank loan.) This meant they were over-capitalised, and in order to satisfy shareholders they needed to make profits that were now unfeasibly huge. So, in a desperate attempt to generate turnover in a collapsing retail market, they cut prices. Raleigh dropped the price of its cheapest model from £20 to £10, and then again to, essentially, anything it could get. Humber reduced the price of its standard roadster to £4. The same happened across the whole industry. Raleigh was one of the most successful companies in Britain in 1897, but by 1898 it was on the verge of bankruptcy.[15]

Meanwhile, over in America, none other than Colonel Albert Pope chose this moment to start an export drive.[16]

The imports were cheaper, partly because they were mass-produced. Most of the domestic makers, like Raleigh, were still wedded to the idea of batch production, where a smallish number of bikes were made, then the design was revised, and some more were made. It produced a high-quality, up-to-date product, but at a price that no one would now pay.

A senior director at Raleigh complained, 'The better class of rider, instead of buying the highest-grade machines, are satisfied with a cheap machine. They also make their machine last two seasons, instead of, as heretofore, having new machines each year.' That wasn't the only problem: 'Hundreds of the swell class of rider is [sic] switching their allegiance to the motor cycle.'[17] Pope's imported Colombias fitted the new mood perfectly.

Any chance of re-establishing what had, for a while at least, seemed set to become the very affluent normality for the bicycle as a luxury item was finally snuffed out by first the motor bike and then the car, which came along a few years later and took whatever place cycling might still have had as a novelty entertainment for the rich. The turn of the twentieth century saw a perfect storm of economics, technology and class snobbery engulf bicycle riding. It completely changed the character of cycling and of cyclists, and did so over the course of no more than a couple of years. Cycling began to evolve in a more rational direction, one that happily involved many fewer maypoles, no soft balls, and had no use whatever for The Hungarian Band. In short, cycling was taken over by rather more dependable hands.

From the contemporary accounts, and even those of many historians, you'd be forgiven for thinking that the only people riding bicycles in the 1890s had titles and tiaras. It's understandable – it was very odd, but also very picturesque, and frankly rather funny. But as an under-current, other things were happening. Counter-jumpers were on bicycles, cads were on castors – and these less aristocratic riders generally eschewed doing lengths of the leafy byways of Battersea Park to roam further afield. And it wasn't just men. Women did the same.

One of the compulsory stopping-off points for any history of cycling and cyclists is H. G. Wells's *The Wheels of Chance*, published in 1896. It was one of two cycling novels of the era, the other being Jerome K. Jerome's less-celebrated follow-up to *Three Men in a Boat*, featuring the same cast, published in 1900 and called *Three Men on the Bummel*. (The latter book's fortunes were not helped by the fact that no one knew, or knows, what a 'bummel' is – on the last page, Jerome finally tells the reader that it's a journey without a purpose, of undefined length and which finishes where it started.) It tells you a certain amount about the status of cycling in the 1890s, and the status of cycling for most of the period since, that if you put them side by side on a shelf you will have before you almost the entire library of classic cycling novels.

The Wheels of Chance is the better book. For all that, its longevity probably has more to do with its place in cycling than in English literature, because it tells you rather more about cycling in that era than it does about the human condition. The main reason to read it today is for its unfussy evocation of the open roads of a quiet rural country, and the freedom that the safety bicycle had brought to relatively ordinary people. 'Pinewoods and oak forest, heathery moorland and grassy downs, lush meadows where shining rivers wound their lazy way . . .' It was an era when cycling could offer an escape from the city for the urban dweller that nothing else could. Bike riding was independent, simple and, if it wasn't yet quite cheap, it would be soon.

The plot is not a complicated one. The hero, Mr Hoopdriver (yes, that's his name), is a draper's assistant (yes, the quintessential counter-jumper). He had only just started cycling but decided to take his brand new £40 bicycle on a tour of southern England for his annual summer holiday despite the fact that, in the early chapters at least, he fell off it fairly regularly. Along the way he meets a lone woman, also on a bike, and wearing (then radical) bloomers. She has fled her stepmother's home in Surbiton, and is now being pursued by a bounder who offered to help her establish herself as an independent woman but who, inevitably, had less honourable plans for her. Hoopdriver, of course, saves her, then nobly rides away, back to his job in London, like a tweedy Superman. The whole thing could be turned into a slightly silly opera with minimal adaptation.

Hoopdriver is middle class, perhaps even lower-middle class, and his station in Victorian Britain is far from that of the participants in the society craze. But Wells still feels it plausible to have him mistaken for a duke on the strength of being on a bike. For a man such as Hoopdriver to take up cycling was still to trade up in class. His relationship with the woman (she's called Jessie Milton, but seems normally to be referred to by cycling critics as 'the New Woman') is confused by his attempts to oversell himself – he fancied himself easily confused with the heir to a baronet. Socially Hoopdriver was trying to head in one direction while cycling was heading in the other. Within a year or two, Wells could have written a cycling novel about a bicycle leading to an earl being mistaken for a draper, but of course no one would have read it, so he wrote *The War of the Worlds* instead.

Jessie is at least as interesting as Hoopdriver. A New Woman was a specific phenomenon, one that was closely associated with cycling. To the New Woman, the bicycle was more than a way to promenade in Battersea Park, or something to decorate with flowers. These women were independent-minded, pro-suffrage, early feminists. When they took up cycling, the mobility it offered made them even more of an affront to convention. The New Woman was subject to every reaction from patronising amusement to political concern to outraged horror, largely because she was everything a woman was not supposed to be. Such issues, of course, encompassed a much wider battle than just riding a bike, but the era has been a subject of fascination for cycling historians because cycling can be painted rather nobly as an enabler of real social change.

Cycling has been of much interest to feminist historians for exactly the same reason. There were all sorts of debates about women on bikes. They started with outright rage at the very idea. The first woman to ride a two-wheeler in Ireland, for instance, was Pearl Hillas, who rode around Dublin in 1888. The *Social Review* said that such was the 'anger and horror' that many furiously suggested her father ought to lock her up and throw the bicycle (and perhaps the key) in the Liffey.[18]

To shore up social convention there were medical experts to make dark predictions as to the fate of any female rider's reproductive health. The female pelvis was apparently very susceptible to bending under pressure – an unexpected bit of news to anyone who's ever had a baby, I imagine. To deal with the question of whether anyone would even want to reproduce with a cyclist, a

British doctor called Shadwell invented 'bicycle face' – a permanently engraved expression of strain and effort, complete with bulging eyes and clenched jaw, caused by the dual strain of both balancing on a bike and pedalling it, and to which there was naturally no cure.[19] 'Bicycle hands' were enlarged and lumpy and flattened, just like 'bicycle feet'. Special saddles and raised handlebars had to be devised because of the terrible danger of 'accidental sexual stimulation' (or perhaps more threateningly for world order, 'deliberate sexual stimulation').[20]

But the most visible battleground of early feminist cycling was dress. When Hoopdriver first encountered Jessie Milton, pretty much the first thing he noticed was what she was wearing: 'Strange doubts possessed him as to the nature of her nether costume. He had heard of such things of course. French, perhaps.'[21] She was wearing bloomers. I tend to associate bloomers with saucy *Last of the Summer Wine*-era comedy. In the nineteenth century they were a lot less frivolous. Unless you've waded through it, you would simply not credit the sheer quantity that was written about what women wore to go cycling during the 1890s. From a modern perspective the arguments and outrage and genuine disgust that women's outfits were capable of generating looks like an episode of collective insanity.

To set the scene – skip ahead if you're a costume drama fan – Victorian women were conventionally required to wear skirts that reached the ground. A Victorian gentlemen was more than capable of being titillated by an ankle. The skirt was invariably combined with a corset and a hat. None of this makes life easy for cycling – or, for that matter, anything else. A woman on an upright bicycle wearing a full skirt and a hat had the aerodynamic drag of a wardrobe with the doors open, and, like a penny-farthing rider, could be reduced to a standstill by a very modest headwind. The corset was part of the conspiracy, since it limited the amount of effort the rider could put into overcoming all that wind resistance before she passed out. A woman could be independent minded in conventional dress, but it was a lot harder to actually go anywhere.

One answer was for convention to get off its high horse, and let women who sought the freedom of cycling dress a bit more rationally, the better to be independent and mobile. The other was to make them put up with it, and hope that they'd moderate or abandon their ambitions. The extraordinary vehemence of the argument reflected a much bigger social debate happening in microcosm.

It was a very British argument. In France, there had been women riders since the dawn of cycling (and even racers, like Miss America) and while it certainly wasn't respectable, neither was it regarded as the sort of national scandal that would make a gentleman bite through the stem of his pipe in horror. Contrast that with the reaction in Britain when Tessie Reynolds rode from Brighton to London and back in 1893. Women riders weren't totally new – the first women's club had been formed a year earlier – but they didn't have the sheer attitude of Reynolds. She completed the 120 or so miles in around eight and a half hours, which was pretty sharp going any way you measured it, and she did it on a man's bicycle while wearing what was becoming known as 'rational' dress, in this a case a long jacket and a pair of loose-fitting below-the-knee breeches with stockings.[22]

At the office of *Cycling* magazine, this blew the editor's hat clean off his head: 'Every cyclist who truly loves the sport, every lady rider who has striven, in the face of many difficulties, to spread the gospel of the wheel amongst her sisters, every wheelman who has managed to retain a belief in the innate modesty and sense of becomingness in the opposite sex, will hear with real pain, not unmixed with disgust, of what it would be moderate to call a lamentable incident that took place on the Brighton Road last Sunday . . . We were just spared seeing her, but we heard from various sources that her attire was of a most unnecessary masculine nature and scantiness.'[23]

A whole industry grew up around women's cycling attire, from the conventional to the scandalous. There were screens designed to doubly protect the ankles of those who rode in a full skirt from impertinent eyes – the effect was much as if the woman in question had crashed her front wheel through an umbrella – and a 'saddle mask' to protect the rear. 'McNaughton's Bicycle Attachment' was a special women's mudguard that was shaped like a great eagle with outstretched wings, and was attached to the back of the seat tube. The head and neck extended over the rear wheel to protect the rider from anything thrown up from the road, the wings sheltered the full width of the back of the skirt and the legs folded down to form a bike stand. (I'm not making this up.)[24] There were skirts with leaded hems to ensure they didn't blow anywhere, and, I imagine, to give the ankles of the wearer a damned good bashing if she tried to walk in a hurry. There were voluminous divided skirts that attached to the ankles. There were skirts with highly complicated drawstring systems that converted them into something approximating baggy bloomers when a cord was pulled, rather like a sail being furled.[25]

It has to be said that the majority of women stuck with convention. Those who did not tended, in the end, to go for the straightforward bloomers, which were simple, sensible, and scandalous. Anything other than a normal skirt was a public political statement, so there wasn't much point in some sort of compromise. And, as with any public political statement, there were consequences. Women in 'rationals' were mocked; often they were jeered in the street, or even threatened. Two female tourists wearing them were pelted with mud and rubbish by an angry mob in Cork – this as late as 1899 – and it was far from a unique occurrence. And it wasn't just street yobs who took exception: an otherwise perfectly respectable girl found herself expelled from her school for having attended a cycle show in rationals in her own time.[26]

An especial source of anger at the time was the refusal of hotel and innkeepers to serve women in rationals. This was the subject of a much celebrated – and much misunderstood – court case. In 1898, Lady Harberton, a very substantial and middle-aged example of aristocracy, arrived at the Hautboy Hotel in Ockham in Surrey in what were described by witnesses as 'exceedingly baggy knickerbockers'. I've seen a picture of Lady Harberton modelling the garment in question. 'Extremely baggy' only begins to cover it. She looked like a tweed galleon in full sail. To the untutored eye she displayed all the dangerous liberal tendencies of the Albert Memorial.

The Hautboy Hotel's landlady saw it differently, and refused to admit Lady Harberton to the coffee room. She showed her to the public bar instead – a calculated insult, since the public bar was for working-class chaps to wear flat caps and drink ale, talk about dogfights, and ferment revolution. It was no place for a viscountess. The national Cyclists' Touring Club took the landlady to court for refusing to serve one of its members.[27] The CTC lost – the landlady had, after all, offered to serve her, just not where she wanted to be served. But the publicity was immense. The case was very widely reported, created a great deal of interest and debate and was the most high-profile event in the whole late-nineteenth-century saga of liberal women in dangerous trousers.

In the end, while the CTC had put a lot of money into the case and wanted to actually win, Lady Harberton and her associates were probably content. She was a committed *agent provocateur* – she was fond of walking up and down Oxford Street in knickerbockers and without a corset, with the intention of attracting attention. Her visit to the hotel was not an unhappy accident. She was an officer in the Rational Dress Society, and she went there because she was aware of previous rational-wearers having had trouble. Indeed, four years earlier she'd been refused service herself, on the basis her skirt didn't quite reach the ground and her 'full-length gaiters' were not to the landlady's taste. It was, in short, a set-up. Lady Harberton was quite a force when she was in full spate, and it's possible that the judge had some sympathy with the landlady.[28]

(Lady Harberton's enthusiasm for trousers should not be confused with zeal for social equality – one of her justifications for trouser-wearing was that if her housemaids wore them, they'd spend less time knocking her china and bric-a-brac over with their skirts. It would also probably be fair to say that her main interest in cycling was not as a means for getting about, but as a means to promote rational dress. She was, in the nicest possible way, a career troublemaker.)

By the time Lady Harberton went to war in her knickerbockers, contemporary accounts suggested that women were already winning. While some women could get pelted with mud in Cork in 1899, in other areas, especially Surrey, they could wear knee breeches without attracting much attention other than from a handful of committed reactionaries. There was a women's club in Newcastle for rational wearers only, which was well supported and seems to have attracted no outrage at all. There seems every chance that acceptance would only have spread.[29]

And then, it all went away again. The rational dress movement went into retreat. By 1903 women riders were almost universally back to skirts. The handful that weren't were of an older generation – ironically, rational dress became, if anything, a little old-fashioned. And cyclists and cycling were changing once again. Women's liberation was an upper-class and middle-class cause. As cycling became increasingly a working-class pastime, and even as rational dress became an entirely acceptable thing for women to wear, skirts were reasserted as the norm. They were still the main dress for women riders in 1916.

In truth, it was the First World War that changed women's dress, as it did for much else in gender politics.

Cycling had still done its part – being an independently minded and indecently mobile woman was never quite as scandalous again, because the world had seen such women riding through villages and towns, and the sky had not fallen in. In ten years or less bicycles had gained women a freedom they'd never known. Susan B. Anthony, the American who played a pivotal role in early feminism and suffrage, said that cycling had 'done more for the emancipation of woman than anything else', and, as the twentieth century dawned, there would have been few who would have argued with her.[30]

CHAPTER 8

Twentieth-Century Racing and the Loneliness of the Time Triallists

If you look back across the whole sweep of road racing through the twentieth century, the most puzzling aspect is just how bafflingly bad the British were at it. A fan born at just the wrong moment could have waited almost a lifetime for a world champion. A Tour de France winner took nearly two lifetimes to appear. The first Olympic road race champion from the UK in the history of the Games was Nicole Cooke in 2008. Up until then the entire medal haul from the road racing side of the sport, in 112 years, was three bronzes and one silver.

It's not as if racing wasn't something British riders wanted to do – the early racing scene was, as we've seen, vibrant, successful and even rather profitable. It was well supported by the public, it was a source of fascination in the press. To look at the pattern set by the early years, one would have expected James Moore's triumphs to set the tone for continued international glory. Yet by the end of the twentieth century, if you measured things by men's international road racing, as most fans do, Ireland, with a fraction of the population of the UK, was substantially the more successful nation. And Ireland had had, for obvious geo-political reasons, an almost identical start in cycling life.

Like so much else in UK cycling, the answer to a century of underachievement lies in those formative years of the late nineteenth century. The technology was new, the sport was young and growing fast. Anything must have seemed possible . . . before it all crashed headlong into the unshakable conservatism of the National Cyclists' Union, and the least radical 'rebel' sport has ever known, Mr Frederick Thomas Bidlake.

The pivotal event in this story can be nailed down to within a few hours, and its location to a few hundred yards. On the morning of 21 July 1894 on the Great North Road, Bidlake was being paced in a road race by Arthur Illsey and J. W. Stocks. Near the 57th milestone – on the modern A1 road not far from Huntingdon – the three of them overtook a carriage being driven by a woman (or, and this is relevant, a 'lady'). The horse panicked, and depending which telling of the story you believe, some permutation of the horse, carriage, woman and riders ended up in a heap in the ditch.[1] (The whole episode is one that has been recounted frequently down the years but from rather minimal contemporary sources, so the details will remain forever rather sketchy. The problem was that, of course, no one realised the significance of the incident at the time. It was a commonplace. But in any event, it's safe to say there was some considerable unhappiness.)

The woman, uninjured but distinctly annoyed, complained to the police. The police were not fans of racing on the highway, and there was always a certain amount of cat-and-mouse between race organisers and the cops. For example, the race that had been organised to prove the merits of the Rover safety bicycles had been advertised with a decoy course specifically to put the police off the scent. The police made clear their irritation, with an implication that a more interventionist stance would be the consequence.

There was a lot of general public hostility to what were called 'scorchers' – fast riders. It has a familiar ring to it. Bear in mind that breeches, stockings and riding jackets may look quaint now, but to many the open-road racers were very much the equivalent of a group of 18-year-olds racing between traffic lights in highly tuned hatchbacks on a Saturday night. Scorchers alarmed pedestrians, frightened horses, and indeed frightened all sorts of people who were unused to the idea of someone propelling themselves almost silently at 20 mph or more in a world that until very recently had proceeded at walking pace.

In what looks like an early instance of Stockholm syndrome, the National Cyclists' Union resolved the stand-off by banning all racing on the road. Their fear was one of bad PR: that all the respectable bits of cycling – the early touring, the promenading, the flower-bedecked musical rides and maypole dances – would be dragged down if the NCU acknowledged the legitimacy of riders whom the public recognised only as scorchers. There was no thought of defending the idea of a right to race on the roads, perhaps because road racing still very much played second fiddle to track racing. But it seems not to have occurred to the NCU that the riders who enjoyed road racing might not feel terribly inclined to just give up because the NCU said so.

The rebellion was a terribly, terribly well-mannered one. F. T. Bidlake and his club, the North Road CC, organised a time-trial race. Unpaced, which eliminated any groups of riders, and with riders starting one at a time, the whole idea was to avoid attracting any attention. The races were unannounced and unadvertised. If a policeman or anyone else should coincidentally turn up, unless they stood by the road for the several hours that a race might take and started to notice a pattern emerging, all they'd see would be a few solitary riders clipping along. It was a rebellion so subtle that no one really noticed or cared, so naturally it worked rather well.

The whole idea of an unpaced time trial wasn't new, but up until then it had been an occasional format. What Bidlake did was create a formal, regular sport out of adversity. By the time the NCU and the police worked out what was going on – which was really only a couple of years later – the hoo-hah from the initial incident had died down, and everyone just managed to rub along perfectly well.[2] In 1922 Bidlake was instrumental in forming the Road Racing Council to administer time trialling, and the whole thing was formally above board.

In the short term, Bidlake's 1895 race was successful in preserving racing on the road. In the long term it was possibly the greatest setback the sport ever experienced in the UK. In the rest of the world, in Europe and in Ireland, even in the Isle of Man, road racing developed into primarily a massed-start discipline: everyone setting off together, first man and bicycle across the finish line the winner. It's what everyone recognises as a bicycle race, from Eddy Merckx to Freddie Mercury. In the UK, Bidlake's time-trial format made it easy for the authorities to ban massed-start racing totally. Massed-start racing didn't so much get driven off the roads as scamper off them of its own accord.

In the 1890s it didn't matter very much. It was a technical difference as much as anything else, because road racing was not a fast sport. On rough dusty roads, on single fixed gears, on more primitive machines and in a world before speeds were high enough for aerodynamics to dominate, the tactics and drafting that came to define massed-start road racing were in their infancy. Road races, especially those over difficult terrain or roads, tended to quickly fragment into small groups or individuals – a bit like cross-country mountain-bike racing or cyclocross today. You could all start together or you could start one at a time, but the chances are that the result would be very similar.

From there, though, the sports diverged. Well known for their strength on the track, in the 1890s British riders were a presence in world road cycling as well. George Pilkington Mills won the first edition of Bordeaux–Paris in 1891. Arthur Linton finished fourth in the first Paris–Roubaix in 1896, and won Bordeaux–Paris in the same year. (This was the last British win in a Classic road race until Tom Simpson won the same race in 1963.) At the 1896 Olympic road race in Athens, Edward Battell won the bronze medal. The sport was weighted towards continental Europeans, partly through force of numbers, but there were British riders making the effort to get to the races, and punching above their weight when they got there. But from then on, the two worlds drifted apart.

The rift was deepened by the rigid British adherence to amateurism. When Battell won his bronze medal in the 1896 Olympics he was a butler at the British embassy in Athens – like his colleague Frank Keeping who won the 12-hour track race. Both of their entries into the Games were over the objections of many of Athens's British residents and diplomats, who felt that as butlers they were by definition not gentlemen, and so could not be considered amateur.[3] If you're wondering how the ability to decant claret conferred an unfair advantage in a bike race, you clearly haven't understood class and sport in Britain in the 1890s.

As professional massed-start road racing became the pinnacle of the sport elsewhere, in Britain amateur time trialling came to dominate. Its origins meant it developed into a strange, secretive sport. It happened early in the morning, in locations that were given only in a code. The cycling press was not allowed to mention where and when races would happen, only report results after they'd occurred.[4]

The quest for fast times above all else meant that the riders sought out the flattest, straightest, smoothest roads in the land. The Great North Road through Bedfordshire; the Bath Road near Newbury and Hungerford – entirely unremarkable places like these became the meccas for the sport. The race distances were almost always a nice round number, because time trialling was as much about setting records and best times as it was about winning: 25 miles, 50 miles, 100 miles; 12-hour racing and 24-hour racing was common.

More often than not there wasn't even a headquarters or a changing room – riders would simply gather as unobtrusively as they could on the roadside verges near the start timekeeper. The courses were a simple out-and-back. The competitors rode to half distance, turned around a marshal standing in the middle of the road then rode back to finish opposite where they had started.

The photos of races usually show the riders at the turn, frequently taking a drink from a helper. Riders always wore full-length black alpaca tights and jackets, because that was what the rules required. In the photos the riders are as likely to be turning round the marshal in either direction, because the roads were so quiet that it didn't really matter what side you were on. There was sometimes a tiny handful of spectators standing watching, but often there was no one apart from the rider, the marshal, and perhaps a helper or timekeeper – otherwise just an empty, dusty road with telegraph poles stretching into the distance. The challenge was to ride alone, and that was exactly how it was. It was a sport you could only do for love, because you couldn't conceivably do it for anything else. It clashed with the rest of the world, but it chimed with a certain British view of things. The discipline that could only have come to be in the mid-1890s, when cycling was, for want of a better word, posh. Even the rebels had taken their blank sheet of paper and devised a strictly amateur sport of the utmost respectability.

Time trialling quickly became the accepted compromise between competitive young men and easily scared horses. On the other hand, massed-start racing remained not just neglected, but essentially taboo. In 1914, when it was suggested that the Isle of Man (outside the NCU's jurisdiction) might host the World Championships complete with massed-start racing, Bidlake deemed such a notion, 'A superfluous excrescence . . . Unpaced, solitary speed-men perform magnificently, unobtrusively, with no obstructive crowds and give no offence. I can't believe that our roadmen want to alter all this.' This was not an opinion that would have met with much argument from the racing fraternity.

From a racing point of view, time trialling isolated the UK from the rest of the world. It was insular, eccentric, and it made it all but impossible for British riders to compete on a world stage on the road. The reasons that it took until 2012 for Britain to produce a Tour de France winner in Sir Bradley Wiggins can be traced back to F. T. Bidlake's incident on the Great North Road without any terrible over-simplification of cause and effect. In a fine example of holding a grudge, one old bike racer I interviewed recently said, 'The bloody North Roaders. If it hadn't been for them and their forelock tugging we'd have had a Tour champion a hundred years ago.'

It is, however, only fair to say that one of the reasons time trialling was so successful at driving out demand for massed-start racing was because it worked rather well. There was clearly something going for it, since it went on to form the bedrock of racing in the UK for the next hundred years or more. Time trialling was accessible, simple, cheap and very popular. It fitted in nicely with the life of a club, who could organise events with a minimum of effort, meaning there was a huge choice of races over different distances and different courses, from the beginning of the season in March through until October. If you wanted to see your heroes win the Tour de France, a sport that was limited to time trialling was a disaster, but if you wanted to go bike racing yourself, it was a triumph.

I ought to declare an interest here, in that I spent most of my bike-racing career as a time-trial rider. That world still exists, almost unchanged. It's still often a sport of the early mornings, and of long straight roads – as often as not the very same roads it started out on. I live only a few miles from the start line of Bidlake's first time trial, and until a couple of years ago there was racing every weekend on what was to all intents and purposes the same course. The Great North Road became the A1, a dual carriageway that bypassed its villages, while the signposts grew from painted wooden fingers to billboard-sized sheets of aluminium. But still, not long after dawn on a Sunday morning, time triallists would gather quietly at a village hall, and then set out to test themselves against the old road and the watch.

A 120-year time-lapse film would show huge changes to everything around that road, but the riders would remain more or less the same. One of the histories of the sport, by Bernard Thompson, is called *Alpaca to Skinsuit* and charts 50 years of the time trialling, but the title reminds us that the clothes have been as big a change as it's seen. I've sometimes wondered if anyone ever bought a house in one of the villages that serve as race HQs for time trialling without knowing about us. What would they have made of an unexpected invasion of bike riders at 5 a.m. on a Sunday, and of the fact that by 9 a.m. we would all quite probably have gone again?

My first ever race was on Bidlake's old course. The sport still uses the once-secret codes to define courses. By the time I raced on it, time-trialling's original course was known as the F1 – 'F' for the area of the country just north of London, and '1' for the first course in the area. The 25-mile variant I was racing on was the F1/25. The 50-mile version was the F1/50, and so on. Other areas of the country use different codes – in Yorkshire (an area known to us time triallists by the letter 'V') you get courses like the V718, a ten-mile course near Hull. The logic of it has always escaped me. I think the '7' is for Hull, and maybe the '1' is for ten miles. I've no clue what the '8' means. I could ask someone from Yorkshire, but it would spoil the slight air of mystery, which I rather like.

The official reason for retaining the secret codes is that they enable officials and timekeepers to distinguish between different courses located in the same area – near Port Talbot in South Wales the R25/3H, R25/3L and the R25/3G are almost identical, but with differing start and finish points of a few hundred yards. Near Cambridge the E2/25 and the E2/25b were, until the courses were re-coded, several miles apart. The codes were changed for the benefit of idiots like me who would enter a race on one course, and turn up to the headquarters for the other one.

I think the truth is that time trialling's participants still quietly enjoy the feeling of exclusivity that the codes give them. The race details don't tell you where the race is any other way, and there's no earthly reason why they shouldn't at least include the name of the nearest town. The sport's not a secret any more, it barely was even at the beginning, but in some ways it behaves as if it is. Until the 1960s race information and results were posted to riders marked 'Private and Confidential'. Entry via the internet is a recent innovation. Until just a couple of years ago the only way to enter an 'open' event was to fill in a fairly hefty entry form and post it to the organiser along with a cheque, to arrive no fewer than 11 days before the event. But the cheque was usually only for about £10, and you can't really argue with that. Stamps constituted about 5 per cent of my race entry outgoings for a season.

The prize money on offer in time trialling is in line with the entry fees. When Sir Bradley Wiggins rode at a local time trial a few years ago a reporter for a national paper who wrote a short feature about it was so astonished by an event prize list that went '1st: £50.00, 2nd: £25.00, 3rd: £10.00' that he assumed the decimal points were typos. I was able to assure him that they were not, and that it was a decent payday with the decimal points exactly where they were.

At least prize money is now permitted. Until the 1970s, accepting prize money of any sort made you professional. Instead what happened was that a nominal sum was awarded, and to claim it you had to send a receipt for something to that value from your local bike shop to the race secretary, who'd reimburse you. That's if the prize wasn't something random from a local sponsoring business. One of my predecessors as a columnist at *Cycling Weekly* can recall the occasion in the 1970s that a friend of his won a birdcage, clearly the result of a local shop owner looking for something terminally unsaleable to donate to a local race.

Further back, in the 1930s, one rider recalled that piglets were a common prize at track races: 'At the end of the meet we would head for home on the track bikes. In those days there were only paper bags, no plastic, and the pig would be in one of these, hanging by the handles over the bars. Its front feet and head would be poking over the top of the bag. All was well until the pig got overexcited, probably speeding down a hill. The excitement would be too much for the pig's bladder-control and in no time the bottom of the bag would be soaked. The race was to get home before the bottom gave way completely, and the pig would land on the road and head off as fast as its legs would carry it, chased by the family, who would have to take turns carrying it under one arm while riding home.'5

By the time I was racing not only were riches available in £50 instalments, but no one minded if a sponsor paid you to ride. There was even quite a bit of press coverage in the magazines and, eventually, online. In an era when cycling in the UK was growing, but didn't yet have international stars for the press to focus on, there was an opportunity for riders who liked riding against the clock to make a career of time trialling, as I did, for a few years at least. F. T. Bidlake would have loved the idea that his sport was still running 120 years after he waved off the first rider at his inaugural event. And he'd have banned me for life on the spot for accepting money to do it.

CHAPTER 9

1900–1920: Cycling and Moting

For all of cycling, the sport and the pastime, most of the first half of the twentieth century was a strange period of near stasis. The 15 years that preceded the turn of the century were a headlong helter-skelter of invention and change that built to a crescendo . . . and then suddenly cycling burst through into silence. The infatuation of the fashionable ended. The aristocrats left. The more socially ambitious elements of the middle classes drifted away after them. It felt like the history of cycling had stopped. Suddenly bicycles were just bicycles, and their riders were just cyclists.

It's true that the technology was mature. I've ridden bikes from the 1890s and the early 1900s, and apart from their age they are entirely unremarkable. In 2015, to coincide with Sir Bradley Wiggins's attempt on the world hour record, I made an attempt to beat the first official hour record, the 35 kilometres set by Henri Desgrange in 1893, using a period bike. There were only three things that really gave it away. It had a rather upright riding position, inherited from the penny-farthing where the saddle and the bars were necessarily very close together. The chain was very wide, at about half an inch, and a bit unrefined. It looked like it had come from some piece of ancient agricultural equipment, and beyond whatever other merits it might have had, it was an outstanding means of transferring oil from its loving owner's shed onto almost everything I owned.

The bike also had a mounting step by the back wheel just like a penny-farthing, because, through habit, that was how the first safety bike riders got on board. But it looked exactly like the peg you get on a BMX for doing tricks, so I chalked it up to the Humber bicycle company being a century ahead of the game.

I spent an hour riding round Herne Hill track at a pretty decent pace on this old machine, and the experience was not much different from going out to race any bike that didn't quite fit. I found that when I leaned forward to try to ape the semi-aero riding position you see in old photographs, my hands were oddly far back – the arm position was akin to doing dips on parallel bars. All the while, though, the overwhelming feeling was one of normality, of a modern bike. Maybe of a modern bike that hadn't been designed for racing, and which had grown a little bit loose around the bearings. But there was nothing very strange about riding it. (I didn't break the record, though I'm blaming that on my rather heavy road tyres. It's counterintuitive, but early tyres were very good. For some applications they were at least as good as modern ones, and Desgrange's track tyres would certainly have rolled faster than mine. Without that disadvantage I'd definitely have stuck it to the 122-year-old bloke.)

Without relentlessly changing technology to drive interest, and with the slump caused by a saturated market, the excitement and novelty went out of cycling. Cycling stopped being something you'd do for the sheer thrill of your amazing new circus skill, and became something you might come to love for better and more grown-up reasons. Bicycles and cyclists were settling down together, and finding their real purpose.

The chronicling of the bicycle and its glories changed too. The society cycling journals, published and edited by the gentry, vanished one by one. Especially unfortunate in its timing was *The Hub*, founded for women cyclists in the summer of 1896. In a masterclass in missing the crest of the wave, *The Hub*'s very first issue artlessly reported that London's Hyde Park was entirely and mysteriously devoid of cyclists. The society ladies who were to be its subject, its market and most of its contributors had upped and gone.[1]

The leather-bound cycling manuals disappeared too. So did the jolly accounts by the aristocracy of their tours of the Black Forest and such like, with their dedications to the Prince of Wales. Instead, cycling literature became dominated by plainer magazines, especially *Cycling* magazine, founded in 1891, and one of the small handful of cycling periodicals to make it to the twentieth century intact.

History in this form immediately had less sweep. Self-conscious narrative was displaced by detail; cycling became everyday, and the concerns of cyclists were suddenly about the best way to oil a chain, and not so much about the place of the bicycle in the history of the world. The same thing happens to most of the world's great inventions, but it usually has the grace to happen a bit more slowly.

‖ ‖ ‖

The assumption of most of us is that the car killed off cycling. It did nothing of the sort, because nothing killed off cycling. Cycling continued to grow into the early years of the twentieth century. Lower prices and large numbers of second-hand bikes meant thousands could be cyclists. Even in 1898, in the midst of the falling roof-joists of 'the slump', a record 50,000 cyclists and their bikes passed through Waterloo station over Easter on their way to the coast.[2]

You would only be able to float an argument that the car (or anything else) killed off cycling if your interest extended no further than the lives of people with titles and/or townhouses in Belgravia. Even then, there were plenty of members of the upper class who continued to ride. However, the view that the car in the first years of the twentieth century was an essential part of cycling's 'downfall' is not even rooted in class snobbery, it's rooted in just about the only thing shallower: fashion snobbery. Cycling stopped being the thing to be seen doing because poor people could now do it too. That's all.

But fashion, finally, is where the car comes into the story. Motoring *was* the thing to be seen doing, despite the small numbers of cars on the road. By 1900 there were still only about 8,000 cars in the UK. Even in 1905, the number was still only around 15,000 – although reliable statistics for very early car numbers are very hard to find, and some sources suggest the number of registered cars was even lower than this. Whatever the exact number, there certainly weren't enough of them to kill off anything other than by actually running it over. (Something which, it must be said, happened quite frequently.)

Not only were there not a lot of cars, the speed limits for them were low. The 'great emancipation' of 1896, when the speed limit of 4 mph in the country and 2 mph in town was lifted (along with the man with a flag) was a liberalisation that extended merely to a not awfully Mr Toad-esque 14 mph. The rather pleasing response of the Surrey police to this was to dispatch 125 officers on bicycles to apprehend speeding motorists. I do very much like the picture of a motorist being pulled over by a uniformed bobby on a bicycle. On the other side of the argument, the AA employed patrols of cyclists to warn motorists of police speed traps. The boot was not quite as firmly on the foot of the motorists as subsequent history might have led many of us to assume.

Early motorists actually owed a lot to cyclists. The cyclists were the ones who had pushed for proper maintenance of the old roads, and had prevented them disintegrating into the total disrepair that would otherwise have been the consequence of the railways. The roads were falling apart when local National Cyclists' Union branches started to demand the enforcement of the laws mandating their repair. In Birmingham in 1888, for instance, no fewer than eight local surveyors were summoned before the courts to explain the state of the local roads.[3]

Sometimes affairs were less confrontational. In Surrey, between 1890 and 1908, cyclists got together to raise money for 'road menders' feeds' – essentially a charity to provide meals for road menders.[4] The Surrey road that was the focus of the fundraising was the one through Ripley, a stretch of highway famed throughout the country for its incomparable smoothness, and so well known that riders would travel for miles just to ride a few turns up and down it. H. G. Wells used it for a meeting between Hoopdriver and Jessie in *The Wheels of Chance* – like Albert Pope's carefully curated street in Boston, it showed what was possible. (Ripley is just off the A3 from London to Portsmouth. If you fancy a proper cyclists' pilgrimage, go and have a drink in the Anchor, which was the hub of Ripley Road cycling. Part of the pub's popularity was due to its having welcomed cyclists from the very beginning of the pastime when other hostelries were often more hostile. It's never too late to show your appreciation; extra marks, obviously, for turning up in plus-twos or bloomers.)

It wasn't just the roads. The country inns, like the Anchor at Ripley, would have struggled even more badly than they did in the years between the stagecoaches and the motor car if it hadn't been for the cyclists. Signposts would have been even more neglected than they were; there would have been fewer mechanics in far-flung villages. Almost the whole infrastructure required to go for a drive in the countryside without getting lost, breaking down and starving to death had been kept in business by cyclists. Even the idea of 'going for a drive' took its cue from cycling in the first place. In this context it's not surprising that a large number of early motorists were cyclists – just as a very large proportion of cycle manufacturers went into car and motor bike production in the 1900s, with varying degrees of success.[5]

Cars in the early 1900s were regarded as more like enhanced bicycles than anything else. (I use the word 'enhanced' with some caution, lest I find my lawn occupied by vengeful cycling campaigners.) Certainly cars weren't billed as competition. *Cycling* magazine was welcoming enough to change its name in 1900 to *Cycling and Moting*, 'moting' being the most popular of the names for the new activity. The assumption was the cyclists and motorists ('motists'?) were cut from the same adventurous cloth. The key question revolved around whether you were the sort of free spirit who wanted to have a picnic on Brighton beach. How you got yourself and your sandwiches there was a footling side issue. The roads were for everyone, rich and poor, cyclist and motorist, with a parp of the horn and a ring of the bell.

In 1906 the Cyclists' Touring Club sought to change its constitution to allow the admission of motorists. It would become simply 'The Touring Club'. The judge who presided over the case turned out to be rather more far-sighted than the CTC's committee: Sir Thomas Warrington foresaw that cyclists and motorists would one day end up on different sides of the argument.[6] As if to underline this opinion, the very next issue of *Cycling and Moting* abruptly returned to its original title, with no editorial comment on the change, as if the whole thing had simply never happened. (There is an alternative reading of the CTC argument. The CTC had been founded as a distinctly posh organisation, and many of its members were exactly the sort of cyclist who, as they got older, would take to motoring with great aplomb. I imagine they liked the raffish look of the goggles. So the enthusiasm for motoring may have been because the members of the club at that time were actually moving away from cycling rather than because they wanted to extend a welcoming hand to some other chaps who also liked to drink warm beer at country inns.)

What the car did do was take the upper classes away from cycling. Without it, after the price-crash and the slump, and the arrival in cycling of a distressingly broad cross-section of humanity, there's every chance that upper-class cycling would have survived and maybe even come to thrive again. After all, they can't all have been doing it just because the Prince of Wales liked watching Miss Snell's ladies throwing soft balls to each other. Some of them must have come to actually like it. They could, I'm quite confident, have found a way of cycling that would have allowed the maintenance of the maximum possible class snobbery while minimising contact with counter-jumpers and men who repaired water closets. But you could do too many of the good bits of cycling with a car – the countryside, the inns, the sightseeing – and it was even more tempting to travel by car when motoring was novel and very fashionable. Depending on how you feel about the upper classes awheel, the timing of the car's arrival was either disastrous or miraculous.

So, it was a combination of circumstances that left cycling destined to become an activity for the middle and working classes, and as time went by, bike riding became more closely identified with the workers. That's not to say it was in any way less valuable for that, or that it was somehow disreputable. If the society craze had done nothing else, it had left cycling as respectable, especially for women, and as an inexpensive recreation and a means of independent transport, the workers had much more use for cycling than the aristocrats ever had.

The traditions of touring grew and matured. When the Shops Act of 1911 provided for a half-day holiday in the week, cycling received another boost. Clubs thrived, and time trialling kept growing. The industry recovered from the disaster of the 1890s, and towns like Birmingham, Coventry and Nottingham did well from the bicycle. The number of makers fell but their size grew – between 1897 and 1913 the number of cycle makers in Birmingham fell from 308 to 160, but the proportion of the workforce they employed had risen to an incredible 27 per cent.[7] By 1914 Raleigh, which had teetered on the edge of the abyss in 1898, was the biggest bike manufacturer in the world.[8] The car had influenced cycling in the UK, but it certainly hadn't killed it. If anything it had made it the great pastime of the ordinary people.

The downside was political. Cycling was starting to lack advocates among the ruling classes. And one day that would come to matter.

ǁ   ǁ   ǁ

Cycling might have lost one sort of political player, but it attracted some new ones. There were several points in the twentieth century where cycling and politics became very closely linked.

A few years ago, having grown tired of what seemed like altogether too much travelling to get to higher-profile bike races in far corners of the country, I decided I'd stick to competing in some smaller local races for a couple of months. One of the first local races I did was that of the Fenland Clarion Cycling Club. It was a very pleasant race, friendly and well organised. Unfortunately the field was a little weaker than it might have been if I'd taken myself to one of the bigger races, so I won by more than was, I think, polite. This made one or two of my fellow competitors rather angry with me, and it was suggested that I might like to go back to my wind tunnel, and perhaps, this time, stay there.

I'd long since grown used to 'Clarion' in the name of a cycling club: the Fenland Clarion, Bolton Clarion, North Lancashire Clarion, and quite a few more. Very little surprises you with club names, because cycling clubs are fond of a bit of poetry. 'Somewhere-or-other Wheelers' is common; the Hitchin Nomads organised the first race I ever rode – they were from Hitchin, but lacked a regular meeting place; the Velo Club Free Press was named after a Cambridge pub ('the Free Press' being, in itself, an odd name for a pub); the San Fairy Ann CC was named phonetically for the French '*Ça ne fait rien*' – the 'it doesn't matter' cycling club borrowing a phrase that soldiers brought back from the First World War, and which was once a commonplace verbal shrug.

Road names are common, too: like F. T. Bidlake's North Road CC, which was named for the road out of London, and which was founded to promote cycling on what's now the A1; the Bath Road Club, named for what's now the A4, and which ran what was for many years perhaps the most famous time-trial race of them all, the Bath Road 100.

So at first glance, 'Clarion' seemed to fit with this slight eccentricity. The only clue that there was more to it came in the annual race handbook, where there was always an advert for the *National Clarion*. It was headed by an old hand-drawn logo of a goddess in billowing robes blowing a long trumpet, surrounded by banners saying, 'Socialism, the hope of the world,' and 'Fellowship is life; lack of fellowship is death.' Not many clubs ever advertised, and those that did tended to lead with their cycling, so the *Clarion* advert was a bit of a curiosity.

Strangely, the *Clarion* started out as a newspaper. It was never supposed to have anything to do with cycling at all. It was founded in 1891 by Robert Blatchford, a man with no real interest in cycling but a considerable interest in socialism. He was the son of an actress, and he'd spent his youth travelling northern England on the back of a cart full of props and costumes. He ran away from his mother's itinerant lifestyle and became a soldier, then a journalist, but remained in his attitude to life a drifter and a bit of a chancer.[9] He was also fiercely patriotic – a trait that now seems an odd fit with socialist politics, but was rather more common at the time. Blatchford's socialism was inspired by the slums of Manchester and by William Morris, and Morris's 'fellowship is life; lack of fellowship is death' was also the message of his paper. The *Clarion* was moderately popular, especially in its early days, although it would be fair to say that at no point did the editor of *The Times* anxiously draw a graph of its sales on his office wall and worry about how to deal with it.

Blatchford and his paper's socialism was not that of smoky rooms and interminable doctrinal debate. It was about fellowship and the open air – the chance to get out of the cities and back into the countryside for a bit, in good company and good spirits. The paper had politics to underpin it, but its actual content included news, stories, puzzles and jokes of highly variable quality. To call its outlook 'fun for all' would be to trivialise it, but if the emphasis goes on the 'all' that wouldn't be so very far away.

So perhaps its appeal to the cyclists shouldn't have been a surprise, but it was. The National Clarion Cycling Club was founded as early as 1895, but it was the early twentieth century before it started to hit its stride, growing to 77 local Clarion clubs by 1897, and then to a remarkable 230 in 1909.[10] The outlook of the Clarion clubs fitted the cycling that took over from the craze years, as bike riding became accessible to skilled workers with some disposable income. The beer flowed freely, and the politics was not an aggressive part of one of the weekend tours or Easter holidays, when the clubs headed out of the northern industrial cities to the Peak District or the Dales. These were people who wanted to just get on with a socialist life rather more than they wanted to ferment revolution.

The Clarion organisation was pleasingly chaotic. National AGM meetings sometimes ended up being organised by someone randomly picking a place and a date, without reference to whether there was anywhere for those attending to stay, or even if there was a hall available for the meeting. One AGM, much to the satisfaction of almost everyone involved, took place in a churchyard, because no one arranged anything else. At another, a hopelessly incompetent national committee was re-elected 'in the hope they'll do better next time'.

This was exactly as Blatchford wanted it. Enjoying good company came first, and since there was every chance that an attempt at decisive administration would just make enemies of friends . . . well, decisive administration could go hang. Disorder, in its theory and its practice, was what Blatchford relished, and it was key to the Clarion's appeal, because fellowship was what mattered. It took until 1903 for anything vaguely resembling a proper conference to happen at all, and by that time the annual meetings had over a thousand Clarion riders in attendance, from a total membership of around 7,000.[11]

I say 'Clarion riders' – they called themselves 'Clarionettes', which sounds like a brass clarinet, or like a group of grown-ups begging not to be taken too seriously. They called their traditions 'Clarionese'. Their traditions could be rather odd: one Clarionette seeing another Clarionette out on the road would shout, 'Boots!' as a greeting, the other would shout, 'Spurs!' as a reply.[12] The origins of this strangely specific bit of Clarionese are not entirely clear.

Socialism was still central to club activities. It was a socialism that was vaguely defined, but both the *Clarion* paper and the club had very little urge to try to delineate it any better by endless argument. That wasn't what the Clarion was about. There was no hierarchy, there was no very specific political goal, because such things would breed resentment and tension. Friendly disagreement was much preferable to unfriendly compromise. You couldn't be off-message, because the Clarion took care to ensure that no one really knew what the message was.

The chaos didn't mean that they didn't campaign, though. The Clarion Scouts – a more evangelist subset of the disorganisation – distributed campaigning literature and stuck up posters. There was a sort of 'flying-speaker' service – the Clarion would provide a socialist orator to any public meeting that had a use for one, in the same way as modern campaign groups can provide someone to answer the call of a *Newsnight* researcher at a moment's notice. Speakers regularly rode up to 50 miles each way to meetings. It's hard not to be impressed by the idea of riding perhaps three hours into a headwind on a winter afternoon, delivering a rousing speech, and riding home again in the dark.[13] Such activities weren't entirely ineffective either. It's possible to trace a thread through the Clarion's campaigning and its role in the formation of the Independent Labour Party of the early 1900s all the way to the British Labour Party of the twenty-first century.[14]

Until the 1950s the Clarion ran 'Clarion Camps'. First at Bucklow Hill, then Handforth and Marston, all in Cheshire, and finally in Lancashire's Ribble Valley, the Clarionettes built clubhouses, camping grounds, orchards and kitchen gardens, and held concerts, games and sports. It was an example of the same outdoor instinct that led, in the first half of the twentieth century, to the Scouts, the Ramblers and the Youth Hostels. It was another way, perhaps the best way, to express socialism as something workers could just get on and do rather than something to talk about. It was Blatchford's ideal of fellowship.

It was also important that the camps included women. The bicycle was viewed by the Clarion as an essential part of female liberation. Bicycles allowed women to be mobile, to travel on equal terms with men, which made the bicycle a political artefact on its own. 'Beneficial though women's suffrage has been,' said Blatchford, 'I would place it second to the pneumatic tyre in the general life of our working people.'[15] (A comment with a strange echo in Billy Connolly's joke that, 'Marriage is a great invention, but so is the bicycle repair kit.')

The Clarion's women staffed the 'Clarion Vans', caravans that toured north-west England and South Wales, distributing literature and promoting the Clarion's brand of socialism. These never-ending tours, with a rolling cast of Clarionettes, lasted for almost 20 years.[16]

The Clarion clubs are still going. At the turn of the twenty-first century there were around 800 members across 18 clubs. There are even new clubs still being formed – Malmesbury Clarion CC was established in 2012 – but the Clarion's high point, at least in terms of membership numbers, was just before the First World War, with somewhere between 7,000 and 8,000 members, spread over 200 clubs. From then on, with the exception of a brief revival in the early 1930s, the Clarion has been growing smaller. The politics took a back seat many decades ago. In the 1930s Blatchford recalled how the decline had set in: 'All went merrily for some years and then a number of earnest young men joined up, and there arose a demand for "organisation". I pointed out that fellowship was a genial crowd of congenial spirits, and that it was impossible to organise friendship. But the fellowship was organised, and its glamour slowly faded.'[17]

The *Clarion* newspaper suffered badly in the First World War, when its patriotic outlook and support for the war jarred with the more international vision of socialism that had come to prevail, and it closed in 1931.

The Clarion clubs captured the mood of cycling in the 1900s. Cycling had moved on from being a thing of fashion, from the expense of the early bikes, from being boxed-in by class. If you're of a sentimental disposition, it gives you a nice warm feeling to claim that the

Clarion captured the mood of cycling for all time. There is something about the ideals of friendship, equality, non-conformity and activism that almost anyone might feel pleased to have as their own. After all, who would want to carry a torch for their opposites?

While the Clarion was at its height in the years before the First World War, a rather less liberal (but often just as chaotic) organisation was equally interested in the bicycle. The British Army had noticed that a bike was cheaper than a horse, easier to repair and marginally less prone to outbreaks of hysterics at the sound of gunfire. The army seemed blissfully unconcerned by any issues of practicality should a battle be held somewhere other than a paved parking lot, or by the fact that, should the worst come to the worst, a bicycle was a damn sight harder than a horse to cook and eat.

There was even a drill book for cyclists. It was the work of an officer whose only experience of cycling had been on a penny-farthing. This attracted the sarcastic attention of none other than H. G. Wells, who was always keen to start a fight with the British Army. Wells was quick, for example, to point out that the pages dealing with how best to carry a sword while riding a bicycle were, perhaps, a little outdated. He also suggested that the tactics of the pikeman, on which most of the book was based, were not a very obvious starting point, and that some experiments with cyclists in simulated battle might be more useful.[18] The British Army, on the whole, rejected these criticisms. So the 14,000 army cyclists who headed to northern France with a bicycle in 1914 could be confident they wouldn't come to any harm by getting their sword tangled in the spokes of the front wheel.

Wells was right, of course, but only in the same sense as an expert would likely tell you there is a right way and a wrong way to get hit by a falling piano. The argument about the best formation for an infantry unit to adopt while mounting a bicycle bayonet charge was rendered somewhat moot by their sheer uselessness in the mud and the trenches of the First World War. The army had probably been taken in by the bikes used in the Boer War. There, the hot and dusty conditions had been rather better suited to two wheels. Bikes were used for scouting, for carrying homing pigeons, and for delivering dispatches. Lord Baden-Powell had even personally used a bicycle in the Boer War, from which he flew a kite with a camera attached for taking reconnaissance photos, which was as cunning a use for a bike as you could think of. It was to the spy satellite what two tin cans and a bit of string are to the internet.

As far as cycling in the First World War was concerned, there was a bit of messengering and traffic direction in the early days. There was even, rather inventively, some use of stationary bikes for generating electricity in trench dugouts.[19] (Remember that the next time you're on a stationary trainer and think you're having a bad time.) And that was about it.

That was a pity, really. The army had put so much effort into the fighting bicycle. Not just two-wheelers either. They repeated all the mistakes of the early nineteenth century when they combined human power with heavyweight engineering. There was a four-wheeled pedal-powered gun carriage that bore two men and two machine guns. On the flat it was a bit ponderous, but on a hill it was impossible to progress at all, which was hardly a surprise since it weighed nearly a fifth of a ton. On the other hand, when you fired the guns, the lack of any mechanism to deal with the recoil meant it could quite literally fly. For a slightly lighter-weight fighting bike, the army designed a tandem with a machine gun for the stoker to operate. Again, one suspects recoil might have been an issue if you were attempting a broadside while under way, but at least it opened up the possibility of a dogfight on tandems.[20]

Even that wasn't the end of it. There were bicycles adapted to run on railway lines, which shared all of an armoured train's inability to take evasive action or do anything remotely unpredictable but none of the actual armour that might have mitigated this defect. There was even a war reporter's bicycle produced, which had a typewriter welded to the handlebars. The idea was that the reporter, as he rode through the landing shells, could stop 'and record all his impressions of the battle surging around him'.[21] There is no record of any war reporter trying to combine a death wish with their best one-hundred-words-a-minute and actually use it.

It all shows a touching enthusiasm for the bicycle. It was so exciting that surely it could do anything, cheaper, faster, better. But of course none of this stuff was the slightest use. When it came down to it the motor bike, the horse, the tank and even the car were better ways of getting around a Flanders battlefield.

In the Second World War, many of the soldiers arrived on the Normandy beaches with folding bikes. Photos show troops wading through the surf carrying already assembled bikes – their expectation had been that they were going to be able to wheel them down the ramp of the landing craft straight onto the beach and ride off. They just ended up as awkward encumbrances. It would probably be fair to say that France was liberated despite the bicycle, not because of it.

There was some concern back in the UK that German paratroops might make use of bicycles. In a scene that *'Allo 'Allo!* would have rejected as too far-fetched, a War Department information film showed an enemy paratrooper disguised as a nun suddenly whipping a folding bike out from below his habit, and riding off on it.[22] At the same time, bike shops were advised to remove all pedals from stock bikes, and cyclists in general were requested to disable bikes by removing as many critical nuts as they could when they left them, so that any paratroopers who didn't arrive dressed as Brompton-packing nuns wouldn't be able to steal them.

At least the bike-stealing fears showed some insight. Bicycles were key to the Japanese invasion of Singapore in 1942. The Japanese army didn't use folding bikes or parachutes. Instead, a scant 35,000 troops took the colony, and they did it by riding down the excellent roads that the British had built on the Malay Peninsula, using bicycles that they'd stolen from wherever they could find them after they'd landed. They weren't even allowed to bring a bike on the invading ships if they wanted to. A witness described the Japanese carrying guns and equipment, riding three or four abreast in large pelotons, laughing and singing as they went. Just like a club run on a nice warm day.[23]

That was, however, the only properly successful use of the bicycle in war. Despite all the efforts of the British and other armies, aside from the Singapore invasion and Baden-Powell's spy-kite, it was pretty much a bust. The more warlike you make a bicycle the less use it is. It's a nice, if self-satisfied, adjunct to the ideal of the bike as a democratic ideal. In the end cycling was, as it always had been, better at opening up the world in more peaceful ways.

CHAPTER 10

1920–1958: The Tourists

The years between the twentieth century's two great wars don't seem so very far away now, or so very alien. Certainly not in comparison to the years before the First World War. The writing was modern – Waugh, Wodehouse, Fitzgerald; the communications were modern – the telephone, the train, the aeroplane; the music was modern, or at least, fairly modern – it was the jazz age. If you can remember a time before the internet, you're pretty much there.

Above all, there was the sheer pace of everything. The 1920s was a decade in constant motion. In London, even the socialites were obsessed with getting from A to B – a party on a typical night out would jump into a car at the slightest chance and roar drunkenly around London as fast as it could weave through the traffic of other partygoers doing the same thing. Starter in one restaurant, main course in another, pudding probably forgotten altogether in the rush to get to a jazz club. It was fast, exciting, and soaked in post-war delirium.

It wasn't an era where you heard an awful lot about the bicycle. The bright young things were not much for oil lamps and cotter pins, and bicycles had become too useful to be fashionable.

But despite this near invisibility, the period between the wars is often held up as a golden age of cycling. It was certainly a golden age for the bicycle itself. In Britain in the years between the wars, bicycles were sold and used in vast numbers. By 1936 there were reckoned to be ten million bicycles in regular use, among a total population of around 40 million.[1] To keep my anecdotal evidence close to home, my father, who grew up in a working-class street in a town in County Antrim in the 1940s, says he recalls everyone in the street using a bicycle, and in most cases every day. He also told me the story of a summer holiday, sometime during the Second World War, when he was about 11. The holiday was to be with his uncle and aunt and two cousins of about his own age. They got the train from Belfast (still smouldering from the Blitz, I imagine) and the plan was that they'd all cycle the rest of the way to the coast at Ballycastle.

The problem was that they were collectively one bike short. Good manners meant that Dad's bike was lent to one of his cousins. The solution was provided by my grandfather. He ran a grocer's, of the Arkwright variety. He procured for my father the delivery boy's bike, of the Granville variety. You know the sort of thing – heavily reinforced steel frame, huge basket on the front, signs advertising the shop and the week's special offers, a single gear with a badly oiled chain, and brakes that only existed to give you something to do while you waited to arrive at the scene of your accident. The basket was useful, because it offered an opportunity for a further show of good manners, when it turned out to be big enough to carry all his cousins' luggage.

My father, aged 11, rode this dreadnought across the North Antrim Hills to the coast. His cousins obligingly waited for him at the top of the many, many climbs on the route. Two hours there, two hours back the following weekend, and all the bright lights of Ballycastle in wartime in between. Seventy-three years later his indignation still burns brightly.

It was a not inconsiderable feat of bike riding – the bike and luggage probably weighed more than he did. But he would never have considered himself a cyclist, nor would any of the family, and nor, probably, would anyone in the street. It was just how everyone got places. If that meant riding the delivery bike to Ballycastle, well, it was probably better than spending the holiday at home – although, in truth, my father is unwilling to be drawn on this point.

The other mystery in all this is what the delivery boy did, since the shop didn't close for the week. As he hawked groceries around the steep streets of the town, his feelings towards my grandfather must have been almost as dark as my father's.

For sheer numbers of bikes and miles covered, the interwar years were a time like no other. Affordable transport has been the greatest triumph of the bicycle, and never more so than between the wars. It changed lives at a practical level, allowed workers to live in better houses by making for a simple, cheap commute, and even increased the breadth of the gene pool in rural areas by allowing lovers and their DNA to roam a bit further in pursuit of Mr and Miss Right. And it allowed families to go to the coast on holiday. My father and his delivery bike were part of many different histories – of land transport, of the Second World War, of retail, of leisure, even of innovative child-cruelty techniques in County Antrim in the mid-twentieth century. Bicycles and cyclists were part of many stories other than their own.

Yet, even when huge numbers relied on cycling for transport, there were plenty who valued a bicycle just as much for the time you could waste on it as the time you could save. Perhaps simply because there were so many bicycles around, the sport and the pastime thrived. First and foremost, cycling was an escape from the cities. 'Is your life spent among whirring machinery, in adding figures or attending to the wants of fractious customers? Don't you sometimes long to get away from it all?' enquired a Raleigh advertisement from 1923, accompanied by a picture of one of their roadsters. I'm guessing it seemed less patronising then.

Even when the adverts were a bit less clanking, they were still all about escape and gentle adventure. They progressed from a standard form – a side-on line drawing of the machine in question, an exhortation about how much faster it was than every other bike ever made, and a price – to some rather lovely drawings of figures awheel in the great outdoors. They moved from selling bicycles to selling cycling. There's an echo of modern car advertising in that it's about lifestyle rather than performance or specification. Your life would be more fulfilled if you went to see country churches on your half-day, but not half as fulfilled as it would be if you did it on a new Royal Enfield, on favourable finance terms. The artist normally tried to evoke some sort of brand-specific *joie de vivre* with something of breathtaking subtlety, like a jaunty peacock-feather waving around from inside a rider's hatband.

It was all about touring. Touring could be a day out, or a fortnight's holiday. It covered solo wanderings and organised club runs. Some of the club runs could be huge. A rider in her late eighties recalled for me a regular club run from the Barnet area north of London that often numbered over a hundred riders and would set out at nine on a Sunday morning, usually headed for the seaside in Essex. They frequently called at the finish of a time trial to collect the racing men at the end of their event. The racers would put the mudguards and lights back on their bikes, strap their racing wheels to their forks and put their everyday wheels back in, and join the run.

At the seaside, the younger members would probably play football on the beach while the older members would have a cup of tea, and after an hour or two the whole group would head home. They might not get there till early evening, having covered well over 100 miles. There were club members who got through the working week sustained by the dream of Sunday – to ride through the peaceful countryside with their friends, and keep an appointment with a fish supper on the front at Frinton.

Many of the runs were mixed. Women's cycling had advanced from Lady Harberton being ejected from the Hautboy Hotel, to the point in 1923 where Kuklos, one of *Cycling*'s columnists, felt able to say that a woman could ride a bike much as a man could, to the extent that he felt a woman riding in a skirt 'was not a proper cyclist'.[2]

Not only were the club runs mixed, but it wasn't all that unusual for children to be brought along as well. That included those too young to ride. In 1932 *Cycling* magazine published an excellent guide to taking children cycling, suggesting such hair-raising home-baked methods as stringing a hammock between Mother's and Father's bikes. It also offered a set of instructions for making a sidecar large enough for several children from off-cuts of wood and some pram wheels: 'If you choose to build a sidecar, you may prefer first to test it with a bag of potatoes, before entrusting a child to it.' Note, '*may* prefer'. During war years and rationing, you may equally have felt a child would be easier to replace than a bag of potatoes, and decide not to risk fatal injury to the latter by using it as a crash-test dummy for a plywood sidecar. ('Can't you do anything, Doctor?' 'Well, if you have some cooking oil I could make chips.')

The best way to get a flavour of what this sort of club run was like actually comes from the 1950s. Cycling continued very much unaltered through the Second World War, to emerge almost the same as it had been in the 1930s. And in 1955 British Transport Films produced a short film called *The Cyclists' Special*. (British Transport Films was the propaganda arm of British Rail, which continued to make films set in a bucolic, pre-war – pre-both wars – Britain of ox-carts driven by yokels in smocks right up until 1982. Many of its films are available online, including *The Cyclists' Special*.)

The Cyclists' Special of the title was a train, specially equipped with carriages for carrying bicycles, which took several hundred London cyclists for a day's riding somewhere different, somewhere beyond their normal range. So where was this exotic spot? 'A hard-riding London cyclist might reach Brighton, Basingstoke or Bedford,' said the voice-over. 'But if anyone said you could reach Warwickshire, you'd say he was nuts!' Warwickshire was apparently to all intents and purposes the Galápagos Islands. The men wore plus-twos and stockings and smoked pipes. The women wore khaki shorts and smiled self-consciously at the camera. On the train, the editor of *Cycling* magazine, H. H. England, planned the route on a map ('He knows that a tour without a map is like new potatoes without mint,' said the voice-over) while a man called Reg gesticulated with his pipe and nodded in agreement.

From Rugby station they set out, in several groups, to look at stained-glass windows in medieval churches, or to imagine what Kenilworth Castle might have looked like during the civil war. There are shots of bicycles piled neatly against each other by churchyard walls, and cyclists taking photographs of buttresses and making brass rubbings. It looks like a school trip for adults. It took me an embarrassingly long time before the penny dropped that they were only doing the same things I've done in Venice or in Rome.

At the day's end they all caught the train home, 'tired but happy' in a way that seems rather innocent now. It reminded me of the early chapters of children's books like *Swallows and Amazons*, about long days spent outdoors, exploring to no grand purpose, eating sandwiches and macaroons and drinking ginger beer. (And, Lord, how these cyclists ate. Rationing was not long over, and the director took an almost pornographic delight over lingering shots of rock cakes being stuffed into faces that were unsure how to reconcile eating with the apparent need to keep smiling nervously at the camera.)

The *Cyclists' Special* ride was a bit more carefully organised than most, but the majority of riders between the wars and into the 1950s would have been familiar with the basic idea: go and see interesting places, have a laugh with your friends, eat cake, and go home tired but happy. Flop into bed, and then back to the whirring machinery, the columns of numbers, or the awkward customers on Monday morning.

It was in this the golden age of the late 1920s and early 1930s that *Cycling* magazine really hit its stride. It was the essential newsletter, diary and friend to anyone who called themselves a cyclist. These are the issues that it's easiest to lose yourself in. They exude a confidence that came from an assured place in the world.

All the same, some of it seems very strange now. For years the magazine ran an 'asked and answered' column, which answered readers' questions. It was like Google by post, and, on the face of it, not that far away from some current magazines' content. But to save space, *Cycling* didn't print the questions, just the answers. So there would be a page that consisted entirely of cryptic comments like, 'T. F. of Leeds: the size you are seeking is 1½-inches.' There was the disappointing, 'To J. D. of Brighton: we don't know the answer to your enquiry.' The waspishly liberal, 'To E. A. of Small Heath: we do not agree with your views, which are apparently founded upon the belief that opinions contrary to your own should never be expressed.' The intriguing, 'To F. B. of Swansea: it depends exactly where you have inserted the spring.' And the plain daft, 'C. P. of New Cross: write on only one side of the paper, please.'[3] All of this in a magazine that had a distribution of over 75,000 readers, almost none of whom would have had the first idea what any of this meant.

January saw the publication of *Cycling*'s mileage chart for the year – a blank histogram to colour in with each week's mileage. This is a tradition that continues to this day. What they don't do now is the follow-up, where readers are invited to submit their mileage charts for publication and analysis the following year. It's not so much Google by post as Strava by post. A chart is reproduced, with a commentary: 'Mr Reg White from Colchester has sent us one of the best charts we've seen. A fine year's total of 7,000 miles, distributed throughout the year. His best month was July, boosted by an enjoyable tour of the South Coast, although he only managed 300 miles in September, during which month his wife unfortunately passed away.' There were quite literally dozens of these, printed over several issues. Most of them were a lot less interesting than Reg White's.

If nothing else, Strava by post showed that racking up miles is not a modern obsession. In an issue from as recently as 1995, I read an obituary of a rider, of whom the club secretary said, 'He was always the sort of chap who'd take the long way home for extra miles.' It was a high compliment, albeit a hard one to explain to a non-cyclist.

There was tech news – modern concerns like avoiding the evils of 'top dead-centre' with curved cranks, and reports of ever-lighter bikes. The magazine was a much less doubtful reproducer of manufacturers' claims than a modern publication – if a maker said that its new cycling galoshes were 100 per cent waterproof, the magazine was always happy to put its weight behind the claim.

Racing was covered, a mix of time trialling, place-to-place record breaking, and track meetings. This was interspersed with breast-beating every four years about the consistent failure of British riders to pull up any turnips at the Olympics, and suggestions of various schemes to rectify it – some of them as sensible as a series of races around the country to identify new talent; some as strange as compulsory lessons in 'ankling'.[4] Ankling is flexing the ankle to supposedly increase the power of the pedal stroke, and it was an obsession among coaches and cycling magazines for much of the twentieth century, to the exclusion of almost all else. At least it was for the British. The continentals, who actually won the bike races, couldn't have cared less about it, and if you try to explain it to them today they still look at you as though you've lost your mind.

But the heart of the magazine between the wars was touring. *Cycling* was, in many ways, a travel magazine. Every issue had suggestions of where to go – from day trips by train, to three-day 'tourlets' for Easter, suggested as a way to get back into the swing of things after the winter, to longer tours for a week or a fortnight's holiday. The interwar cycling heroes were tourists as well. The magazine's star writers were men like Kuklos (William Fitzwater Wray), Wayfarer (W. M. Robinson) and Hodites (Neville Whall). They wrote about whatever took their fancy, but most of the time that was their recent riding.

Kuklos and Wayfarer and Hodites were famous enough to make a nice supplementary income by the modern-feeling addition of live shows. Fans would travel for miles to see their lectures – on 'Wild Britain', 'Old Inns of England' or 'The Lighter Side of Cycling'. Hodites's lecture, 'Such Roads as This', which packed them in over the winter of 1932–33, was the record of two and a half weeks' touring in the Alps with some friends, riding a nice steady 50 miles a day, '. . . crossing 12 mountain passes across nine mountain ranges.' His lecture was accompanied by dozens of pictures on glass slides – the standard form for the talks. The debut of this new 'lantern-lecture', in the Central Hall in Cambridge, was enough of an event to feature in *Cycling*'s news section.[5]

It's almost impossible to write about this sort of thing without worrying that I'm sneering a little – at the parochialism of the lectures, at their small scale. A slide show of Alpine views followed by a cup of tea was something of a contrast with the fast-moving world of the bright young things in the 1920s. But if it sounds dull, it's only because of my own failure of imagination. I've seen the Alps, and the audience hadn't. For someone whose world was one of flatlands and wheat fields and exposed roads with a view that stretched uninterrupted to the horizon – such as the countryside around Cambridge or many other parts of the UK – the Alps would have been different enough to be worth hearing about. Never mind the views, the very idea of riding uphill for an hour at a stretch would have been so far-fetched as to border on unbelievable. The world was a lot bigger when you got around it by bicycle rather than by Boeing, and it was none the worse for it.

Although I'll level with you on one thing: 'The Lighter Side of Cycling' sounds dreadful in any era.

Still, there were troubles hanging over this golden era. The boom in cycling in the early 1930s was partly prompted by the Great Depression, which had led to an enthusiasm for camping, foraging and generally bumbling about in the hills and forests. The Cyclists' Touring Club handbooks started to recommend less and less expensive accommodation. There was even a row about whether the book ought to list 'tea only' establishments – cafés that would be happy to provide nothing other than tea to go with the packed lunch that cyclists had brought from home.[6] Some felt they should be included because it was what the membership wanted; some were just unwilling to accept that the typical CTC member was now so far from the affluent young men who had founded the club.

Counter-intuitively, towards the late 1930s cycling received another boost as the Depression ended. People had money, but held off buying a car because they were damned if they were going to do that just so the government could requisition it and use it for defeating Hitler. But even I'm not going to try to sell you that one as 'The Lighter Side of the Nazis'.

The mutual accommodation and the sharing of personnel between cyclists and motorists of the early 1900s didn't last for very long. Between 1919 and 1926 car ownership increased from 70,000 to a million. By 1934 that had doubled to two million and, as a result, that year alone saw an incredible 7,343 deaths on the roads of Britain. That's an average of 20 a day[7] – compared to around 1,700 annually now. There were about a tenth the number of cars that there are today, so to put that another way: back in 1934 each car was on average 62 times more likely to be involved in a fatal accident. Cyclists were particularly vulnerable – the total killed on the roads in 1934 was 1,536. It was even worse for pedestrians.

Not that this produced any agony in political circles, perhaps because we'd come a long way from the sort of era when anyone could claim that every member of the House of Lords was a cyclist. For purposes of sheer hooting horror, it's hard to resist quoting Colonel Moore-Brabazon, who was Churchill's Transport Secretary during the Second World War. It would be fair to describe him as pro-car. It would also be fair to describe him as a bloodthirsty loon. In 1934, he told the House of Commons: 'It is true that 7,000 people are killed in motor accidents, but it is not always going on like that. People are getting used to the new conditions. No doubt many of the old Members of the House will recollect the number of chickens we killed in the old days. We used to come back with the radiator stuffed with feathers. It was the same with dogs. Dogs get out of the way of motor cars nowadays and you never kill one. There is education even in the lower animals. These things will right themselves.'[8] The same man also asked why everyone was so exercised about 7,000 deaths on the road when there were 6,000 suicides a year 'and nobody makes a fuss about that.'[9]

(In 1949, Moore-Brabazon went on to have the huge Bristol Brabazon airliner named after him. It had a fuselage wider than that of a 747, but was designed to carry just 80 passengers, who could enjoy a separate 37-seat cinema, two bars and a promenade deck. It was so big that a village near Bristol had to be levelled to create enough space for it to take off. It was an over-privileged white elephant for a Britain that had vanished about 30 years earlier, and it seems to me that the manufacturers could not have named it after anyone more appropriate.)

On a weekly basis, *Cycling* contained accounts of riders killed – by the careless, by the stupid, even by drivers so drunk they thought someone else was driving. The majority of the editorials concerned safety. Even where a conviction resulted, punishments were universally condemned as inadequate. This, from 1934, feels very familiar: 'Magistrates hesitate to take away a motorist's licence, they say, because it might cause him inconvenience. Inconvenience indeed! Let us hear no more of this disgraceful sympathy for the living person whose behaviour was such that life and death was involved in the mere act of permitting him on the highway.'[10]

It wasn't just the appalling casualty rate. There were fumes, there was the aggravation of being honked at to get out of the way. Even in the 1920s there were complaints that cyclists were being forced off the main roads and onto the byways. The way the roads were used changed more dramatically over a few years than it had in decades. For instance, I was surprised to discover that through all the centuries until the 1920s there was no obligation to keep to the left-hand side of the road in the UK. The only custom was to pass an oncoming vehicle on the left. That wasn't going to last long with the fast moving car. Everyone else had to not just get out of the way, but get out of the way on a permanent basis. When the new *Highway Code* was published in 1931 it was mainly concerned with reminding the cyclist that he was a nuisance.[11] Ten million cyclists versus two million cars, but it was already clear who had won.

In fact, the cyclists didn't win many victories. They sorely lacked supporters in the political world, so all they could do was campaign from the outside. They managed to avoid being banned from the roads altogether and banished to cycle paths. But as a victory it came mainly because no one really cared enough about cycling to fund a network of paths in the first place. They managed to see off some half-hearted attempts at registration and a cycling test, and they saw off an annual bicycle tax.[12]

Some of the arguments seem strange now. The Cyclists' Touring Club's main battlefront of the 1920s and thirties was rear lights. They were against them. Very,

very firmly against them. Their stance was that avoiding a collision was the responsibility of the overtaking vehicle, and that a compulsory rear light put some of the onus for avoiding a collision on the cyclist, and was thus an encroachment on a cyclist's basic freedom.[13] (On the other hand, the CTC was firmly in favour of headlights on cars, which weren't a requirement until some namby-pamby health and safety consultant changed the law in 1907, thereby taking all the delightfully mysterious thumps and bangs out of a evening's moting.)

This rear-light battle lasted for more than 20 years before it was finally lost in 1939, when wartime blackout regulations meant that car headlights were rendered almost useless and even the CTC conceded that some compromise was needed. William Oakley, the official CTC historian, had lived through the era and was clearly still livid about the whole thing almost 40 years later in 1977. Of the CTC leaders in the 1930s, he said: 'They were the leaders in a bitter fight against the insidious attacks of a mechanised Moloch, and its willing servitors, that was destined to order the lives of all mankind. Human sacrifice in slaughter and disablement on the roads was mounting and would continue to mount, inexorably. They had lost the Battle of the Rear Lights, but at least they had stood up for the rights and welfare of the weak against the massed forces of intolerance, of magistrates, local authorities, police, parliament and bureaucracy.'[14]

What Oakley lacks in cool understatement he more than makes up for with his summoning up of the depth and passion of the arguments about the roads between the wars. The CTC case seems almost laughable now, but at the time it was no more outlandish than the current debates about compulsory hi-viz clothing. In truth, what the loss of the battle of the rear lights shows is that the basic idea of how roads worked in the 1930s was changing, from something consensual to something much more adversarial. It wasn't a change that was good for cyclists.

CHAPTER 11

1942–1959:
The British League
of Racing Cyclists

You can say what you like about Adolf Hitler, but he was the midwife to modern British bike racing. Without him, there would have been no Bradley Wiggins, Chris Froome, Victoria Pendleton . . . or if there had been, at the very least it would have happened very differently. I accept that this revelation will probably not swing the balance of history's judgement, but thought that at the very least I ought to mention it.

Hitler is relevant because the 1936 Olympic Games was the key to all of it. The road race at the Berlin Games was a massed-start event. All the Olympic road races since

1906 had been time trials, much to the satisfaction of Britain, which was the only nation on earth that had made time trialling its speciality (not that Britain had actually won any of them). When the news of the format for Berlin reached the UK the National Cyclists' Union, the Road Racing Council and *Cycling* magazine (hereinafter known as 'the establishment') had a collective fit: 'The strongest possible protest ought to be made by the English delegates both to the UCI and the Olympic committees against the recent decision that the Olympic road race is to be a massed-start affair. The Olympic Games were the last stronghold of the genuine international trial of road riding ability, free from tactics or bunching.'[1]

Road racing in the UK had picked up after the First World War exactly where it had left off, which is to say it still lived in the shadow of the accident with the woman and the horse on the Great North Road at the end of the previous century. There was time trialling, and there was nothing else. While the rest of the cycling world had come to love the 'bunched' race for its tactics and its intrigue, for the fact that success required both riding strength and racing intelligence, the British had no truck with it. The whole idea of a tactical road race went against what had become a deeply held principle that the strongest rider should always win, and if that irked those who were looking for entertainment, then those who were looking for entertainment were welcome to go and find another sport to watch.

This they did, and in their droves. Road racing in Britain remained a secretive backwater. As a set of instructions to competitors at a Catford CC 50-mile race in 1932 said, 'In the interests of the sport, competitors are earnestly requested to avoid, whenever and wherever possible, any semblance of a race.' Tens of thousands of spectators might have turned out to watch the very first road races, but by the 1920s they had all successfully been bored into going away.

In what might as well have been an attempt to make time trialling even more impenetrable to the casual spectator, the British Best All-Rounder Competition was founded in 1930. It was a virtual championship, allowing riders spread out over the country to compete for a single title by ranking them according to their average speed over their season's best 50-mile, 100-mile and 12-hour events, wherever those races had been held. Despite the element of Strava by post, it quickly established itself as the biggest prize in British bike racing.

As grand championships go it was wonderfully understated. The format meant that the big-name riders frequently never met head-to-head at all. You could win it without ever actually winning a race. The key events were impossible to predict in advance, because weather and road conditions played such a role in fast riding.

eyes it seems likely that Hansen was just better – as far as most of Scandinavia was concerned he was the surest bet at the whole Games, and the British officials were entirely unable to point to a shortcut he might actually have taken.[4]

A colossus Southall may have been, but the mere prospect of the 1936 Olympics was the end of him, and all like him. In 1933 he was sent to the Worlds in France to ride a massed-start race with a view to having to ride the same event three years later in Berlin. He took nine shades of a walloping, and was never quite the same again. The circuit's modest hill battered him – each time the bunch came to it, the continental riders picked up the pace and 'honked' up it, getting out of the saddle and accelerating to try to drop weaker riders. ('Honk' is a word that seems to have completely vanished from cycling in the last 20 years. I've no idea why – it doesn't even seem to have been replaced by anything else, except perhaps the moronic 'dancing on the pedals'.)

Southall could only ride up the climb steadily, the way you must in a time trial to avoid going into the red. His bike might have had two gears, but he only had one. After grinding up every climb, he had to chase back to the bunch on his own, and eventually the elastic snapped. He might have been the superman of the wheel in England – so good that no honest man could best him – but he wasn't even able to make it to the finish of his first international massed-start event.[5] It turned out also to be his last. Within a year he'd abandoned his amateur career and turned professional, with the aim of setting place-to-place professional records. He set nine over the next two years, but he never rode for his country again.

The first massed-start race on British roads since the 1890s seems to have been in 1932, when a club ran an event on the Bath Road as a massed-start affair, apparently more or less on a whim. It was reported in the press ('There you are,' said the starter, 'they've all gone, and there wasn't half the usual congestion') but everyone seems to have tacitly agreed to look the other way rather than take the more traditional cyclists' disciplinary action of banning anyone who had the slightest thing to do with it for ever.[6]

The first officially sanctioned massed-start race was at Brooklands motor circuit in 1933, organised as a selection trial for the Worlds. All the country's top roadmen turned up for it. Almost none of the riders had ever seen a massed-start event, let alone ridden one. So, armed with considerable fitness, fuelled by the competitive desire to represent their country, and in a state of almost complete practical ignorance, they all blazed away for 100 kilometres of the least competent racing in the history of cycling.[7] There were crashes, random attacks, the repeated chasing down of teammates, more crashes, lamentable bike-handling, huge pointless efforts on the front of the bunch . . . Tactics weren't so much a mystery as an irrelevance, and if you'd suggested co-operation to catch a breakaway, you'd have got much the same reaction as if you'd suggested co-operation to catch syphilis. It was the sort of shambles a modern group of under-ten racers, every single one of whom is pretending to be Mark Cavendish, would be ashamed of.

An unknown rider from Wolverhampton called Percy Stallard won several intermediate prizes, and, although he didn't finish the race, that was enough to secure his selection. Stallard liked massed-start racing, and, despite being no great shakes as a time triallist, he was reasonably good at it. The cut and thrust and the stop-and-go suited his physiology; the combative racing suited an aggressive nature. At the 1933 Worlds that Southall failed to even finish, Stallard finished 11th to score the best British result. He came home a very vocal advocate of massed-start racing.

Slowly, with one eye on those Berlin Olympics, things began to move. More racing was organised at Brooklands in 1934. Partly on the basis of his rides there Stallard again went to the Worlds in 1934 in Leipzig, and finished seventh. His British teammate Charles Holland finished a pretty impressive fourth. Back home, the establishment wasn't impressed. 'This is not the kind of championships to interest this country at all. That we might get a finisher with the leaders occasionally does not justify all the bother and interference with the legitimate English racing programme,' said *Cycling* magazine.[8]

There was still no massed-start racing on the open roads. What few massed-starts there were happened on motor-racing circuits or occasionally on airfields – rather sanitised environments compared to ordinary roads with real climbs, sharp corners and rough surfaces. The NCU was not prepared to hear of it moving to the public roads for fear it would bring down the rage of the police, the magistrates and the public.

The Isle of Man, still outside the NCU's jurisdiction, offered a solution. The island was as keen on attracting tourists then as it is now. A race round the TT circuit was arranged in 1936, attended by many ambitious British riders. It was notable mainly for an extravagance of crashes – 31 riders managed to hit the ground in just 38 miles of racing, from a field of only 81.

Which might have been excusable if they'd all come down at once, but they did it in a series of instalments that showed their serious lack of experience of real-world conditions. Eight riders crashed in the first few hundred yards. Four more fell at five miles when they failed to collectively ride around a parked lorry. A few miles further on someone's chain broke, causing them to swerve – another ten went down. Thus it continued in a succession of bangs and thumps and cries of alarm. Of the 81 starters, just 48 made it to the finish line, and eight ended up in hospital.[9] Charles Holland won, underlining his emergence as the first real star of British massed-start racing, and as a man with an uncanny talent for threading his way unharmed through the crash-filled chaos of early British massed-start racing.[10]

And the 1936 Olympics? Narrow twisting roads meant that it was also something of a crash-fest. Again, Holland ducked and weaved through a chaotic last few kilometres only to be edged off the podium and into fifth place in a bunch sprint. It was a remarkable result. Holland had been almost entirely unsupported by his team because the British hadn't yet worked out that riding as a team was how you won a massed-start race. The squad management wouldn't have cared about it even if they had understood it, and unlike riders from other nations Holland was racing on a single gear because that was the British way.

It might have been a turning point. As well as having the skills to be perhaps the finest road rider of his generation, Holland was also a fine time triallist – he won the Best All-Rounder title in 1936, to make himself a distinctly establishment rider. He'd already got a bronze medal from the 1932 Olympic team pursuit, he played cricket when he wasn't cycling, and he even went touring. You'd have had to be psychopathically reactionary to regard him as a rebel. In a more normal time and place, he might have been an effective poster-boy for massed-start racing. But this was Britain in the 1930s, where 'psychopathically reactionary' was a phrase that had probably been used in the job descriptions for most of the cycling establishment, much of which was just plain terrified at the very thought of bigger and more exciting races. They still stuck to F. T. Bidlake's view: 'The game of road racing [time trialling] is well played and has been well played for many years, and will still be capable of being carried on provided only it does not cause a nuisance or obstruction.'[11]

In respect to the faintly ridiculous secrecy surrounding cycling events on the road, Bidlake was critical of other sports – motor cycling, athletics – for promoting events designed to attract interest: 'Athletic folk might take the hint and follow the cycling example and avoid preliminary publicity for their performances.'[12] No one appeared to notice that none of the other events that used the highway seemed to cause any great annoyance, at least outside major cities. Out in the countryside it's hard to see how the disruption could have been more than trifling, but there was a very real concern that a handful of complaints might lead to the banning of all road racing, or perhaps even all cycling. So a fearful, trembling sport remained in its covert, early morning world of secret codes and unannounced races, plain black clothing and an almost complete absence of public interest.

On the other side of the Channel, the Tour de France was exactly the sort of popular, high-profile brouhaha that the establishment was petrified of. They were probably less than delighted when, in 1937, Charles Holland turned professional and headed for France to join the circus.

This was a Tour from an earlier age. Rather than devising the stages to suit the racing, and using sometimes lengthy transfers to get the riders from the end of one stage to the start of the next, in this era the Tour was a race that pretty much lapped the nation's borders and coasts. It was over a thousand kilometres longer than a modern race, and demanded almost 70 per cent more time in the saddle. It went straight through the Alps, and straight over the Pyrenees. It slogged for days across the mind-numbing plains of northern France, and slogged back the other way up the Atlantic coast on heavy roads and in energy-sapping crosswinds.

Holland survived 14 days and 3,000 kilometres of monster stages and brutal mountain roads that were like nothing he'd ever even seen before, let alone raced on. As an unsupported rider with no team and no manager to find him food and hotels and pass up drinks, his ride around France was magnificent. But on the third of the three separate stages held on 17 July (for a total day's racing of 325 kilometres, please note) he punctured, and in the course of replacing the tyre, his pump broke. It's hard to think of anything more trivial, but with no team to help him there was no coming back from it. He was left stranded by a Pyrenean road on the way to Luchon with his flat tyre and his useless broken pump.

When Holland did finally get a borrowed tyre on the rim, inflated with a borrowed pump, the occupants of a press car attempted to push him to the finish – a contravention of the rules that appalled him so much that he put his brakes on to stop them. His Tour was over.[13] It was the last mountain stage. There were only six days to go and, compared to what he'd already ridden, they were six fairly straightforward days at that.[14]

Cycling at least had the grace to celebrate him: 'We can take pride in his glorious failure, knowing that alone as he was, the victor's laurels could never have been his had he been the greatest stayer, the fastest sprinter and the finest roadman in the race . . . [Holland] demonstrates that no matter what the sphere of competitive cycling we have ambitions to contest, Englishmen can be developed who can rank with the best.'[15] It was to be 18 years before there was another British rider at the Tour.

By the time that happened, though, things had changed somewhat. Back in 1933, when the NCU selected the outsider Percy Stallard for the Worlds, they were inviting on board a man who was quite certainly the most disruptive individual ever selected for a national team. Whatever the opposite of clubbable is, Stallard was it. Spikey, confident and determined, he was not happy with the idea of massed-start racing consisting of riding round motor circuits or an occasional trip to the Isle of Man. He enjoyed it, and he was rather good at it, and he thought it simply ridiculous to suggest that Britain was so different from every other nation on earth that to hold massed-start events on the open road would bring the sky crashing down on all cyclists.

After years of persecuting officials, in 1942 Stallard got bored and decided he'd had enough. He was frustrated at being stuck in Wolverhampton in a reserved occupation (as a cycle mechanic – note the importance of bicycles on the Home Front). He was frustrated that there were so few racing opportunities, since most of the airfields he normally raced on were given over to the war effort. And, above all, he was frustrated at the very, very quiet wartime roads, and how perfect they were for racing.

Stallard organised his own massed-start, open-road event, under the auspices of no authority at all, and with the permission of no one except for the local police. He told the police that such races were commonplace in Europe, and usually went off without a hitch. They said they were happy to help. And so arrived the revolution. On 7 June 1942, Stallard's race ran from Llangollen to Wolverhampton, '. . . by the kind permission of the chief constables of Denbighshire, Shropshire, Staffordshire and Wolverhampton.' The sky stayed firmly where it was. The race was a huge success. The riders loved it, the crowds at the finish loved it, and the profits went to charity. The winner was E. A. Price of the Wolverhampton Road Racing Club and, in the spirit of the occasion, he donated his prize to charity as well.

The NCU's interpretation of 'the spirit of the occasion' was rather different. They banned Stallard from membership and from any of its races, which simply guaranteed that he would form a breakaway governing body. They also, in the spirit of the occasion, banned all the riders in the race, and all the officials named on the programme. This ensured Stallard had a ready membership for his new outfit, and some officials.[16]

The NCU badly underestimated Stallard. Many of the governing body's officials predated cycling's change to a working-class sport, and probably misjudged the Wolverhampton rider on the basis of class snobbery as much as anything else. But while the handwriting in Stallard's frequent letters to them left something to be desired, you don't run bike races on penmanship alone. That was the establishment's first mistake. Their second was to fail utterly to grasp that what bike racers wanted had changed. Time trialling in secret and dressed in black, like a group of paranoid spies, was no longer enough. Their third mistake was a failure to anticipate that men returning from the war would be in no mood to be told what to do by a cadre of non-combatant officials, retired bike racers and journalists, when there was no better justification for it than that it had always been done that way.

Thus was born the British League of Racing Cyclists, created to promote massed-start racing. There was an immediate civil war within British cycle racing, because you couldn't be a member of both groups. You couldn't even choose to be a member of neither and plan to stay a racing cyclist, since any loose association with a rider or riders from one organisation would bring down upon you an instant ban from the other. To equivocate was to risk being banned by both of them at once.

Even Percy Stallard managed to be banned by his own league in 1943, after he'd criticised the quality of the organisation of some of its events.[17] (The criticism in question was, it has to be said, pretty trenchant. Peter Bryan, a Leaguer who would one day go on to edit *Cycling*, explained that Stallard getting banned by his own side was probably inevitable because of Stallard's huge self-confidence working in tandem with his simply phenomenal ability to make enemies.[18])

At the dispute's cuter end, a group of Leaguers on a ride who saw a group of NCU riders shouted, 'Up the League!' while the other group shouted back, 'Fuck the League!'[19] At its less cute end, clubs were torn apart as members' sympathies divided, old friends ended up on rival sides and, quite literally, not speaking for years.

It wasn't just the racing, it was cultural. The heroes of the establishment were men like Frank Southall. The heroes of the Leaguers were men like Fausto Coppi. (I say 'men like Fausto Coppi' . . . there are, of course, no men like Fausto Coppi, but you know what I mean.) The establishment riders and officials were from a black-and-white age; the Leaguers were, to be blunt, cool. They wore sunglasses, they had brightly coloured jerseys. They bought the French sports paper *Miroir-Sprint* if they could find it, whether they could read French or not, and looked at the pictures in coffee shops. They were a type of rider that's still quite familiar in Britain, even if the context has changed. They would have bought Rapha jerseys in bulk if there had been such a thing.

The sheer venom of the dispute was extraordinary. Years ago, when I was a young university lecturer, the head of my department once told me that 'Academic politics can only afford to be as poisonous as they are because the stakes are so small.' There was an element of this to the cycling civil war. But I only have the nerve to mention this now, at a point where I'd be able to outrun most of its surviving protagonists.

A full account of the war would be both long and bewildering. It is such a confusing tale of acrimonious chaos that it would also be all but impossible to make it accurate. The swirl of claim and counterclaim, of propaganda and outright deceit, is an exhausting prospect even now. One old Leaguer claimed that it took him two years to physically recover from the front-line stress of being an official in the organisation, and anyone who has tried to wade through it all will know how he felt.[20] I doubt you could have a battle like it these days, because no one would pay you to do it, and no volunteer would have the time to spare.

There were points where all bans were rescinded, only to be almost instantly re-imposed. The BLRC found the energy to add fighting internal battles to its agenda. *Cycling* announced it was going to start including BLRC results, but it turned out it was only doing so to further its interests in a diversionary skirmish with the time triallists' organisation about the Best All-Rounder competition. The stories feel of a piece with the sort of post-war industrial disputes that rumbled on for decades fuelled by animosity rather than grievance. Animosity was, of course, one of Percy Stallard's specialities.

The eventual result was that the battle almost bankrupted both the NCU and the BLRC. They were forced to their knees by penury, and in 1958 they agreed to merge to form the British Cycling Federation. There was no realistic choice, but still, Stallard never forgave the betrayal. He did sports administration with the same aggressive win-at-all-costs style as he rode those first massed-start races. Years later he maintained that even if the two organisations had had nothing left to argue over, they should have stayed separate all the same, and tried to drive each other into the sea.[21]

It's hard to know what would have happened without the civil war. It was divisive and destructive, but it did at least bring Britain into line with everywhere else. Fifty years late admittedly, but who knows how much longer British racing would have been stuck in a nineteenth-century time-warp otherwise? It could, in all seriousness, have been decades. It might not have happened even now. By the 1950s, increases in road traffic would have made the argument a much harder one to start, let alone win, because the police would have been unlikely to take the laid-back attitude that they did in 1942. Percy Stallard might have been a cantankerous old bastard, but British bike racing would have been very different without him.

From an international point of view, while BLRC riders were not eligible for international selection – that was still in the gift of the NCU – they managed to build relationships with some promoters, notably in the Warsaw Pact nations. These promoters ran the Peace Race, an eastern European version of a Grand Tour. It was promoted from 1948 until 2006, and through most of its history was primarily run for the benefit of the Soviet hard-nut 'amateurs' who had built up a deep experience of racing for 200 kilometres a day on a diet of nothing but cabbage soup and steroids.

In 1952, to the surprise of many, the Peace Race was won by a Scottish Leaguer called Ian Steel. It was Britain's first victory in international road racing since the 1920s, and the first in a massed-start race since the nineteenth century. Just as remarkable, the BLRC riders won the team classification. These were both truly outstanding achievements, ones that to this day fail to get the attention they deserve – popular history always gauges success by the Tour de France and the World Championships and by almost nothing else. To take on the eastern Europeans in a race from Warsaw to Berlin to Prague and win was the mark of real quality.

Yet it was more than that. The NCU saw which way the wind was blowing, and dropped its bar on BLRC riders being selected for international events in 1953. If they hadn't, there was a serious danger that the BLRC would have ended up being recognised as the UK's governing body instead of the NCU, and that would have been a victory for the upstarts from which the establishment would never have recovered.[22] Steel's Peace Race victory was a turning point that made it possible for British riders to ride as professionals at events like the Tour de France. It was another staging post on the way to Wiggins's win at the Tour in 2012.

Meanwhile, back home, the BLRC had started the Tour of Britain, which begat the Milk Race, which begat the PruTour, which became the modern Tour of Britain, mercifully without becoming the Tour 'de' Britain anywhere on the way. It grew rather quietly. Its origins were in the Southern Grand Prix, the first stage race ever run in Britain, which happened over the August Bank Holiday in 1944. The first stage began in Lewisham, south-east of London, which in the late days of the war was where German flying-bombs that hadn't quite got the energy to make it to London tended to land. At the scheduled start time Lewisham was still smouldering quite badly from a recent arrival. The officials moved the whole race a few miles up the road and onto a slightly different route, with marshals having to ride to their new stations and having to go nearly as fast as the race to get there in time. It was fitting, though probably not universally popular, that Percy Stallard himself won the first stage of the first British stage race.[23]

On the second stage, the bunch was distracted by the sight of an RAF fighter shooting down a doodlebug flying-bomb more or less directly overhead. There was a mighty explosion. As burning shrapnel fell around the peloton, one rider enquired tentatively as to why they were having a bike race in a war zone, and should they not perhaps be in an air-raid shelter? This was generally considered not quite in the spirit of the event. The race continued, through a series of bangs and explosions, small earthquakes and columns of smoke.[24] On one lap through the town of Tonbridge there were cheering

CHAPTER 11

crowds out. On the next the streets were entirely deserted, except for a few air-raid wardens. By the subsequent lap the crowds were back following the all-clear siren sounding. The riders spent the night in a marquee, kept awake by the falling bombs. After the three stages, the winner was Les Plume, of Manchester, who was the man who had wanted to be in an air-raid shelter on stage two.

The following year the BLRC went a step further and ran an amateur five-day race to celebrate the end of the war. It ran from Brighton to Glasgow, and the organisers even managed to find some French rider (also from a breakaway governing body) to give it some Gallic flare. It was still a trifle home-spun. No one had ever organised or, for the most part, even seen anything that ambitious, and no one had any idea how it would work. There were strange rules – in any towns or villages, for instance, the race was neutralised and the competitors had to ride in single file. For weeks before the race, the officials were consumed with bagging enough ration coupons for the support vehicles' petrol and the riders' food. Still, 20,000 spectators turned up to watch 92 riders leave Brighton and set off into the unknown.

The whole thing was a weird mix of the formal and the chaotic. Before the start of the second stage in London, the organisers went to Buckingham Palace to deliver the text of a Loyal Address to the King. That was followed by a formal reception for officials in the City of London. Meanwhile, the riders got bored with standing about in freezing cold and torrential rain waiting for everyone to sort themselves out and come to wave a flag at them, and started the second stage of the race themselves. The officials were left scrabbling to catch up with their race and get to the finish in Wolverhampton.

It wasn't the last time the race looked after itself – on the fourth stage, from Bradford to Newcastle, the riders were left to find their own way for most of the day, while the officials took the train to the finish, hoping that someone might turn up in Newcastle to time the riders in. (Thankfully someone did.) When the race got there the riders had to pass a hat around to see if they could gather together enough money for the event to keep paying its bills. This was immediately followed by another full-dress civic reception.[25]

There was a wondrous make-do-and-mend feel about the whole thing. One of the motivations for riders to race hard was that there was no official accommodation in the stage towns. If you got there early you had the pick of what boarding houses there were, as long as you didn't spend too long hanging around at the finish congratulating yourself. If you arrived late you might end up sleeping in a barn. Arrive really late and you might not have been that lucky – many riders ended up sleeping under hedges. There wasn't much food going either. If you were a mediocre racer, it could be a seriously hard way to spend a week.

There were five different organisers for the event, who didn't meet at any point prior to the start. Most of the stages hadn't been ridden in advance, and half the time the organisers themselves were hazy about where the race was meant to go. Stages were often many miles longer than the riders had been told. For instance, the final one, from Newcastle to Glasgow, was officially 100 miles. It was actually 150. That's not a marginal difference, especially when the riders discovered that quite a bit of the section through the borders was on an unmade road. A stage that might have been expected to last for five hours actually lasted for almost eight. The winner of both the last stage and the overall race was Robert Batot from France. Along with his team, he had spent almost the entire race threatening to pull out because of the lack of organisation.

All the same, the race grew. It acquired sponsorship from the *News of the World* in 1947, though they pulled out after a year because of the constant bickering in the BLRC. The *Daily Express* took the race over in 1951, before pulling out in 1953 for exactly the same reasons as the *News of the World*.[26] And then the BLRC approached the Milk Marketing Board, and created the Milk Race. This was a perfect match, and led to a sponsorship tie-up that lasted 35 years from 1958 until 1993. Its brand was so strong that I've met non-cyclists in the last year or two who assume it still happens.

My own first direct contact with serious bike racing was the Milk Race. It turned up in Durham when I was a student there – it was the start of a stage that was going to noodle around the north-east for 200 kilometres or so before finishing in Sunderland, not that I cared. It may have been the grey morning, or it may have been the race had barriered off my route to a lecture, but at that moment my future career didn't sell itself to me. It was a race full of scrawny men in funny-looking caps. They were riding the skinny-tubed steel road bikes of the era that, however modern they might have been, still managed to look old-fashioned. This was all the more the case the less you knew about the sport, and I knew less than nothing. As the race rolled out and the stage began, I muttered a curse on it and all who participated therein, and prayed that I would never in my life lay eyes upon another bloody bike race. It wasn't my most clairvoyant moment.

The Milk Race did perhaps more than anything else to normalise massed-start racing in the UK. It was popular, it was big. It was no longer even remotely possible to stick to the pre-war arguments that it was going to be the ruin of cycling in the UK.

The British Cycling Federation that was set up as part of the NCU and BLRC's truce is now called British

Cycling. British Cycling had, and occasionally continues to have, travails of its own, although they've been minor compared to 1942 to 1958, and they haven't much impinged on the normal daily life of a cyclist in the UK. The emotional divisions took longer to heal. The sport in the UK is still divided between time trialling and massed-start road racing, administered for the most part by different, if cooperative, organisations.

As a rider it's easy to switch from one discipline to the other. Yet when I started racing in the mid-1990s there was a certain tension. The feeling among many of the old Leaguers was that they'd experienced a takeover by the NCU, rather than a merger. It's not impossible that this was because as an administrative entity the League, even when it was clear it was winning the argument, used to have committee meetings that were almost indistinguishable from blood sport. The old NCU could at least occasionally agree with itself, even if it agreed with no one else.

What the Leaguers often failed to notice was that, culturally, their brand of racing had won hands down. Children from cycling families hadn't grown up dreaming of being a British time-trial champion since somewhere around the era of Frank Southall. Britain's first full Tour de France team, in 1955, had firm roots in the BLRC. The League changed everything, and changed it to the extent that by the 1990s to be a time triallist was to be always aware you weren't one of the cool kids.

Cycling Weekly still covered domestic time trialling as lovingly as it always had. Massed-start racing was covered in roundup reports that started with words like, 'Meanwhile, in bunched racing . . .' which still gave the impression it was a bit deviant. But no one else thought that.

Percy Stallard died as recently as 2001. He was still reported to be bloody cross about almost everything.

II   II   II

A fair question at this point, after the NCU and the BLRC, Charles Holland and Ian Steel, would be: what about women and racing? After all, it was women's adoption of the bicycle that had propelled it to the height of fashion in the 1890s, and the bicycle that did so much for early feminist politics. We had Tessie Reynolds, we had Miss America and we had, well, um, lots of slightly pervy Frenchmen staring at women competitors in the 1870s. So what happened about women's racing? The blunt answer is: not very much.

In the interwar years there were several women's clubs formed for those who wanted to race, like the Rosslyn Ladies' Cycling Club, founded in Essex in 1922 (and which thrives to this day). But while by 1922 a woman on a bike was no longer automatically causing any sort of scandal, she could turn it in to one very quickly by trying too hard. This was an era when it was not unusual for men, infuriated by the sight of women riding at a pace that was insufficiently sedate, to throw stones at them. Incredibly, *Cycling* had staged a not noticeably ironic debate in the letters page only a few years earlier about whether women ought to be subject to a speed limit 'so we can better appreciate their charms'.[27]

The Rosslyn Ladies weren't easily discouraged, and promoted some early races. The first women's 12-hour time trial in 1924, and the first women's racing at Herne Hill Velodrome in 1927 were both the work of the Rosslyn.[28] But just because women were as well capable of racing then as they are now doesn't mean there was a lot of official encouragement. The UK was not alone in this. The women's World Championships didn't start until the same year as the BLRC and the NCU merged, 1958. That it happened at all was very much down to another British racing woman, Eileen Gray. Even then, the organisers managed to have an official banquet at the 1959 women's Worlds to which women were not admitted. There were no women's events in the Olympics until 1984. That's right, 1984. That was a single, rather short, road race. The first women's Olympic track event had to wait until 1988.

In the UK, things did improve after the Second World War, at least a little. While the BLRC was not overly concerned with women's racing (the thought of a women's racing sub-committee might well have pushed them over the edge), time trialling had more or less the same events for women as for men, and did so from the mid-1940s. The Women's Cycle Racing Association was formed in 1949, and ran the first massed-start National Championships in 1956.

The one upside was that magazines of the era actually gave at least as much prominence to women's racing as they do now – in truth, probably more. They did the same with the numerous women's record attempts. Considering how reactionary the cycling press could be about almost everything else, it seems like something of a welcome aberration.

The lack of opportunity was a pity considering the quality of some of the riders. Eileen Sheridan, for instance, should clearly have been a huge star of the sport. Having won all there was to win as an amateur in the late 1940s she turned professional to attack road records – much as Frank Southall had done 25 years earlier. In fact, the famously terse Southall became her manager. She followed up her amateur career by breaking all the records there were.[29] Her record for 1,000 miles lasted from 1954 until 2002. But she had no other outlet for her prodigious talent.

A little younger and therefore a little luckier was Beryl Burton. Her story is better known today outside cycling than it once was – her reputation has risen with the sport's fortunes to the extent that I'm tempted to say that no one has ever been more famous for their obscurity. Even so, however good you might think she was, she was better. She won everything domestically, and won it over and over again. She won the Best All-Rounder title for 25 consecutive years from 1959 through to 1983, starting when she was 22 years old and finishing aged 47.[30] In total she racked up 97 domestic time-trial titles – her nearest challenger of either gender to this day has just 56. Not only had she physical talent to burn, she was one of the most ferocious competitors that any sport, any time, anywhere has ever seen.

When Mike McNamara set the British men's 12-hour record in 1967 he had a bit of the shine taken off it by the fact he was caught and passed by Burton on her way to setting a women's record that was almost a mile better. That she offered him a liquorice allsort as she passed, because she couldn't think of anything else very useful she could say, is part of cycling's folklore. He ate it. Johnny Helms, for many years the cartoonist in *Cycling Weekly*, said he should have saved it so it could be displayed in a darkened room where the unworthy could pay homage.[31] The record she set still stands, 50 years later, and there's no immediate sign of anyone breaking it.

Burton was better off than Sheridan had been, in that there were at least the first beginnings of an international scene for her. She won seven World Championship titles between 1959 and 1967, and a considerable collection of other medals and honours. But there wasn't a professional tour, where she could have converted her talent into real fame and fortune. Instead she spent her career as an amateur, riding for the local Morley Cycling Club and working as a market gardener. The idea that Britain's greatest cyclist spent so much of her time growing rhubarb in Yorkshire's rhubarb triangle has been, for years, the subject of rather patronising marvel.

There were just a handful of chances to race outside the UK in a year, which is why Burton is as much remembered for her dominance of the domestic scene as for anything else. Though it's too easy to dismiss that – at the time, the domestic races, for both men and women, still offered quite a lot of glory, and certainly more than they do now. On the NCU and establishment side of the sport there was still a strong flavour of the isolationism of the interwar years, when traditional British time trialling against your honest British fellows was a truer test of ability than shifty foreign racing against, frankly, God knew what sort of cheats and shysters. (Remember this is an era when *Cycling* was still rather prone to reporting the Bath Road 100 over three spreads at the front of the magazine, and the Tour de France at the back under the heading, 'Foreign Racing'.)

People did care more about all of Burton's achievements at the time than common mythology suggests. She was at least as big a star in the sport as Tom Simpson.

Uniquely, she got two pages in *The Golden Book of Cycling*. She won the Bidlake Prize – for an outstanding contribution to cycling – three times, also a unique achievement. Magazines and newspapers were agog at her rides. She was a draw at any race she did, and I know time-trial riders of a certain generation, of both genders, who feel they were in some way anointed when they were caught and passed by her.

Burton's problem was simply that women's racing was too small for her. All the glory it had to offer was less than she deserved. I imagine the sport would still be too small today. I can't imagine Burton doing the photoshoots or the sponsor PR that are part of being a modern sportsperson. She'd want to be out on her bike, or better, winning a race. And there would never be enough of them for her.

CHAPTER 12

1957: 'Most of Our People Have Never Had it so Good'

For the nigh-on 60 years between 1893 and 1952 almost every weekly issue of *Cycling* carried at least one drawing by Frank Patterson. Often there were several – a large full-page one, and more to illustrate the articles of Wayfarer or Kuklos. It doesn't require an art critic to recognise a Patterson drawing at a glance: black and white, drawn with a very fine pen, shadows and dark colours always executed with a dense packing of the thinnest of straight parallel lines rather than cross-hatching or shading. You never need to check the flowing signature that is always tucked away among the lines at the bottom, often as not blending quietly into the foliage or the road surface of the foreground.

The subject matter of Patterson's work is remarkable for its consistency. They are typical cycling scenes, or at least typical scenes from a certain sort of cycling. They are most often of a solitary cyclist riding on a lonely road, maybe through a recognisable village with a well-known church or an inn in the background, or maybe just through the fields or woods of early twentieth-century Britain. He would usually wear the plus-twos or plus-fours and the jacket and cap of the tourist, and carry a saddlebag. Very occasionally he would be a time triallist, but if he was it meant only an alteration of costume and attitude. He was still alone with the road. Patterson's riders hardly ever have any passing witnesses.

The drawings were never of groups of riders, or club runs, or (certainly not) a massed-start race. While sometimes there were two riders on a tandem, or a husband and wife putting up a tent for the night, their bikes neatly parked against a tree, there was never much feeling of companionship about them. There was certainly never any hint of humour. They depicted the unobtrusive and purposeful riders the cycling establishment admired, out to enjoy the small pleasures of the countryside, to stop at an inn or (latterly) a café, and to ride home in time for bed and back-to-work Monday morning.

Patterson was hugely popular. It was because his work showed cyclists the things they liked best about themselves: their ability to steadily cover miles and miles of empty road, their appreciation of the landscape, and their modest self-reliance. Patterson showed it to them in a simple, unfussy style. His scenes were so familiar that it would have been easy to project yourself into the white spaces of a Patterson drawing, and to feel the road beneath your tyres and the sun against your face. It's not even all that difficult now, changed though the lanes and the landscape might be.

The irony was, of course, that Patterson wasn't a cyclist. He wasn't alone in this – one of the magazine's last touring correspondents was Ragged Staff (Rex Coley), whose touring stories were often as not accomplished by train, particularly towards the end of his career. Patterson lived a life as isolated as the cyclists in his drawings, on an all-but inaccessible farm in Sussex where he and his family existed somewhere between self-sufficiency and survivalism. He might have had a feel for the poetry of cycling, but he had precious little interest in it, and no interest whatsoever in meeting cyclists or fans. He rarely if ever left his farm, and his work was drawn entirely from postcards and photographs, which the staff of the magazine would collect and send to him. He reproduced them, added a cyclist, packaged them up and sent them off to London.[1]

Most of the thousands of originals have disappeared now – art critic Tim Hilton estimated that there might have been as many as 26,000 of them in total.[2] Hilton suggests some were destroyed by a fire during the Second World War. Others were very probably discarded in the numerous office moves the magazine made in the years afterwards, and from conversations with past staff it seems the few that remained were more than likely stolen by a 'researcher' who'd been given access to the archive.

There are ways in which the quiet disappearance of Patterson's legacy is appropriate. Social classes changed, fashions came and went, but the decades of his drawings were the decades of a certain sort of cycling. Patterson drew the long, long golden age of club runs and of touring and of amateur time trialling as the pinnacle of a racing man's ambition. For many, his drawings are the only way to see that kind of cycling now. And when Patterson died in 1952 the era was finally, quietly, coming to an end.

If you wanted to find a man who could have blended into a Patterson drawing effortlessly, even as that period drew to its very close, you could do no better than Ray Booty. On Bank Holiday Monday, 6 August 1956, on a course on the Bath Road, Booty became the first rider to beat four hours for 100 miles in an out-and-back time trial. He rode the course in 3:58:28.

It was time trialling's four-minute mile, and the tall, elegant Booty was an easy fit as the sport's Roger Bannister.

Sixty years later Booty's 100 is still the most famous of all time-trialling records, and his name is one that anyone interested in the sport knows. Back then his ride even made some of the newspapers, though not as prominently as time-trialling folk-memory might hold. That's because while Booty was a massive star, he was a massive star in a sport that in 1956 was still 50 per cent NCU secrecy, 50 per cent BLRC infighting, and as a consequence almost ignored by the mainstream sports press.[3]

When I met Booty many years later he was modesty personified. He certainly didn't seem to have any complaints, despite the fact that if he'd achieved anything similar in a slightly less strangely managed sport than cycling he'd have been as much a household name as Roger Bannister. He was kind enough to have a word for me on my own racing – 47 years after his ride I too held the 100-mile record, for just a few months in 2003. It was a record that passed mostly unnoticed even by my competitors, but it hadn't escaped him.

Booty was among the last of a type of rider that stretched back to Southall and even to Ion Keith-Falconer. He was of amateurism and real cycling. He actually spent the week before his record ride working in Reading near the course, but still rode home to Nottingham on the Friday night because the forecast was fine, and he didn't want to miss a good weekend's touring with his club. He rode the 100 miles back from Nottingham to Reading the Sunday evening before the race, and paid ten shillings to stay in a bed and breakfast. On his way home after his shatteringly hard ride, he managed to get a lift as far as the town of Nuneaton. Then he rode the remaining 40 miles home, and enjoyed the ride. All on the same bike that he raced. When I met him he said he still had it, and still rode it occasionally.

He could have been a pro, but that never seemed to interest him. He won the Empire Games (massed-start) road race in 1958, but then faded away from the sport. It's hard to see him as a pro, despite his huge talent. He used to carry a stove in the panniers that he strapped to his racing bike to ride to events, and not infrequently offered to make tea for anyone who might want a cup after a race. He was far from alone in this. I don't know if he did so after his epic Bath Road 100 – his B&B might have been a bit of a step up from the camping that was a familiar part of a distant race, and a stove might not have seemed necessary. I very much hope he did, though, simply because I like the idea of the new British record-holder celebrating by making a round of tea for everyone. It would be nicely emblematic of that kind of cycling and that kind of rider.

Outside of the strife-riven racing politics, cycling in Britain in the late 1940s and early 1950s picked up from where it had left off before the war: club runs, children in sidecars, and all the rest of it. The nation put its signposts back up, so tourists didn't get lost so often. You could go back to the coast, much of which had been off-limits during the war, or at least off-limits to anyone who included 'riding over a landmine' as things that would spoil a ride. As rationing ended, there was even sugar for a cyclist to put in his tea.

Times were, if not actually 'good', at least better than they'd been. There was a lot of optimism – while the racers bickered, CTC membership rose in the late 1940s from 34,000 to 50,000.[4] The cycling press predicted boom times ahead. 'Cycling will advance in popularity to saturation point,' declared *Cycling*. 'That will be the time when there are no non-cyclists left.'[5] There was no stopping cycling.

If only that had been true. Bicycle sales started to falter in the early 1950s. The industry blamed, among other things, National Service, which diverted the young from cycling. Sales tax was levied at 33 per cent on bikes, which didn't help.[6] There was a certain amount of hand wringing. Saturation point looked a little further down the road.

All that, though, was small-arms fire compared to the atom bomb that was heading for cycling. When Harold Macmillan stood up at a Conservative Party rally in Bedford in 1957 and said, 'Most of our people have never had it so good', what the British people heard was, 'Buy a car. Buy it now. You deserve it. This whole island is going to be just like California. Didn't you hear me? I said, "Buy a car."' If you look at a graph of car ownership in Britain through the twentieth century you'll find it ambles along doing nothing especially extraordinary until the mid-1950s. At that point it turns and roars abruptly off the top of the scale. It took about 60 years for the UK to get from zero to four million cars. It took only another six to get to ten million. At the start of the 1950s fewer than 20 per cent of British households had a car. By 1965 that figure was 50 per cent.[7]

All those cycle tourists? Well, here's the thing. For decades the proud assumption had been that their cycling was motivated by a simple love of the world's greatest invention, and by the nobility of travelling by their own honest sweat. But it turned out they weren't all that interested in cycling, after all. All they wanted to do was get out of the house and go somewhere. And if they could do that in a Morris Minor, well, so much the better. I mean, they could listen to the radio and take a proper picnic and the baby didn't have to travel in a sidecar made from a packing crate.

No one really saw this coming. They probably should have done. There was a repressed demand for cars from before the war – those families who hadn't bought one then for fear it would be requisitioned by the government. Post-war, pent-up aspiration, a booming economy and the sudden arrival on the market of cars like the Mini, which were both cheap *and* desirable, led to the explosion in motoring. The first motorway opened in 1958, and by the early 1960s the traffic jam had thoroughly arrived. British transport had changed out of all recognition in less than a decade.

CTC membership dropped to 18,000. The total miles ridden in Britain fell from 12 billion in 1951 to not much more than two billion by the early 1970s.[8] It was a rout, a comprehensive defeat by an enemy that no one was even worried about because everybody had convinced themselves that cyclists wouldn't want cars even if they could have them. It was classic class-cringe: cars were for posh people, not merely for people who could afford them.

Peter Hopkins is a cyclist from Staffordshire, who re-founded the Oxford University Cycling Club in 1958 – it had been in abeyance since before the war because the sort of young men who went to Oxford had long since stopped being the sort of young men who rode bicycles. Peter was from a working-class background, and arrived at Oxford via the post-war Education Act and a Midlands grammar school. He was exactly the sort of young man who rode a bicycle, just like his family, just like his friends in the club back home.

Peter managed to gather up some like-minded grammar-school boys and got the club restarted. In 1958 even a club full of students at Oxford University still had touring runs: meet at Martyrs' Memorial at 9 on Sunday, lunch in Banbury, tea in Chipping Norton. The club had racers too – they'd meet up with the tourists after their event. You know the routine. Ray Booty would have fitted in. It was the sort of club that was on the edge of disappearing.

When I asked Peter about what happened next, as the 1950s turned into the 1960s, he said, 'It was a dreadful era for cycling. It turned out to be a myth that all these people loved cycling. It was just that in the years after the war they hadn't had any choice. I bought a car, but I kept cycling because I loved to do it. But there weren't very many others like me. So many riders just disappeared.'

So much of what had been normal cycling disappeared too. Touring especially suffered, and with it the sort of club life that people had taken for granted. 'The all-round clubs vanished,' said Peter. 'When I went to Oxford the clubs were big, there were pure tourists, racers, people who did a bit of both. Racers would join up with the touring run at their lunch stop after racing. But that all stopped. All the club runs turned into what I used to think of as a racers' training run.' Even how cycling looked changed. 'Tourists used to ride in fairly normal clothes,' Peter pointed out. 'It wasn't even that unusual to see a tourist wearing a tie. But it became more and more about racing, and riders started wearing racing-type kit whether they were racing or not.'

It's true that the cyclist's relationship with clothing has changed. At a vintage cycle run I went to a couple of years ago period dress was encouraged. A handful of people turned up in period racing kit – wool singlets and shorts – but most wore fairly normal-looking period suits, probably with plus-twos as the concession to athleticism. They replicated exactly the look of the old photos, and complied with the advice in the old manuals and magazines: 'starched shirts have no place in athletic pursuits'; 'celluloid collars are particularly popular with tourists'; 'a lounge suit cannot afford adequate ventilation'; and so on. One book even offered the very sound but still pretty strange-feeling advice that 'a leather golfing-jacket is not well suited for cycling'.[9]

'Cycling shrank. And it just became seen as so downmarket,' said Peter. 'There was a real snobbery about it. When my wife went to a work-related conference in the 1960s she drove there with her bike, so she could go for a ride or two while she was there. The manager of the hotel made her hide the bike round the back, because he was scared that guests would see it. That was how it was.'

Britain had emerged intact from a war that had been won with the aid of a great deal of innovative technology. After years of the hardest of hard times, the New Elizabethans wanted to look forwards, not backwards, and the future they saw was about all that technology: jet aeroplanes, fast cars, motorways, hovercraft, space travel. This was a nation that was seriously contemplating levelling large areas of cities to build elevated roads. Machines with a capital 'M' were in; bicycles with a very small 'b' were not. They didn't seem to fit any more. They were just too simple and too human.

If you look at highway and urban planning of the 1960s it's clear the assumption was that as prosperity increased, cycling was going to just vanish, at least as any serious means of transport. It was designed out as more and more roads were based around solely the needs of the new motorists.[10] An official report prepared for the UK government in 1963 even suggested banning cyclists entirely from primary routes.[11]

Already the black-and-white world of Frank Patterson – of tourists ambling around country churchyards in plus-twos, of shop boys on delivery bikes – was receding into the past. To remain a cyclist through all this took a real love of what a bike offered that nothing else could. To be a cyclist in a world of cyclists was one thing; to be a cyclist in a world of Minis and Morris Minors was quite another.

Before he retired, Peter Hopkins was an English teacher. One of his pupils was a cycling friend of mine, Ken Platts. Ken went on to be a British international bike racer, but his introduction to the sport was through school touring trips that were organised by Peter. Ken was still a tourist who'd never raced when he arrived at college in Cambridge in 1970. 'I was still wearing tweed plus-twos and stockings and a jacket,' he told me. 'And I was certainly not alone in that. There were still some proper touring runs happening in some clubs, and I used to do a lot of youth hostelling – North Wales, northern Scotland – and there were riders there in their fifties and sixties who'd been doing that sort of touring since well before the war. And I slotted right in, because I was doing the same thing. But it was changing very fast. More and more it became about racing, and youngsters coming into cycling in the late sixties and seventies probably had racing as their first experience of it, not the sort of touring trip that Peter was running.

'The youth hostels started to disappear, and the roads got busier and busier, which took a lot of the pleasure out of touring. I can remember doing mile after mile in the mid-sixties without a car passing. But within a few years that changed. I was amazed on a tour in the seventies when we were turned away from a café – they said they were setting up to serve lunch and couldn't let us in, but it was obvious it was because we were on bikes. I used to ride to work and back, about 12 miles each way, which was almost unheard of by that time. I think everyone just put me down as bit of an odd ball.'

Cycling had become something for children, or for the poor, or for the strange. The great pastime had passed away. You'd have been forgiven for thinking it would never return.

CHAPTER 13

1960–1990:
An Ugley Situation

Miraculously, cycling did not die. Through the technological, social and political upheavals of the 1960s and 1970s it was almost invisible, but it was still there. There were even some properly great moments. Tom Simpson won the World Championships in 1965, and with it the high-profile BBC Sports Personality of the Year Award. Simpson beat Jim Clark to the award, and Clark had done nothing less than win the Formula 1 World Championships *and* the Indianapolis 500. Beryl Burton won the Worlds as well, and was runner-up for the BBC Sports Personality Award two years later. But like the rest of that era's small handful of cycling highpoints, these fizzed only briefly in the public imagination.

For the most part, cycling retreated into the kind of anonymity of which the National Cyclists' Union had dreamed for so long. It was ironic that the Union was no longer around to enjoy it. To be a cyclist in the middle of the 1960s was, in much of the public mind, to be something between at worst a tramp and at best a Luddite. The cyclists shrank into something not so very far away from a secret society.

It's an era that hasn't completely vanished. In the late 1990s I won an event called the Ugley Men's Road Race. It took its name from the small Essex village of Ugley, a place where you can't wave a bicycle pump without hitting an ugly pun: the Ugley Women's Institute, the *Ugley News*, the Ugley Farmer's Market. The Ugley truth is that it's a rather nice village, full of rather nice people who are numb to the puns.

On the slightly less lovely side of Ugley you can find several old-fashioned-looking bungalows, sitting in neat plots on a thin slice of land between the M11 motorway and the railway line from London to Cambridge. These are the club huts. They're owned by various cycling clubs from east London, about 30 miles away. Generally dating from the 1960s, they're on sites subject to planning laws that allow them to be used only as 'sporting dormitories' – they can only be occupied on Friday, Saturday and Sunday nights. In the early days of cycling it wasn't unusual for well-to-do clubs to have a country base as well as a city clubroom, and the huts are a mid-century reinterpretation.

The Ugley Men's Road Race was based at one of the huts – I can no longer remember which. It might have been the Lea Valley CC, or the Shaftesbury, or the Easterly. Not, I think, the Victoria, or the Eagle, or the Crest. I've lost track, because there were a lot of races that started at the huts. It was cheap and easy – the huts as race HQ and changing rooms kept the costs of running an event down, and we all knew the circuits. Most Sundays through the season, at 9 or 9.30 in the morning, you'd find the regulation 60 riders standing in the road outside, listening to the race briefing before clipping in and setting off to the start.

The huts themselves had bunk beds, a kitchen, and a sitting room with posters of a random selection of notable bike riders of the last 20 years, and lots of old magazines. The furniture was of the donated variety, the carpets floral where they weren't threadbare. There were never enough loos to deal fragrantly with 60 nervous bike racers. If you were racing, for an extra £4 or so on top of the entry fee, you could stay the night. I never did, because I had the feeling the previous evening's hospitality would not be compatible with being up bright and early and springy-legged. At an Ugley race I was once in a breakaway with one other rider who, at about 3 kilometres to the finish, said, 'Look, just go now, mate. I won't chase you. If I have to sprint I'll be sick.' The previous evening at the hut he had singlehandedly accounted for two bottles of red wine and waved away all offers of assistance with them. In the circumstances his riding was astonishing.

The huts were built as, in essence, a refuge. Some of them replaced earlier wooden structures. Maybe there was a hint of the old Clarion Camps, a place in the quiet of the country where cyclists could go to be cyclists. The locals were used to them, the Essex–Cambridgeshire–Hertfordshire borders were good for riding, and it was a place in those hostile years where no one demanded an apology.

Most of the huts are still there now. A couple of them have been sold, and planning sought for a change of use. The ones that are left are used, often as not, by the children and grandchildren of the riders who built them. The clubs still ride (or sometimes drive) up on a Friday night, stay for a night or two, and ride the same roads they've done for decades. I've lost count of the number of events I did from the huts over 20 years of riding – all of them low-key, all of them friendly, and all of them, like the huts themselves, a bit of cycling that's survived from an era cycling was lucky to get through. It feels wrong to arrive at the huts on a carbon-fibre bike. If ever anywhere cried out for a proper old steel bike handmade by a bloke called Stan from Stoke, with holes drilled all over for lightness, and a full Campagnolo groupset, it's the huts.[1]

Racing was most of what happened during the 1960s. There was a bit of touring, yes, but as the decade wore on, cycling became more and more racing focused. The magazines thinned out the touring articles, the reviews of panniers became fewer and further between. In came blow-by-blow accounts of British races – both time trials and massed-start. There was more training advice, diets, reviews of race bikes and lightweight kit. Interviewers stopped asking riders what their favourite tour was, and started asking for their 'week in training'. For years *Cycling* magazine ran a series of winter features about the training of the top 12 finishers in the time triallists' Best All-Rounder competition. I'm hard pressed to imagine they were interesting even at the time. ('My wife works at a baker's, so every night before training I have a grand feed of buns. Then I do my 40 miles as hard as I'm able. I do that every night from October till April. In April I up it to 45 miles.')

The press was just following its audience. Racing hadn't really increased – though it was at least now run by a unified organisation – it was that everything else had almost gone. Racers were less fickle than tourists. Most of the riders who loved cycling enough to stay were the ones who liked to do it hard, for whom the effort was the joy. You couldn't ride a bike race on a motor bike.

The outlook remained insular. The press now gave the Tour de France an annual look-in and it was no longer confined to 'Foreign Racing'. The World Championships was covered. But other than that? The establishment's magazine *Cycling* ran page after page on races run by British clubs, contested by British domestic amateurs and the occasional scraping-a-living professional. Even as late as the 1980s, when a reporter new to the magazine suggested he might go and report on the Belgian Classic Gent–Wevelgem in his own time and at his own expense, he was told not to.[2] This was despite British riders like Tom Simpson and Barry Hoban having become contenders in much of the continental programme.

Other magazines did try to take a broader view. *Sporting Cyclist* started life attempting to avoid taking a side in the old NCU–BLRC war in 1955, and covered continental racing with a lot of interest and no small amount of knowledge. Compared to *Cycling* it was a lot more modern in feel. But it was never profitable, and it didn't survive the downturn of the 1960s – in 1968 it merged with *Cycling*. Its journalism is still rightly sought out by anyone trying to get a grip on the British continental stars of the era, because it actually understood what they were doing and what it meant. But at the time, *Sporting Cyclist* was a bit of a third wheel.

The truth was that after decades on its own, and despite the victory of the BLRC, British cycling was more comfortable with its own stars and its own races and an idiosyncratic world view that found no dissonance in simultaneously believing that British racing was the finest in the world and accepting that British riders usually struggled to compete on the world stage.

The acceptance of domestic massed-start racing didn't really change this. Ian Emmerson OBE has been among the most prominent and prolific race organisers in the UK since he took over the Lincoln Grand Prix in 1963 at the age of 19. He ran it for over 50 years and made it the biggest one-day race on the UK calendar. 'There were a lot of static years in British racing,' he told me. 'You could maybe find somewhere to read about things like the Tour de France, but there wasn't anything like TV coverage, you couldn't watch it. The British races had the advantage that you could go and actually see them. The world of cycling in Britain was smaller, so the domestic races were much bigger.

'At a modern Lincoln Grand Prix we get crowds of maybe 10,000. Crowd management has become one of the things we have to plan. But I've got photos of the finish of the race from the 1960s where there are maybe 50 people. They're different sorts of people as well – most of the 1960s crowd had come on their bikes, the bikes are parked by the road and they're all in cycling kit. But, like a modern crowd, they'd come to see the riders they'd heard of and read about.'

It was just that back then the riders they'd heard about were from the secluded world of British racing. The big-name teams were not professional outfits, they were clubs, like the Manchester Wheelers, whose riders won the Lincoln and almost everything else. The same clubs ran ordinary club runs, and had a weekly social in a pub. Even the domestic professionals spent a lot of their time riding fairly unremarkable races organised by the clubs.

The upside was that on quieter roads, in a low-key sport, the job of an organiser was rather more straightforward. Emmerson told me that when he started running races, he simply took the forms to the police station, and had them approved there and then. A few stewards were needed, and at that point he had everything in place. 'Now, it's an 18-month job,' he said. 'Meeting after meeting after meeting.'[3]

That old-school simplicity meant that there was at least plenty of this isolated racing. David Taylor was, for many years, a cycling journalist. Like many, his interest was sparked by watching the racing that was based round a local park, in his case in Finsbury in north London. He joined a BLRC club in neighbouring Islington in the 1950s: 'We'd got about 70 members, and we'd have teams at maybe six different massed-start races every weekend – certainly in sheer numbers of events cycling was doing all right. There were always races at Letchworth, at Royston . . . we raced on a circuit at Stapleford Tawney aerodrome, where the racing didn't stop just because a plane was taking off. It was like the war was still on.'

The racing might have been local and aimed at amateurs, but it wasn't especially easy. There was a Tour of Essex, which had a 215-kilometre stage on Saturday, a 40-kilometre time trial on Sunday morning and a 144-kilometre stage in the afternoon. All of that was on top of the fact that almost everyone in the field would have ridden out to the race from London, probably 30 kilometres each way – a total distance over two days that wouldn't disgrace a modern Tour de France. 'It was still like the 1920s, nothing had changed,' said Taylor. 'Still sleeping in a barn the night before a race if you couldn't afford to stay in a pub. The races often finished somewhere completely different from where they'd started, and if you got dropped by the race you'd got no idea where you were. It might have been a bit defeatist, but I remember taking a map in my jersey pocket so that when I got dropped I could at least find my way home.'[4]

The racing was good, there was lots of it. There were stars and water-carriers, and dropped riders scattered all over the country all wishing they'd been realistic enough about their chances to bring a map.

There was even quite a reasonable-looking professional scene – in 1966 the British Cycling Federation had 66 professionals registered in the UK, and the scene offered enough domestic racing to sustain them.[5] The problem with all of it was that no one outside an increasingly small world even knew it existed. The professionals in the UK had only occasional contact with professionals from Europe. Generally they just raced against each other.

The riders who did make it internationally generally didn't achieve that by just moving up the amateur ranks until they attracted the attention of a professional team, the way a rider in Italy or France might do. British riders of the 1960s, 1970s and even 1980s who made it usually did so despite being part of British racing rather than because of it.[6] From Tom Simpson in the late 1950s to Sean Yates in the early 1980s, they packed their bags and their bike and went to France or Belgium. It was a clean break from racing at home, and they all but started again from the beginning. Most of them sought a place in a good amateur team – the ACBB (Athlétic Club de Boulogne-Billancourt) based in Paris was always a popular destination, with a history of taking in English-speaking riders. Sean Yates, Paul Sherwen, Stephen Roche, Phil Anderson, Robert Millar, Paul Kimmage and Graham Jones were all ACBB 'graduates'. From there they worked their way up, just the same way as the native riders.[7]

It was a hard school. None of their achievements back home counted for much. Almost all these riders have stories of living alone in unheated flats, isolated by lack of language skills, having to bash their way around large numbers of races so they could win enough to eat. When Tom Simpson moved to France in 1959 his letters home detailed the prize money, not the victories. Simpson was more motivated than many to make the French move work, because he was also dodging his National Service draft. If he'd gone home he would almost certainly have been arrested.[8]

The riders needed to survive long enough to get a pro contract. Winning helped both sides of the equation – you could afford food, and you'd attract the teams. Fail to win, and you could starve in obscurity and no one would even care. For the most part the foreign legions on teams like the ACBB either got a contract quickly, or not at all. And there were plenty who came under the heading of 'not at all', and came home defeated. Sometimes they could settle back into the domestic scene; at least as often they drifted away from the sport entirely. After all, the reason they'd gone in the first place was that they weren't satisfied with British racing, and it can only have seemed even more parochial after a taste of what the rest of the world had to offer. Someone who took their chances across the Channel was never going to be the same again, whether they succeeded or failed.

That was the way it stayed. There was a little bit of a push towards France for a few riders in the 1980s, when changes to social security policies meant that the 'dole-pro' option – ride full-time while claiming unemployment benefit – was closed off to them and some decided to roll their dice on the other side of the Channel.[9] Most of them still came home empty-handed. The reputation of French racing for chewing up the best and spitting them out was enhanced with every one of them who came back.

British racing had managed to move seamlessly from an isolationism driven by arrogance to an isolationism driven by an inferiority complex without passing through any sort of normality. It was a considerable achievement, and it's a context worth remembering when contemplating the achievements of those who did have the determination and confidence to take a chance on the big time.

Yet, just because the sixties, seventies and eighties were the bleakest era cycling had known, especially for the non-sporting bits of the pastime, doesn't mean there weren't outbreaks of optimism. In fact, there were outbreaks of optimism about every three weeks. There was a perpetually renewed faith that whatever low things had reached this month must surely be the nadir, and that things were about to take a swing for the better. A world view more sensitively attuned to reality would have been that there was no situation so bad that it couldn't get worse.

The keepers of the faith had a conviction that if only they could find a new way to present cycling then all would be well. There was, for example, the small-wheeled bike. The first one of these was designed by Alex Moulton, and was rather clever, using a suspension system to compensate for the harsher ride of the small wheels.

Raleigh picked up the idea. Moulton's idea was that smaller wheels would be lighter and more aerodynamic. The Raleigh marketing department's idea was that small wheels would be 'fun'. In practice the Raleigh version, lacking the suspension Moulton had engineered to make the whole thing work, had to rely on large bouncy tyres to prevent the road vibration making the rider numb from the nose down. The knock-on effect was that the bikes were notable mainly for being slow and uncomfortable. But it's easy to be clever about it after the event – a lot of cycling's problems were about image, so trying to change that image made sense.[10] It wasn't entirely ineffective either – Raleigh didn't exactly face down the motor car, but they did sell quite a few small-wheeled bikes.

All the same, a different approach to changing cycling's image worked better elsewhere. There was a big boom in bike sales in the US in the late 1960s and early 1970s. It began with kids' and teenagers' bikes like the Schwinn Stingray, which was pretty much what Raleigh were ripping off when they came up with the Chopper of so many 1970s childhood dreams.

Compared to the Chopper even the small-wheeled bikes of the 1960s were triumphs of functionality. The Chopper's centre of gravity was too far back, the saddle chafed, those ape-hanger handlebars were just stupid and, more directly to the point, there was no chance whatsoever of nine-year-old-me getting one for Christmas. Instead I got a Vindec Viking, which was a rip-off of the rip-off, and had gained nothing in aesthetics along the way. It was clearly a common-or-garden girl's bike with an undersized front wheel, some hasty fashion-chasing add-ons, a saddle blatantly modelled on something from the Tower of London, and a coat of rust-coloured orange paint that subtly changed to actual rust over the course of no more than about six months. It was so wildly unstable that it was the only genuinely homicidal inanimate object I've ever encountered, and I count myself lucky to have survived it.

In the US, though, the Stingray had quite an impact. It managed to nudge bicycles out of 'children's toy' and into 'teenage toy' – they became an acceptable way to get to school. The style even appealed to adults looking for toys. Peter Hopkins – he of the re-founding of the Oxford University club – recalled meeting an American cycle-tourist in the late 1960s 'with an incredible bike, done up to look like a motor cycle, with a fake petrol tank. It must have weighed a ton'.[11] The Stingray kicked on into sales of adult ten-speed racing bikes – between 1969 and 1973 US sales of those rose from 600,000 to 8,000,000, and for the first time since the 1890s most of the bicycles sold in the States were for adults.[12]

The US boom didn't last. It was killed off by the oil price shocks of the 1970s and their effect on disposable income. By 1977 sales had more than halved again. There is an irony in the effect of the oil price hikes. If you want to understand something about the way cycling was changing, you'll want to know that in the UK at exactly the same time the oil price hikes were seen as great news for cycling. Cycling historian Andrew Ritchie said, 'Now, in the 1970s, the internal combustion engine looks like it might be on its last legs. The bicycle is booming all over the world. Its future looks extremely bright. For cyclists the old pride of independence is still alive and well as they contemplate the coming transportation revolution, and the possibility that governments may recognise the value of the bicycle and appreciate its sanity and humanity.'[13]

Many others reflected the same very noble sentiments. They were wrong, and wrong twice over. It was just another bit of the cyclists' irrepressible optimism and profound state of denial – the internal combustion engine was not doomed, and even in the short term its problems were not good for cycling. The US was showing the way things were heading – cycling was ceasing to have anything much to do with transport. Bikes were no longer interchangeable with cars, they were now interchangeable with music centres, video games and televisions. Cycling was coming to have more in common with jogging or hiking or fishing than with motoring.

Cycling was quietly becoming more desirable, but it was happening at least in part because bikes were ceasing to have an air of utility about them. It was a fundamental change in direction.

But one that was hard to detect without the benefit of hindsight. In the UK there remained a determination to make cycling relevant the way it once had been. After the small-wheeled bike for the swinging sixties came another attempt to reinvent the bike for the space age, with a push by some campaigners towards recumbents and especially towards human-powered vehicles with enclosed fairings. HPVs could be much faster than upright bikes, at least on the flat. They were reasonably weatherproof, but at least as much of their appeal was their smooth aerodynamic shape and their sheer modernity. They had an air of a sci-fi pod about them, like something out of *Blake's 7*.

The standard manual for cyclists in the 1970s and 1980s was Richard Ballantine's *Bicycle Book* – a gloriously eclectic mix of campaign polemic, workshop manual and practical guide to riding on hostile roads. The first edition, for instance, included an alarming set of instructions for using a bicycle pump to kill an aggressive dog.[14] Ballantine was a huge fan of the HPV, and very persuasive on their benefits. Reading his books in the 1980s I could quite fancy myself HPVing to school. But HPVs were still about modernising the bike to compete with the car, and that game had been up for years. In all the time I've been a cyclist I don't think I've ever seen an HPV other than in an exhibition, or in a record attempt.

Changes were coming, but they weren't really based in technology. The bike was going to remain very much as it was. It was who was going to ride them and why that was going to change, and America in the early 1970s was a better (if far from perfect) place to look for the future than Britain in the early 1950s.

CHAPTER 14

1992–2016: The Life of Lottery

I took up cycling in the mid-1990s. Very shortly afterwards, the activity in the UK experienced its biggest boom since the 1890s. The two events are most likely a coincidence. I mention them together only to admit that I'm now dealing with a story I've been standing in the middle of for the last 20 years, and that it would be foolhardy of me to claim that I can try to make sense of it without being prejudiced by my personal experiences.

The sport that I came to was old cycling. It was the rump of what had been going on for a hundred years. Whenever anyone accuses me of being a cyclist just because all the middle-class creative types are into it, I can assure them that when I pulled on my first terrible

1990s Lycra jersey I was definitely joining a sinking ship. 'Back then,' I tell them, 'whenever I told anyone I was a cyclist they almost invariably said, "You mean a motor cyclist?" and looked embarrassed for me when I said no.'

It wasn't even the fashionable side of the rump. Not for me the scrawny world of British bunched racing. I initially joined the underclass's underclass, and became a time triallist. The old-fashioned sport appealed to me, not least of all because I turned out to have a considerable talent for it. F. T. Bidlake would have approved of me. Frank Southall would have understood what it was that I liked about the lonely, early morning roads. Charles Holland would have thought I had some ability, but was irrecoverably square. Percy Stallard would have simply and quietly added me to his long, long list of enemies and idiots.

The BLRC and the NCU's war was 40 years past, but there was still a division between road racers and time triallists. Despite the fact that most riders competed in both disciplines, you always ended up branded as one or the other. Maybe part of the problem was that time trialling still just about held the whip hand in *Cycling Weekly*. While I quickly expanded my repertoire to both sides of the sport, I was always a better time triallist – and the exploits of riders like me, riding the long flat main-road time-trial courses, were documented in detail every weekend. They gave away a double-sided poster of me once, and I didn't even have the good grace to be sheepish about it.

Cycling in the 1990s was inclusive. The numbers of people who wanted to race were sufficiently small that no one was really ever turned away. Certainly there was no dramatic stratification of the sport, no layers and layers through which to work your way up. You could get a ride in some of the biggest races in the country off fairly modest reserves of ability and dedication, which meant that for a new arrival in the sport you could compete with your heroes almost before you'd even worked out who your heroes were.

What it was not, was successful anywhere outside the network of village halls that were its Old Trafford and its White Hart Lane. International pro cycling was still a different thing, unconnected to us by anything except admiration. The only race you could see on television was the Tour de France, and that in a 30-minute highlights programme each evening that contained, on a good day, about 15 minutes of actual footage. We were grateful for it.

Even in the 1990s, continental racing remained uncompromisingly foreign – European riders with unspellable names and deep tans, in teams with sponsors that, for the most part, we'd never heard of. The Motorola outfit had a lot of UK fans in the 1990s, partly because they were American, but mainly because at least we knew who Motorola were. But Banesto? Polti? Mercatone Uno? GAN? Le Groupement? No idea. (A bank, a vacuum cleaner, a supermarket, an insurer and a dodgy pyramid-selling scheme, it turned out.) The ability to distinguish one oddly designed jersey from another, and knowing how to pronounce the team names, was like being able to speak a foreign language. It was the same exotic attraction that pulled people to the BLRC in the 1950s. When the pros came to the UK for events like the PruTour, a short-lived version of the Tour of Britain, we went to watch, and to notice how the pros seemed to glow with an inner light.

The glow wasn't just stupendous quantities of highly experimental drugs – it was the reflection of all our admiring gazes. We wanted to be just like them but, as had been the case since the 1950s, the only way to have made the leap would have been to pack up your bike and your UK career, move to France, and more than likely starve to death in an unheated room above a provincial bike shop. I knew several talented riders who, just like their predecessors, agonised about whether to take the chance. Almost none of them did, scared off by French food, the fear of ferocious French racing, the isolation and even the worry of working a launderette in a foreign language.

I didn't move to France, so at least I didn't starve to death in month-old underpants. I moved to London, where my underwear was spotless, but where riding a bike felt like an extreme sport. To ride a bike in London then was to mark yourself out from normality. There was a man across the street who rode a penny-farthing to his job in the City every day. He wore a suit and carried a polo mallet so he could prop himself up with it at traffic lights, and perhaps just occasionally stab it vengefully through a sunroof. He was only marginally odder than the rest of us. The roads were hostile, bike lanes were non-existent, and the only way to stay safe was to be fast enough and aggressive enough to ride in the middle of the lane at the same speed as the traffic. In a way I quite enjoyed it, and was good enough at it to not get knocked off very often, but it was a young, fit person's game – it wasn't really a mode of transport at all.

In short, cycling in the mid-1990s was still on the same trajectory it had been following for decades. The only way to tell it wasn't dying was that if it had been going to do that it would have done so already. But we were bumping along the bottom. Cycling wasn't a sport or a pastime that anyone aspired to; it was something you were born into, or stumbled into, and found you liked.

Then everything changed. Between 2005 and 2015 membership of British Cycling increased from 15,000 to over 100,000 – a mere 600 per cent. The total distance cycled increased from around 2.5 billion miles in 2005 to over 3.5 billion miles in 2015. The value of the UK bike market increased by over 50 per cent. By 2016 8,000 riders an hour were crossing Blackfriars Bridge in the London rush hour – 71 per cent of the traffic.[1]

In competition Britain became the main medal-winners in Olympic track cycling, produced the world's leading international road team in Team Sky, and saw its riders switch abruptly from also-ran status at the Tour de France to dominance of the event in the space of just a few years.

But you don't really need the statistics. Just look around you. A sport that used to be a) invisible and b) unsuccessful even if you could find it has become a major force. As a hobby, it's saved a whole generation from the trauma of golf. As a means of transport, it's come back to become a key part of planning, or at least it has in London and one or two other cities.

You can see all this in much sharper relief if you've been a cyclist all the way through. Anyone who's come to cycling during the last ten years might assume it's always been there, and it's always been like that. No. It's changed. Or maybe what it's done is change back. There are echoes of the past, not least the enthusiasm for heading out of the cities to ride in the countryside on a Sunday morning, which has such a strong resonance with the penny-farthing riders of the 1880s and the club runs of the 1930s. The class orientation has regressed as well. Cycling has gone back upmarket. H. G. Wells's Mr Hoopdriver and his quiet pride at being mistaken for an aristocrat no longer seems quite as laughable as it did in the late twentieth century.

Something that is not a throwback is the motivation of the Sunday riders. Somewhere along the line cycling, for most of its disciples, stopped being about adventure and started being about fitness and about sport. The degree of adventure changed over the decades. It moved from the properly dangerous and novel explorations of what a man on a bicycle could safely do in the 1870s and 1880s, to the relatively safe adrenaline rush of the toffs learning to ride in Battersea Park, to the tourists of the mid-twentieth century. 'Adventure' is probably a bit much for the latter, but it was still the case that what motivated them was curiosity, an urge to go places and explore.

Many, if not most, of the modern weekend riders are more motivated by pushing themselves, seeing what they can achieve. Formal racing isn't what they're doing, at least not for the most part. It's usually more personal than that, a rider on their own, or with a few friends, pushing themselves into the red for the pleasure of it. The word 'suffering' is one they use approvingly, and use a lot. Where there is no suffering, there is no joy. There is a love of the sport of cycling, an admiration for its heroes, and a desire to understand them better by exploring the depth of effort that a bike can demand.

Depending where you stand on it, the modern-day cycling fraternity are either a noble brotherhood of masochists, or a grown-up versions of children who just want to run and run until they fall over and lie panting and looking at the sky. Whichever, cycling today is a world away from loading your children into a plywood sidecar and heading out to ride 80 miles in seven hours on a Sunday with the local club. So, to put it in a sentence, different people are doing it differently for different reasons, and they're doing an awful lot of it. And golf is the loser.

What happened? Why did cycling, in all its manifestations, suddenly leap dancing from its grave? It's complicated, but a good place to start is at the Barcelona Olympics in 1992. I'm talking, of course, about Chris Boardman, who became Britain's first Olympic cycling champion in 72 years.

It was a victory that no one really expected. At least half the attention ended up focused on what he was sitting on, which was the first widely seen example of a bike designed in a wind tunnel and built in carbon-fibre. The bike was, by Boardman's own account, barely capable of holding itself together long enough to reach the finish line, but to the rest of us it looked as though it had arrived through a portal from the middle of the twenty-first century. Black, organically curving, it looked as though it had been sculpted by the wind itself. Everyone else's bike instantly turned to scaffolding tubes.

Boardman's bike might have been sex on wheels. But, other than a nifty bit of PR for moving cycling's imagination on from flat caps and whippets, it wasn't really the important bit of Barcelona. Nor was it essential for what happened next that Boardman himself went on to forge the most high-profile British bike-racing career since Tom Simpson, although it certainly didn't hurt. No, probably the most critical element in the package was his coach, Peter Keen.

Keen was an atypical cycling coach for the era. It went without saying that a full-time coach was almost unknown, and most of the part-timers were old racing men cut from the same cloth as the old trainers of nineteenth-century professionals, whose speciality had been keeping their charges out of the pub long enough to do some bike riding. The image was of wiry middle-aged men barking orders in northern accents and exhorting performance through whatever traditions performance had once been exhorted from them.

Keen, on the other hand, was a university sports science lecturer, and he approached coaching exactly the way you'd expect of a young academic. The press had pictures of Boardman training on a static bike in a laboratory, while Keen stood beside him holding a clipboard, surrounded by assistants who scurried around in white coats tending to computers that drew graphs and anxiously watching machines with blinking lights.

Other sports had been working this way before, but cycling was old school and, frankly, financially badly off, so for us this was all very new indeed. To say there was a degree of scepticism would be to considerably understate the mirth with which a lot, perhaps even most, of the general cycle racing fraternity greeted this sort of thing. Cycling was tough and it was simple. The logic of the age was still that if you wanted to go quickly you simply racked up as many training miles as you could, and then tried bloody hard in your races. If you weren't going fast enough you tried even harder. Coaching cycling in a white coat was like going down a mine in a ball-gown. You had to accept that people were going to laugh until beer came down their noses.

There was actually an interesting counterpoint to the Keen and Boardman approach at the time, in the shape of Graeme Obree. If Keen and Boardman were new cycling, Obree looked a lot like old cycling. He was a self-trained, self-motivated Scot, who built his own racing bikes using bearings cannibalised from his family washing machine, and occasionally incorporating bits of metal he'd found on road sides. He was reportedly capable of pushing himself so hard in races that he coughed up blood. He did not train in a laboratory; he trained according to his own instincts in the rain-soaked hills above the Ayrshire coast, and was fuelled by marmalade sandwiches. Robert Garbutt, a former editor of *Cycling Weekly*, described

Obree as 'A time traveller – he was a man from 1910. In a lot of ways he was in it for the adventure and the discovery.'[2]

The irony was that despite superficial appearances, it was Obree who was the more innovative – he had an open-mindedness to wild ideas and an intuitive grasp of both engineering and physiology. His inventiveness with aerodynamic riding positions was such that the world sport's governing body kept having to devise new rules to keep him at bay. But the superficial old–new culture clash made for a delicious rivalry with Boardman, who was very clearly a bit put out by a competitor who apparently fitted so well with a version of cycling that he and Keen were working so hard to get away from. (Boardman did later admit that Obree was the more original rider – 'a genius' was one of his subsequent descriptions.[3])

Nonetheless, it was Keen who was key to much of what happened next. Having achieved some fame as coach to Boardman, in 1997 he was asked to take over as head coach of the British Cycling team. Up until then the funding available for the team was enough to buy most of the international riders a team jersey. That was about it. Otherwise, it was their own bikes, their own shorts, often their own travel expenses. Mechanics were usually volunteers from a bike shop somewhere, and they had something of a reputation for retiring to a local bar for an extended beer tasting of an evening, leaving the riders to clean their own bikes. One former rider reported giving his bike to the mechanics at the end of a long, arduous, wet stage of the Peace Race in Poland in the 1970s, and getting the reply, 'I'm not cleaning that. It's fucking filthy. Do it yourself.'

At the same time as Keen took over, National Lottery funding arrived in British sport like a liberating army. The quietly spoken man in the white coat suddenly had £2.5 million at his disposal, a budget increase of something like 5000 per cent. There wasn't even an infrastructure in place to spend it, so he had to create one, create it very quickly, and make sure it would win Olympic medals, since they were the only currency the Lottery was interested in.

Keen did what you'd expect a scientist to do, and worked out what the most efficient way of turning cash into medals was. He quickly concluded that track medals were 'cheaper' than road medals, because vast swathes of the cycling world didn't really care very much about them. International pro road racing was a whole industry, with a budget of millions and a huge roster of top athletes. Track cycling was rooted in amateurism, a bit make-do-and-mend, generally underfunded and clearly offered opportunities for a team with money and ambition.

As if that wasn't persuasive enough, of the 18 Olympic events in cycling, 12 of them were on the track, and none of them were as fiercely contested as the four that were on the road. Six of those medals were in timed events, like the pursuit that Boardman had won in '92, which involved no real tactics, just pure speed. They were particularly amenable to the sort of scientific approach that Keen liked. They were put at the top of the list.

The decision to focus on the track was made even easier by the recently completed Manchester Velodrome, which had been built at least partly on the wave of interest created by Boardman's Barcelona medal.[4] Basing a programme there had the considerable collateral benefit of establishing a unified training base for a squad to work from. It meant that the whole organisation, athletes, coaches, and support staff, could be based under one roof, where Keen could keep an eye on all of it. It also, of course, reduced the opportunities for the existing coaches to muscle in on the act, which it's hard to imagine wasn't seen by Keen as at least a marginal benefit.

As a question of pure economics, it wasn't a hard decision, but it was a hugely unpopular one. It wasn't at all what people had expected. Keen was still essentially down a mine in a ball-gown. Despite the noble traditions of track racing, road racing was what mattered to the cycling public, and they would happily have traded 50 track medals for a couple of Tour de France stages. The fact that there wasn't such a deal on the table, and that even if it had been the Lottery fund that handed out the cash wouldn't have been impressed, was neither here nor there. Even if they'd been told that the best way to win at the Tour de France would be to start off by funding track, winning medals, securing more funding, reinvesting, and so on, they wouldn't have liked it. Road mattered, track did not, and that was the end of that.

Still less did the objectors like the centralised pro-gramme, nor the new-fangled sciency coaches employed to run it. Almost instantaneously the number of staff involved in running competitive cycling at British Cycling increased from three to 34. Sid Barras, a former professional National champion, complained that British Cycling had 'more coaches than Wallace Arnold', a line that so neatly caught the mood that people are fond of repeating it 20 years after he said it, 17 years after the programme's first Olympic medals, and 12 years after the Wallace Arnold bus company vanished from the roads.[5]

Happily for Peter Keen the plan worked. Just three years later at the 2000 Sydney Olympics, Jason Queally won a gold medal in the one-kilometre time trial. To make it even more high profile, it was the first British gold medal of the Games. It was exactly the sort of controllable track event that Keen had targeted, and Queally, who'd come to cycling only a couple of years earlier, was exactly the sort of athlete whom Keen's programme was trying to develop. There were medals in three of the other targeted events. In an era when British sport's idea of a major Olympic medal haul was 'any', it was a roaring success for cycling.

It wasn't just the change to track racing, the no-cash-unless-you-win-medals culture meant there was a new ruthlessness about the system. I can offer some personal insight into this, since I got the soggy end of it. In the early 2000s I was a very successful rider domestically in the UK. I was invited to train with the national squad immediately after the Sydney Olympics, with a view to going to the 2004 Games in Athens as part of the pursuit squad.

I'm prepared to bet that ten years earlier I would have become a fixture in the squad, for no better reason than my domestic dominance would have meant I was given a swing at whatever exciting trips to big races were going. One or two of my rivals had spent the previous few years going to World Championships, taking a hiding, collecting a few autographs off the famous riders responsible for their humiliation, and coming home to swank around in that solitary team-issue jersey and tell you about meeting 'Lance'.

In this new world, on the other hand, after a bit of familiarisation with track racing (which was new to me), I was given a target to hit, calculated in relation to the current world record. I didn't hit it. And just as swiftly

I was standing back outside the Velodrome in the east Manchester rain, my bike in my hand.

Selection was no longer a question of what a rider deserved as a reward for their dedication and their local results. It was a question of 'Can this hairy bag of meat get on a bicycle and win us a medal?' If the answer was no, nothing else mattered. If the answer was yes, no stone was left unturned in the cause of making the hairy bag of meat go faster. It was so very different.

The same approach rolled on into the twenty-first century. Lottery money and medals formed a positive feedback loop. By 2015 the annual budget for British Cycling was over £7.5 million.[6] The team, under Peter Keen's successor Sir Dave Brailsford, got more ambitious, and adapted the same analytical approach Keen had pioneered into preparing riders for the more complicated bunch races and sprints. Riders like Sir Chris Hoy and Victoria Pendleton developed, over multiple Olympic cycles, into some of the world's most famous athletes. Whatever anyone might say now about obvious 'star quality', for those of us who sat around a velodrome with them in the early 2000s, it was really not what we'd have expected.

At its most basic, for those who got onto the squad, Lottery money kept them in the sport and gave them time to improve, where previously they'd have quit when they got tired of being poor. At its most sophisticated, the money paid for a whole sub-group of boffins – led by Chris Boardman – to spend hours in a wind tunnel designing aerodynamic skinsuits and helmets. On the track it all unfolded exactly as Keen had foreseen. Almost nowhere else has a moderniser quite so comprehensively defeated his critics.

The same general method was carried across to the men's professional road outfit Team Sky, started by Brailsford in 2009.[7] It had the aim of winning the Tour de France within five years. Instead it won it in three, with Wiggins in 2012, and repeated the feat three times more, in 2013, 2015 and 2016 with Chris Froome.

In 20 years Britain went from less than an also-ran in international cycling to one of the sport's major forces. By 2016 there had been four Tour de France wins for two different riders, 25 Olympic titles, 46 Olympic medals in total, and numerous World champions, including both the men's and women's road races. Not since 1868, when for a few minutes one spring afternoon James Moore could lay claim to having won 100 per cent of all the bike races there had ever been, had Britain's racing been in such good health.

The other side of the great revival story – that of what we might call the Great General Enthusiasm – is less straightforward. No one paid for it, or at least not in a way that involved keeping the accounts. That it is related to the success of the sport is impossible to prove absolutely, but it's still hard to argue against. The correlation is too close, the coincidence too unlikely, and the number of weekend riders wearing full Team Sky replica kit all the way down to the bike is too hard to write off as a collection of unrelated fashion decisions. But there is clearly more to it than just high-profile success – or the middle-aged middle classes would be spending their Sunday mornings sailing their dinghies and practising their dressage instead.

I asked Chris Boardman himself about it. He's now a policy advisor for British Cycling, and very much the organisation's front man for the media. 'Everything just came together,' he said. 'Readiness met capacity. In 1994 the Tour de France came to southern England. Millions of people came to watch it. And if they loved it, if they were inspired, there was nothing for them to do about it. But when the Tour came back to London in 2007, when the GB team dominated the Beijing Olympics, there was a product in place. There was something for them to do.'[8]

The 'something' was the sportive. The sportive is what drove much of the boom. The concept is easily understood. A road course is designed and signposted – in general the harder the course is the happier everyone will be. The usual expectation is 50 to 100 miles, through quiet roads and lanes, and including as many hills as the organiser can string together. Feeding stations are dotted along the route, and some sort of mechanical backup is provided. Any number of riders from a couple of hundred to (in the case of the RideLondon event) 26,000 set off in small groups to tackle it. It is very simple, and very accessible. There is no racing licence required, almost nothing in the way of rules, and entry is just on the internet. You don't even have to be a member of a club. You just register, pay an entry fee and turn up.

It's not a race. Well, not technically. If it was a formal race, with results and a winner, it would be subject to a lot of racing-on-the-highways legislation, police notification, policing costs, road closures, racing rules, and all the things that make organising a race for anything more than a handful of competitors such an undertaking. A sportive is set out as a challenge – the organisers usually provide gold, silver and bronze time targets (or something similar) to give riders something to aim at, while not offering prizes to podium finishers.

Of course, afterwards, when the organisers send out a list of everyone who completed the course, and how long it took them, it's inevitable that the list ends up being rearranged into speed order. Sportives definitely have a winner, and in most cases the winner will be quite happy to overlook the technicalities and describe themselves as such, sometimes to the extent of sending press releases to their local paper.

The events are timed from line-to-line, rather than first-to-finish, usually by microchip. So you're not at a disadvantage if you start late – your own personal clock doesn't start running till you cross the line. The irony, then, is that a sportive is almost identical to a time trial, just one that's a bit free and easy with the rules about teaming up with other competitors for a few miles of group riding. The similarity with the early-nineteenth-century races, where the field was usually very strung out and a single 'bunch' was a rarity, is striking.

The accusation levelled at sportives when they started was that they were neither one thing nor the other. There was a grumble from old cycling that sportives were not proper races, just glorified club runs with entry fees. But that missed the point – a sportive was sort of everything to sort of everyone. From the perspective of old cycling, one end of a sportive field should have been racing. The other end should have been touring. A group in the middle probably should have been on a club run. Yet there they all were, in the same place, doing the same thing, at slightly different speeds, and for slightly different reasons, but all getting what they wanted with minimal hassle.

The other thing that changed was the participants. Cycling very abruptly stopped being a cheap sport associated with working-class riders. The connotations became those of affluent professionals. The phrase 'cycling is the new golf' became one that we all had to come to terms with, and you could tell a lot about someone by whether they said it approvingly or with a tired sadness in their eyes. In a few short years we went from the point where a cyclist was from the underclass, to the point where senior British Conservative politician Eric Pickles criticised the city council in Cambridge for promoting cycling, on the basis that it was a something favoured by the 'elite'.[9]

(I also feel I ought to say that it seems likely that cycling transitioned from something Eric Pickles would have sneered at for being working class into something he sneered at for being elitist without actually passing through a point at which he would have approved of it. This might mean that hostility to cycling and its relationship with the class system is more complicated than it at first appears. Or, of course, it could just mean that some people don't like cycling and will use whatever brick comes to hand when they're looking for something to throw at it.)

‖　‖　‖

If it was high-profile success that drove the reinvention, it was something quieter and more organic that created Boardman's 'readiness' to meet all that demand. None of it was as instant as it looked. People had been drifting into cycling (or, in a lot of cases, back into cycling) very quietly for quite a long time.

Peter Hopkins said that he felt he could trace the revival back to the 1970s. In the very depths of the despond, he said he started to see his own contemporaries come back. They'd bought the Morris Minor, and left their bicycle to the spiders in the shed. They'd nurtured a family, built a career, bought several subsequent cars, and then one day realised that they hadn't seen their feet for a decade. They tried jogging, and hated it, and then remembered that they used to ride a bike a bit.

True to the idea that we abandoned adventure in favour of fitness, the motivation was health. That wasn't unusual, there was a lot of that around in the late 1970s – it was perhaps the first big health kick for a generation that had been through the fear and austerity of the 1940s and early 1950s, and then took full advantage of the security and prosperity that followed to eat, drink and smoke themselves to a coughing, spluttering, blubbery standstill. There was a jogging boom, for instance, that led to the London Marathon (and many other marathons and mass-participation events), and the foundation of many still-thriving running clubs. Cycling didn't get that kind of critical mass at the time, almost certainly because of the class issues, but the same motivations were there.

There was more than that, though. There was a major change in cycling in the late 1980s, which I would have managed to overlook had it not been for my former editor at *Cycling Weekly* pointing it out. 'Mountain biking,' said Robert Garbutt. 'In the 1980s, mountain biking was just huge. There was a point where nine out of every ten new bikes sold was a mountain bike.' The people who took up mountain biking were not, according to Garbutt, road cyclists. They were new to cycling of any sort. And, crucially, they came in sideways from very, very cool sports like windsurfing, rock climbing or hang gliding. The kind of sports real men did in the 1980s, complete with blond highlights and a smear of dayglo yellow sunblock under each eye.

I remembered this – at the age of about 12 or 13 in the mid-1980s, I raced windsurfers. The windsurfing magazines were full of articles about mountain biking, and all the ways they could improve your windsurfing. They were also clear that mountain bikes were not to be confused with road bikes, nor, more to the point, mountain bikers with road cyclists.

At the same time, the London cycle courier became a style icon. Young, fit and good looking, they had an encyclopaedic knowledge of about half-a-dozen streets around London's Covent Garden, and they rode mountain bikes – despite the fact that road bikes would have been a lot more practical.

I fell for the propaganda, and saved up and bought a mountain bike. It wasn't a cheap knock-off, it was the real deal. I was such an early adopter than none of my teenage friends knew what it was. They were still riding BMX bikes with their knees around their ears and fancying themselves the sharpest-looking thing in the area, even if they struggled to compete with my unbelievable hairdo and my sunblock.

I even did a handful of mountain-bike races in a forest near home. It was only recently that it occurred to me that this was more or less the same sport as the one that I earned a living from a decade later. I'd never really connected the two, and I'm sure that was just as the world of mountain biking wanted it.

The other thing about mountain biking was that, in the early days at least, the racing was informal. You could buy your first mountain bike on Saturday morning and be racing it by mid-afternoon. 'Mountain biking attracted a whole new group,' said Garbutt. 'They were the sort of people who traditional road cycling would never have appealed to. And then we had a couple of bad winters. The more serious mountain bikers wanted to maintain their fitness, so they bought road bikes, which started a crossover.'

There is, here, a subplot about who invented mountain biking, mainly in that riding a bike off-road has a very long history. *Cycling*'s Wayfarer was famous for his off-road stories. Cyclists' Touring Club members weren't at all averse to hitting the tracks and byways and fields, and an association called the Rough Stuff Fellowship was founded in 1955 in the UK with that as its specific mission.[10] But there is a degree of consensus that what we now know as the mountain bike, and the craze that swept up people like me, came from a group who started racing down a steep forest fire road in Marin County in California in the mid-1970s. The road was famously named 'Re-pack', since the hub brakes on their cruiser-style bikes overheated so badly they needed to be re-packed with fresh grease after each descent. The bikes evolved into the early mountain bikes, with knobbly tyres, flat bars, cantilever brakes and over-built frames.

Like so many things in cycling, mountain biking was a temporary boom. But it gave lots of people an excuse to go cycling, and a different demographic (or, more likely, the perception of a different demographic) to go cycling with. It was simple fun, in a slightly chaotic way, like a non-extreme version of an extreme sport. It lacked the rules and strictures of mature sports, the races were casual, and expanded easily into big events with hundreds of riders.

And it wasn't the only thing that started in North America. The organised 'Century ride' was just a simple, non-competitive challenge of riding 100 miles in a day. The earliest events included the Tour of the Scioto River Valley in Ohio, which began in 1962, the Rideau Lakes Tour in Canada in 1972, and the Apple Cider Century in Michigan in 1974. They grew rapidly to include several thousand riders, with feed stations, mechanical support, and so on. It was an idea too good not to steal. On the British side of the Atlantic, the CTC ran a popular annual series of Century rides in the early to mid-1990s. *Cycling Weekly* promoted some around the same time, and found that with a little bit of plugging in the magazine they were relatively easily able to attract 2,000 to 3,000 riders, a considerable total for a new concept of event.

'They were very successful,' said Garbutt. 'So, typically for us, we gave up running them, and went to find something less successful we could do instead. In some ways they shouldn't really work – at first we thought it was just a club run with an entry fee – but it was clear that they were giving people something they wanted. Perhaps the decline of traditional club cycling meant that people hadn't had the chance to ride with a group. Maybe they just wanted some cycling friends for the day.'

The Century still wasn't the sportive, though. There were lists of finishers, but no target times, no individual rider numbers. They were a little bit more touring, a little less racy. The first event that clearly took the shape of a sportive seems to have been the Circuit of Kent in 1997. It appealed to the same riders, but was organised more along the lines of the cyclosportives that had been running in continental Europe.[11] It was organised by the Gemini Bicycle Club, which had riders who'd done European cyclosportive events like the Maratona dles Dolomites or L'Étape du Tour.

The main difference between the continental events and the Circuit of Kent was that the continental events were proper races. They did, and they still do, have full results and prizes. Otherwise, making allowances for the lack of proper mountains in that corner of England, the concept behind the Circuit of Kent did quite a neat job of knitting together the touristy challenge of the Century and the sporting edge of the continental events. It was certainly an idea that found a market. For riders who wanted to get into racing, rides like Kent were more accessible than a full-on road race, which firstly requires a licence, and secondly can be so fast and aggressive that even a fairly fit novice would struggle to stay in the bunch for more than a few miles. An event like the Circuit of Kent was a way for people to ride routes they would never otherwise find, and a way for them to feel just a little bit like a Tour de France hero, hurtling along in a smooth paceline.

By 2016 there were something approaching 800 sportives on the UK calendar, each involving anything from several hundred to several thousand riders. The number of events is still increasing. For something that didn't even exist until 1997, and as part of an activity that everyone thought was beyond revival, sportives have been a roaring success story.

Given that isolationism was such a theme of British bike riding through the twentieth century, it's ironic that the hugely successful sportives don't really connect very well with cycle racing in the narrow sense of formal races. Because you can't officially 'win' a sportive in the UK, you can't use them to establish a career that extends very much beyond your own imagination. The slight strangeness of a non-competitive sporting event means that however popular they might be, sportives on their own won't nurture a next generation of stars.

For that you need to go back to traditional racing. The blessing is that it's done pretty well too. Both massed-start road racing (as championed by Percy Stallard) and track racing require a race licence, which means you can keep track of the numbers – between 2010 and 2015 the number of full race licences issued by British Cycling increased from 16,891 to 28,985.[12] That's an increase of 71 per cent. The number of affiliated clubs has gone up as well – increasing from 1,672 to 2,200 over the same period.

This came as a considerable surprise, because domestic racing has become almost invisible in the UK. Its profile has fallen down a hole between the mass-participation sportives and the international successes like those at the Tour de France or the Olympics. That's probably inevitable, if a little sad. It's the downside of connecting all of British bike racing to the rest of the world: the scale changes. Only the biggest UK races attract much attention now, and even then British bike racing pales into insignificance beside the full-on general sports-media coverage devoted to the bigger international events.

But at least it has at last begun to form a proper pathway for potential pro riders in the UK. Finally, a rider can start off as a talented junior riding local circuit or track races, and get to the top without having to take huge gambles, or having to endure a career whose length was defined by how long they could put up with the poverty. At last, most of eight decades after Percy Stallard started a modernising revolution, Britain has plugged its bicycle racing into the rest of the world.

Meanwhile, the original and quintessential British bike race, the time trial, has followed a slightly different path. It's more or less exactly where it was when I started riding time trials 20 years ago. The numbers of participants have remained pretty much steady, the number of races has declined a little, but overall not a lot has really changed. Time trialling is still a nice, simple way to go bike racing, but as a separate part of the sport run by a different governing body from the rest of UK racing, it hasn't really been well placed to promote itself on the back of all the success. Maybe no one is too bothered about doing so. After all, they would be doing no more than respecting time trialling's own modest and clandestine traditions. (The governing body – Cycling Time Trials – doesn't have any means of keeping track of individual competitors, so the numbers are something of an estimate. They seem to be holding consistently at around 10,000 active competitors.)

F. T. Bidlake might still be able to take some pleasure in the way that his own branch of the sport has continued so true to the course on which he set it at the end of the nineteenth century – but he'd be horrified at almost everything else: massed-start racing in the ascendant; huge sportives roaming the countryside in mighty bunches; professionals at the Olympics. What he'd make of crowds coming out and lining closed roads to celebrate events like the Tour of Britain or the Tour of Yorkshire I can hardly imagine. It may have taken 75 long and tortuous years, but Percy Stallard has finally, comprehensively won. Even if it does seem very likely that he'd still find a reason to be cross about it.

CHAPTER 15

Towards a Cycling Tomorrow

This, then, is the chapter where, by the traditions of cycling history, I declare that the future belongs to the cyclists. Well, we'll come to that presently. Maybe.

The tradition of the upbeat ending shouldn't be a surprise. Cycling history is written not by the victors, but by the optimists. There are more of them. That's because cycling draws people in. It can be almost anything to almost anyone, while still being just 'cycling'. Over the last 200 years it's been an extreme sport, a normal sport, a family holiday, a focus for fellowship, a political tool, a fitness craze, a means of going to war, a focus of national pride, a feminist liberator, a driver of manufacturing revolution, and a minor perversion (well, in Paris anyway). I'm sure there are plenty that I've missed.

Cycling continues to be all of the above and more for someone, somewhere. There is just so much of it that all anyone can really do is look at the way the tides have come in, gone out and come in again. That cycling still exists at all, and even thrives, when it looked so certain to disappear, is a tribute not only to the brilliance of the machine but to those who love it, not just for what it can do but simply for what it is.

The current state of the cycling tide is not what anyone would have expected. No matter how carefully you might comb through all of the optimistic articles and final chapters, you don't find anyone who predicted twenty-first-century cycling, at least not until it had more or less already happened. Cycling has always been unplanned, unpredictable, infinitely adaptable, and just as much now as ever.

The one person who I thought maybe had seen where we were all heading was Simon Mottram, who founded the high-end bike clothing label Rapha in 2004. I can remember Rapha's first press releases, and the first unbelievable price list. I was quite possibly still wearing one of the dreadful multicoloured polyester jerseys that were almost all you could buy, as I hooted with laughter at the thought of anyone paying the sort of money on

Rapha's price list. The kit looked lovely, but it was clear that no one was going to pay that much for it. I could hardly have been more wrong. Rapha became one of the emblems of new cycling.

Mottram told me that he wished it had been foresight, but it had been substantially luck. 'Eighty per cent luck, 20 per cent judgement,' was his estimate. 'We were actually two or three years too early. I just started the company because I wanted something to wear, and almost everything you could buy was pretty terrible.'

What surprised him a little was the crowd that came to the launch of the first range: 'All sorts of people we'd never seen before turned up, with vintage Colnago bikes, retro jerseys and that sort of thing. Architects, creatives, people who adored bikes and the culture of bikes. I think they were always there, just hidden by the idea that cycling was for losers.' Like many of the current riders, they weren't from traditional club culture. They were loners, or they rode with a few like-minded friends. And happily for Mottram they also wanted the sort of clothing he was selling.

The idea of a cycling culture matters. What Mottram's creatives loved was, for the most part, post-war continental racing – Jacques Anquetil, Eddy Merckx, Raymond Poulidor and Tom Simpson. It intersects with the ambitions of the BLRC, and it's not a coincidence that Rapha's designs frequently take their inspiration from racing kit of that era. It was cool then, and it's cool now. There is an enthusiasm for retro that means there are probably a lot more fans of that age of racing in the UK today than there where when it was actually happening.

Other riders take their cue from more recent heroes. Sir Bradley Wiggins didn't just give people an interest in riding bikes, he got people interested in cycling. Events like the Tour de France wear their history very prominently: they have stories, they have heroes, they have heroes with flaws, and they have tragedies. Almost everyone knows about the death of Tom Simpson in 1967, even if it happened 40 years before it occurred to them to buy a bike.

A lot of current cycling, certainly surrounding the sportive scene, could quite well have been invented cold in the late 1990s as a whole new activity, arriving as something a bit like snowboarding. It's got relatively few direct causal connections to anything that happened much more than 20 or 30 years ago. But many cyclists still feel part of something bigger and older. It's why cycling is not the same as going to the gym, or even the same as going for a run, or a walk in the country. If you consider yourself a cyclist, you very probably consider yourself part of a history.

There are, of course, some respects in which it's yet another example of a middle-class appropriation of a working-class culture. Those twentieth-century heroes, like Anquetil or Simpson, were almost always riding bikes because the alternatives were the mines or the fields or the factories. Maybe they enjoyed suffering in the mountains, but more likely they were motivated by the idea of not suffering at a coalface. They'd be a little perplexed by the idea of paying to go on a cycling holiday in the Alps so you could replicate their misery. You could try persuading them suffering is the ultimate luxury, but they would probably tell you that they'd prefer a Mercedes.

Closer to home the BLRC riders who changed cycling after the war were from the same backgrounds, and without them it seems unlikely we'd have very much of what we have now. In fact, the same applies to many of the riders who kept cycling alive during the late twentieth century.

All the same, it's quite hard to find class-based resentment from older riders about the way cycling has changed. There is certainly some puzzlement and even a little regret about some of it, but usually on a more practical level. Common themes are the drift away from club life, the ever-deepening mystery of why anyone would pay to do a sportive on roads they could ride anytime for nothing, and an awful lot of comment on what seem like exponentially increasing prices. But to call it a culture clash would be to overstate matters. It's no more of a culture clash than two generations of almost anything else. At least there is the feelng that cycling is moving again.

It is true that sometimes what two people want from a bike ride is very different. Robert Garbutt told me about going as a guest on a London–Paris ride, organised mainly for very well-off City types. 'It was extraordinary,' he said. 'At the first corner, a left-hander in Esher, 14 people crashed. In the Ashdown Forest in Sussex one guy hit a pothole at the edge of the road and fell. I was 20 riders behind him, and I was the first one who didn't hit him. It was insanely aggressive and competitive. If you told someone not to ride through a gap because there was a hole in the road, they took it as a personal insult and rode through it to prove they knew more than you did. Then they crashed and took five others out with them. It was mayhem. There were some good riders working as ride captains, trying to keep everyone upright, but controlling these guys was a hell of a job. I gave up at Dover and went home. It was probably the only group of cyclists I've met in 40 years who I didn't feel I had anything in common with.'

I suspect these might be the riders Jerome K. Jerome would write about if he wanted to update his observations about the aristocrats in Battersea Park. For their part, most of the City riders were probably equally uncomprehending at the idea of Garbutt wanting to cycle to Paris *without* showing any pressing desire to race anything on two wheels.

Cyclists, all of them, still have much more in common than you might be tempted to think. There are plenty of older club riders who've taken to sportive riding for a lot of the reasons that newer riders do them, and if you go to a traditional club's time trial after work on a summer evening there are usually riders who took up cycling sometime in the previous year, and are delighted to be part of it.

For most (but not all) of its existence cycling has been inclusive, and now seems like a bad moment to go looking for divisions that don't really exist. There still aren't enough of us to have factions, and there is more danger in drawing your definition of the approved kind of rider too narrowly than in drawing it too broadly. Depending on who's talking, the phrase 'He's not really a proper cyclist' can be used about anyone. I've heard it used about an Olympic gold medallist, and I've certainly heard it used about me.

That's doubly the case because perhaps the biggest problem cycling still faces isn't its own internal differences. While cycling has a culture that sets it apart from other comparable activities, the world at large is rather less enthusiastic about accepting cycling as part of normality. For all the upswings in popularity and the reanimation of a whole culture, we're still a bunch of weirdoes as far as much of the rest of the world is concerned. The UK is a long way from a normal, mundane cycling culture, like the Netherlands or Denmark. The 'otherness' of cyclists is a convincing explanation for a great deal of day-to-day hostility.[1]

It also means that, for almost the first time, in recent years utility cycling has started to become part of the sport and the pastime. For the most part someone in the 1930s or 1940s who rode to work didn't reckon that doing so made them a 'cyclist'. They might describe themselves as a 'cyclist' if they needed to distinguish themselves from pedestrians or bus passengers, but that didn't mean they felt much kinship with the tourists, the time triallists, or Wayfarer crossing Welsh mountains in a storm.

But the distinction has never been a very brightly drawn one. I've tried to stick to it more through a desire to write an account of people for whom cycling was an essential part of their identity, something they loved to do for its own sake. That decision was just a personal preference, and reflected my own curiosity about the history of people who felt the same way about cycling that I do.

But however fuzzy the distinction was, it's a lot fuzzier now. The revival of riding a bike to get somewhere (rather than for the fun of it or to get fit) has been a positive in cities like London, even if it's been more fitful elsewhere than many of its London-based advocates like to notice. Where it has caught on, it's produced riders with a much clearer sense of identity as cyclists than their equivalents 70 years ago – which is hardly surprising given that riding a bike has become a positive choice rather than something akin to a default. You can see the difference without looking any further than how a commuter typically dresses – for the most part they wear racing kit, or something modelled on it.

The fortunes of the commuters are closely tied up with the fortunes of the whole of cycling. For a start, the revival in utility cycling is linked to the same racing success as everything else. While it's far from clear exactly how many people watched Bradley Wiggins winning the Tour de France and thought, 'As God is my witness, if a sideburned bloke from Kilburn can win the Tour, I can ride to the office', but Wiggins's win was just the sort of event that gives cycling the general credibility that something has to have before a politician will touch it.

That, at any rate, is how Chris Boardman – now a skilled political operator in the field of cycling – put it: 'Olympic medals and the rest are what mean I can go on Breakfast TV and talk about cycling. They're what mean I can nudge the Mayor of London. Would Boris Johnson have had the balls to push cycling as a positive thing for London without it? I don't think he would have.' Colonel Albert Pope would give a satisfied sigh to hear Boardman say, 'Any publicity is good. You can associate cycling with three Olympic cycles of success, and you can ride to work on the same brilliant invention. You can get the support to have something like the RideLondon festival, where a whole family can get something out of cycling.'

All of this matters to all sorts of cycling, and it matters for the future. If cycling is relying on racing success to sustain interest in sporting riding, full-on racing *and* now commuting, then there is an awful lot of bike riding that is hanging from not very much. Not really. One pro team, one national track squad and half a dozen riders are driving it all. Boardman said, 'Cycling in the UK is quite fragile, really. At the moment it's dependent on two or three things. The longer it survives, the more roots it gets, the more people are invested in it, the more secure it is. We need to get it past fashion, because fashions change, and we've probably only got a couple of years to do that.'

So, then, that's the wildly optimistic ending. Only a fool would, I think, want to predict anything more definite, good or bad. If the last two hundred years have shown anything, it's been that the world of cycling is an unpredictable one. And that is as it should be. Cycling is a democracy and, despite a few spirited attempts, no one has ever really been in control. Cycling and cyclists will always evolve to suit the world around them, and to make the most of it. Just look at the number of golden ages that cycling has been able to claim – the 1890s, the 1930s, the early 1950s, the present day – different people doing different things for different reasons, but all calling themselves cyclists.

I often find myself thinking about those few years in the early 1880s when a man on a penny-farthing was the king of the roads. I have, of course, got the nagging feeling that even if I'd been born at the right time I'd still have been too much of a coward to even try riding one. But, setting that aside, it seems to me that to ride with a few club mates through an ancient landscape on those old roads, rough and dangerous though they were, would have been very close to heaven – assuming, of course, that someone had thrown the club bugle into a river somewhere near the beginning of the day's adventure, and perhaps the club bugler after it just to make sure.

But, really, I wish I could have been everywhere. Maybe I could have crossed the mountains with Hodites, or at least have sat in a fuggy village hall on a winter evening and listened to him tell the story, and then tried to have a star-stuck, tongue-tied conversation with him afterwards. Or gone on the sort of club run that featured a mother and father with their family suspended in a hammock – at the very least it would have improved my odds whenever the run turned into a bunch sprint for a village sign. I even, in a slightly masochistic way, wish I'd been racing bikes in the 1960s and 1970s when, if nothing else, you had a pretty straight idea of who was on your side and who wasn't.

If you ride a bike it doesn't demand any huge leaps of imagination to put yourself in any of these places and times, and know what there was to love about it. It's the same for the other eras, and the other riders. Even if I'd personally draw a line at riding round a wall of death above a lion's den, I can see why you might want to stand and watch, especially if you were the lion.

Bikes and their riders are infinitely adaptable. They flow through the world like a stream, finding their place, thriving when they can, surviving if they have to. So many people have found so much pleasure and so much purpose in something so very simple.

A few months ago I was out for a ride. At a quiet junction of two country roads a few miles from home, I met another rider. He was repairing a puncture, and since his pump was very small and clearly a bit useless, I lent him mine. After he'd pumped up his tyre and put the wheel back in his bike, we leaned against the top tubes of our bikes and chatted for a moment or two. It was the normal stuff: what a lovely day this was, how far had he ridden? Anyone who was familiar with the drawings of Frank Patterson would have recognised us immediately.

As we started to arrange ourselves to go our separate ways, he said, 'What's the best way to get to Cambridge from here?'

'The short way or the long way?' I asked, although I already knew the answer.

'Oh, the long way, I think.'

I see him sometimes out on the roads, and when I do I always wave. And then a few minutes later I remember that he's still got my pump.

Endnotes

1 1817: The Big Bang

1   Stothers, Richard B. (1984) *The Great Tambora Eruption in 1815 and its Aftermath* Science 224 (4654) 1191–1198.

2   Lessing, Hans-Erhard (2006) *Karl Drais – The New Biography.*

3   Ritchie, Andrew (1975) *King of the Road* p. 17.

4   Lessing, Hans-Erhard (2006) *Karl Drais – The New Biography.*

5   Quoted in McGurn, James (1987) *On Your Bicycle* p. 17.

6   *Baltimore Telegraph*, 9 July 1819.

7   McGurn, James (1987) *On Your Bicycle* p. 21.

8   Lessing, Hans-Erhard (2006) *Karl Drais – The New Biography.*

9   Ritchie, Andrew (1975) *King of the Road* p. 34.

10   See Lessing, Hans-Erhard (1998) *The Evidence against Leonardo's Bicycle*, in *Proceedings of the 8th International Conference on Cycle History.*

11   *Glasgow Argus*, 9 June 1842.

12   Clayton, Nicholas (1987) *The Boneshaker* 113 p. 24.

13   Ritchie, Andrew (2002) *The Velocipede of Alexandre Lefebvre and the problems of Historical Interpretation: a Response to*

Jacques Graber's 'the Lefebvre Bicycle' in *Proceedings of the 12th International Conference on Cycle History* pp. 31–43.

14　Graber, Jacques (2002) *And Once Again Lefebvre: Response to Andrew Ritchie's 'The Velocipede of Alexandre Lefebvre and the Problems of Historical Interpretation'* in *Proceedings of the 12th International Conference on Cycle History* p. 54

15　Ritchie, Andrew (1975) *King of the Road* p. 55.

16　Ritchie, Andrew (1975) *King of the Road* p. 56.

2　The 1860s: Parisian Perversions and the World's First Bicycle

1　Ritchie, Andrew (1975) *King of the Road* p. 58.

2　*Girl of the Period Miscellany*, May 1869.

3　*Scientific American*, 9 January 1869.

4　Cosdon, Mark (2009) *The Hanlon Brothers: From Daredevil Acrobatics to Spectacle Pantomime, 1833–1931* p. 31.

5　Goddard, J. T. (1869) *The Velocipede, its History, Varieties and Practice.* Quoted in Ritchie, Andrew (1975) *King of the Road* p. 62.

6　McGurn, James (1987) *On Your Bicycle* p. 44.

7　Ritchie, Andrew (1975) *King of the Road* p. 68.

8　Bartleet, H. W. (1931) *Bartleet's Bicycle Book* p. 4.

9　Ritchie, Andrew (1975) *King of the Road* p. 73.

10　Ibid., p. 70, quoting Mayall's later account in *Ixion – a Journal of Velocipeding* (1875).

11　*The Times*, 20 February 1869.

12　*Cycling*, 26 November 1906.

13　*The Times*, 31 March 1869.

14　Clayton, Nick (1991) *The Cycling Career of James Moore* vol 35, no 25.

15 Ritchie, Andrew (1975) *King of the Road* p. 60.

16 Bacon, Ellis (2014) *Great British Cycling: the History of British Bike Racing, 1868–2014* p. 11.

17 Petty, Ross (1997) *Women and the Wheel* in *Proceedings of the 7th International Conference on Cycle History*.

18 *Bicycling: a Textbook for Early Riders* (Originally published 1874, reproduced 1970) pp. 34–35.

19 *Petit-Journal*, 2 June 1868.

20 Bacon, Ellis (2014) *Great British Cycling: the History of British Bike Racing, 1868–2014* p.16.

21 See Ritchie, Andrew, *The Origins of Bicycle Racing in England 1868–1870* p. 49 in *Proceedings of the 7th International Conference on Cycle History*.

22 *The Field*, 29 May 1869. Quoted in Ritchie, Andrew, *The Origins of Bicycle Racing in England 1868–1870* p. 45 in *Proceedings of the 7th International Conference on Cycle History*.

23 *Liverpool Mercury*, 24 April 1869.

24 *The Field*, 9 June 1869.

25 *Morning Advertiser*, 27 September 1869.

26 Griffin, Brian (2006) *Cycling in Victorian Ireland* p. 178.

3 The Dignity of the Victorian Clubmen

1 Ritchie, Andrew, *The Origins of Bicycle Racing in England 1868–1870* p. 49 in *Proceedings of the 7th International Conference on Cycle History*.

2 Clayton, Nick (1996) *Who Invented the Penny-Farthing?* p. 35 in *Proceedings of the 7th International Conference on Cycling History*.

3 Herlihy, David (2004) *Bicycle: the History* p. 173.

4   Sinker, Robert (1890) *Memorials of the Hon. Ion Keith-Falconer* p. 33.

5   Lloyd-Jones R. & Lewis M. J. with Eason M. (2000) *Raleigh and the British Bicycle Industry* p. 8.

6   Reproduced in McGurn, James (1987) *On Your Bicycle* p. 67.

7   McGurn, James (1987) *On Your Bicycle* p. 53.

8   Street, Roger (1979) *Victorian High-Wheelers: the Social Life of the Bicycle Where Dorset Meets Hampshire* p. 56.

9   Street, Roger (1979) *Victorian High-Wheelers: the Social Life of the Bicycle Where Dorset Meets Hampshire* p. 12.

10   Bury and Hillier (1891) *The Badminton Library of Sports and Pastimes; Cycling* p. 220.

11   Street, Roger (1979) *Victorian High-Wheelers: the Social Life of the Bicycle Where Dorset Meets Hampshire* p. 45.

12   Bury and Hillier (1891) *The Badminton Library of Sports and Pastimes; Cycling* p. 190.

13   McGurn, James (1987) *On Your Bicycle* p. 60.

14   Quoted in McGurn, James (1987) *On Your Bicycle* p. 76.

15   Bartleet, H. W. (1931 – reprinted 1993) *Bartleet's Bicycle Book* p. 6.

16   Ritchie, Andrew (1975) *King of the Road* p. 106.

17   Griffin, Brian (2006) *Cycling in Victorian Ireland* pp. 27–8.

18   Griffin, Brian (2006) *Cycling in Victorian Ireland* p. 29.

4 1870–1900: American Cycling and the Genius of Colonel Albert Pope

1   Norcliffe, Glen (1997) *Colonel Albert Pope: His Contribution to Bicycle Manufacture and the Development of Mass Production* in *Proceedings of the 7th International Conference on Cycle History* p. 75.

2   Epperson, Bruce (1999) *Failed Colossus: Albert A. Pope and the Pope Manufacturing Company, 1876–1900* in *Proceedings of the 9th International Conference on Cycle History* p. 94.

3   Norcliffe, Glen (1997) *Colonel Albert Pope: His Contribution to Bicycle Manufacture and the Development of Mass Production* in *Proceedings of the 7th International Conference on Cycle History* p. 75.

4   Epperson, Bruce (1999) *Failed Colossus: Albert A. Pope and the Pope Manufacturing Company, 1876–1900* in *Proceedings of the 9th International Conference on Cycle History* p. 94.

5   Norcliffe, Glen (1997) *Colonel Albert Pope: His Contribution to Bicycle Manufacture and the Development of Mass Production* in *Proceedings of the 7th International Conference on Cycle History* p. 80.

6   Norcliffe, Glen (1997) *Colonel Albert Pope: His Contribution to Bicycle Manufacture and the Development of Mass Production* in *Proceedings of the 7th International Conference on Cycle History* p. 82.

7   McGurn, James (1987) *On Your Bicycle* pp. 68–9.

8   Norcliffe, Glen (1997) *Colonel Albert Pope: His Contribution to Bicycle Manufacture and the Development of Mass Production* in *Proceedings of the 7th International Conference on Cycle History* p. 76.

9   *The Wheel*, 21 May 1897. Quoted in Epperson, Bruce (1999) *Failed Colossus: Albert A. Pope and the Pope Manufacturing Company, 1876–1900* in *Proceedings of the 9th International Conference on Cycle History* p. 97.

10 Norcliffe, Glen (1997) *Colonel Albert Pope: His Contribution to Bicycle Manufacture and the Development of Mass Production* in *Proceedings of the 7th International Conference on Cycle History* p. 83.

5 1874: The Honourable Ion Keith-Falconer

1   Sinker, Robert (1890) *Memorials of the Hon. Ion Keith-Falconer* p. 33.

2   Bury and Hillier (1891) *Cycling* p. 258, also (1874) *Bicycling, a textbook for early riders* reprinted 1970.

3   Sinker, Robert (1890) *Memorials of the Hon. Ion Keith-Falconer* p. 118.

4   Sinker, Robert (1890) *Memorials of the Hon. Ion Keith-Falconer* p. 54.

5   Bury and Hillier (1891) *Cycling* p. 260.

6   *The Times*, 26 April 1880.

7   Bury and Hillier (1891) *Cycling* p. 270.

8   (1874) *Bicycling, a textbook for early riders* reprinted 1970 p. 77.

9   Bury and Hillier (1891) *Cycling* p. 87.

10   (2004) *The Letters of Rudyard Kipling 1920–1930* p. 124.

11   Moore, Gerry (2012) *The Little Black Bottle: Choppy Warburton, the Question of Doping and the Deaths of His Bicycle Racers* p. 38.

6 Safety Bicycles and Extreme Danger: Mile-a-Minute Murphy and the Lion's Den

1   Ritchie, Andrew (1975) *On Your Bicycle* p. 125.

2   (1931) *Bartleet's Bicycle Book* p. 67.

3   Bury and Hillier (1891) *Cycling* p. 117.

4   (1931) *Bartleet's Bicycle Book* p. 68 *et seq.*

5   Griffin, Brian (2006) *Cycling in Victorian Ireland* p. 44.

6   (1931) *Bartleet's Bicycle Book* p. 74.

7   Griffin, Brian (2006) *Cycling in Victorian Ireland* p. 45.

8   Moore, Gerry (2012) *The Little Black Bottle: Choppy Warburton, the Question of Doping and the Deaths of His Bicycle Racers* p. 99.

9   Westland, Les *Cycling Plus* magazine, January 2000. *New York Times*, 18 February 1950.

10 Rabenstein, Rüdiger (1999) *Sensational Bicycling Acts Around 1900* in *Proceedings of the 9th International Cycling History Conference* p. 67.

11 See Radford, Peter (2001) *The Celebrated Captain Barclay: Sport, Money and Fame in Regency Britain.*

12 Redmond, Patrick (2014) *The Irish and the Making of American Sport 1835–1920* p. 43.

13 McGurn, James (1987) *On Your Bicycle* pp. 65–6.

14 McGurn, James (1987) *On Your Bicycle* p. 136.

15 Both quoted in Meinert, Charles (1997) *Single Sixes in Madison Square Garden* in *Proceedings of the 7th International Cycle History Conference* p. 59.

16 Meinert, Charles (1997) *Single Sixes in Madison Square Garden* in *Proceedings of the 7th International Cycle History Conference* p. 59.

17 For the 1896 Olympic cycling events, see Wallechinsky, David and Loucky, Jamie (2012) *The Complete Book of the Olympics.* Though as fair warning, once you start reading this book, you will probably never stop.

18 Bury and Hillier (1891) *Cycling* p. 99.

7 The 1890s: The Great Society Cycling Craze

1   Petty, Ross (1997) *Women and the Wheel* in *Proceedings of the 7th International Conference on Cycling History* p. 118.

2   Petty, Ross (1997) *Women and the Wheel* in *Proceedings of the 7th International Conference on Cycling History* p. 115.

3   A speech by George Herbert Stancer, a former president
    of the CTC, looking back at his 80 years in cycling in 1958.
    Cycling magazine, 20 August 1958.
4   Jerome, Jerome K. (1926) *My Life and Times* p. 89.
5   McGurn, James (1987) *On Your Bicycle* p. 116.
6   Griffin, Brian (2006) *Cycling in Victorian Ireland* p. 65.
7   *Irish Wheelman*, 15 June 1897.
8   McGurn, James (1987) *On Your Bicycle* p. 118.
9   McGurn, James (1987) *On Your Bicycle* p. 118.
10 McGurn, James (1987) *On Your Bicycle* p. 121.
11 Bury and Hillier (1891) *Cycling* p. 10.
12 Bury and Hillier (1891) *Cycling* pp. 10–11.
13 Griffin, Brian (2006) *Cycling in Victorian Ireland* p. 93.
14 Griffin, Brian (2006) *Cycling in Victorian Ireland* p. 39.
15 Lloyd-Jones and Lewis (2000) *Raleigh and the British Bicycle
    Industry* p. 77.
16 Lloyd-Jones and Lewis (2000) *Raleigh and the British Bicycle
    Industry* p. 33.
17 Lloyd-Jones and Lewis (2000) *Raleigh and the British Bicycle
    Industry* p. 76–7.
18 *Social Review*, 16 January 1897.
19 *National Review*, 1 February 1897.
20 Petty, Ross (1997) *Women and the Wheel* in *Proceedings of the
    7th International Conference on Cycling History* p. 118
21 Wells, H. G. (1896) *The Wheels of Chance* chapter 5.
22 Ritchie, Andrew (1975) *King of the Road* p. 156.
23 *Cycling*, 16 September 1893.
24 Helvenston Gray, S. and Peteu, M. C. (2006) *Women's Cycling
    Attire* in *Proceedings of the 16th International Conference on
    Cycling History* p. 89.

25 See generally Helvenston Gray and Peteu (2006) *Women's Cycling Attire* in *Proceedings of the 16th International Conference on Cycling History.*

26 Griffin, Brian (2006) *Cycling in Victorian Ireland* p. 133.

27 Oakley, William (1977) *The Winged Wheel* p. 14.

28 See Bowerman, Les (1997) *The Long March of the 'Bloomer Brigade'* in *Proceedings of the 8th International Conference on Cycling History.*

29 Bowerman, Les (1997) *The Long March of the 'Bloomer Brigade'* in *Proceedings of the 8th International Conference on Cycling History* p. 75.

30 Reid, Carlton (2014) *Roads Were Not Built for Cars* p. 28.

8 Twentieth-Century Racing and the Loneliness of the Time Triallists

1 Messenger, Chas (1998) *Ride and be Damned* p. 3. Also Woodland, Les (2005) *This Island Race* p. 21.

2 Woodland, Les (2005) *This Island Race* p. 23.

3 Wallechinsky and Loucky (2008) *The Complete Book of the Olympics* p. 521.

4 Woodland, Les (2005) *This Island Race* p. 25.

5 Underwood, Peter (2013) *Dennis Horn, Racing for an English Rose* p. 18.

9 1900–1920: Cycling and Moting

1 *The Hub*, August 1896. Quoted in McGurn, James (1987) *On Your Bicycle* p. 119.

2 McGurn, James (1987) *On Your Bicycle* p. 138.

3 Lacy and Hillier (1891) *Cycling* p. 38.

4   Reid, Carlton (2014) *Roads Were Not Built for Cars* p. 226.

5   See Reid, Carlton (2014) *Roads Were Not Built for Cars* chapter 2.

6   Oakley, William (1977) *The Winged Wheel* p. 20.

7   Lloyd-Jones and Lewis (2000) *Raleigh and the British Bicycle Industry* p. 27 and p. 36.

8   Lloyd-Jones and Lewis (2000) *Raleigh and the British Bicycle Industry* p. 77.

9   Hilton, Tim (2004) *One More Kilometre and We're in the Showers* p. 43.

10 McGurn, James (1987) *On Your Bicycle* p. 135.

11 Pye, Dennis (2014) *Fellowship is Life: the story of the National Clarion Cycling Club* p. 24.

12 McGurn, James (1987) *On Your Bicycle* p. 135.

13 Pye, Dennis (2014) *Fellowship is Life: the story of the National Clarion Cycling Club* p. 28.

14 Jones, Stephen (1991) *Sport, Politics and the Working Class* p. 33.

15 Batchford, Robert (1940) Introduction to *What's all this?*

16 Pye, Dennis (2014) *Fellowship is Life: the story of the National Clarion Cycling Club* p. 34.

17 Hilton, Tim (2004) *One More Kilometre and We're in the Showers* p. 46.

18 Fitzpatrick, Jim (2011) *The Bicycle in Wartime* pp. 86–7.

19 Fitzpatrick, Jim (2011) *The Bicycle in Wartime* p. 91.

20 Fitzpatrick, Jim (2011) *The Bicycle in Wartime* p. 30 *et seq.*

21 *Regiment*, 24 October 1896.

22 Fitzpatrick, Jim (2011) *The Bicycle in Wartime* p. 153.

23 Fitzpatrick, Jim (2011) *The Bicycle in Wartime* p. 134.

10 1920–1958: The Tourists

1 Lloyd-Jones and Lewis (2000) *Raleigh and the British Bicycle Industry* p. 113.
2 Kuklos (William Fitzwater Wray) (1923) *The Modern Cyclist, a Handbook* p. 8.
3 Harvested from several issues, though the last one is in *Cycling*, 20 January 1921.
4 *Cycling*, 10 February 1921.
5 *Cycling*, 16 September 1932.
6 Oakley, Dennis (1977) *The Winged Wheel* pp. 121–2.
7 *Cycling*, 16 November 1934.
8 Quoted in Reid, Carlton (2014) *Roads Were Not Built for Cars* p. 115.
9 Law, Michael John (2014) *The Experience of Suburban Modernity* p. 176.
10 *Cycling*, 23 November 1934.
11 Hodites (Neville Whall) *Cycling*, 16 September 1932.
12 Oakley, William (1977) *The Winged Wheel* p. 29.
13 Oakley, William (1977) *The Winged Wheel* p. 62, as well as most of the rest of the book.
14 Oakley, William (1977) *The Winged Wheel* p. 78.

11 1942–1959: The British League of Racing Cyclists

1 Quoted in Woodland, Les (2005) *This Island Race* p. 40.
2 *Cycling*, 12 August 1932.
3 *Cycling*, 5 February 1932.
4 See *Cycling*, 10 August 1928.
5 Messenger, Chas (1998) *Ride and be Damned, Chas Messenger's Glory Years of the British League of Racing Cyclists* p. 6.
6 *Cycling*, 12 August 1932.

7   Woodland, Les (2005) *This Island Race* p. 41.

8   Quoted in Messenger, Chas (1998) *Ride and be Damned,
    Chas Messenger's Glory Years of the British League of Racing
    Cyclists* p. 6.

9   Woodland, Les (2005) *This Island Race* p. 43.

10 Holland, Frances (2007) *Dancing Uphill: the Cycling
    Adventures of Charles Holland, the First English Rider in the
    Tour de France* p. 97.

11 *Cycling*, 3 August 1922.

12 *Cycling*, 3 August 1922.

13 *Cycling*, 28 July 1937.

14 Woodland, Les (2007) *The Yellow Jersey Companion to the
    Tour de France* p. 188.

15 *Cycling*, 28 July 1937.

16 Hilton, Tim (2004) *One More Kilometre and We're in the
    Showers* p. 52.

17 *Guardian*, 15 August 2001.

18 Woodland, Les (2005) *This Island Race* p. 49.

19 Bacon, Ellis (2014) *Great British Cycling: the History of British
    Bike Racing, 1868–2014* p. 36.

20 Woodland, Les (2005) *This Island Race* p. 49.

21 Woodland, Les (2005) *This Island Race* p. 51.

22 Woodland, Les (2005) *This Island Race* p. 86.

23 Messenger, Chas (1998) *Ride and be Damned: Chas Messenger's
    Glory Years of the British League of Racing Cyclists* p. 29.

24 Messenger, Chas (1998) *Ride and be Damned: Chas Messenger's
    Glory Years of the British League of Racing Cyclists* p. 30.

25 Messenger, Chas (1998) *Ride and be Damned: Chas Messenger's
    Glory Years of the British League of Racing Cyclists* p. 46.

26 Bacon, Ellis (2014), *Great British Cycling: the History of British
    Bike Racing, 1868–2014* p. 40.

27 *Cycling*, through much of June and July 2015.

28 *Cycling Weekly*, 24 November 2015.

29 Woodland, Les (2005) *This Island Race* p. 170.

30 *Cycling Time Trials Handbook 2016*.

31 Woodland, Les (2005) *This Island Race* p. 174.

12 1957: 'Most of Our People Have Never Had it so Good'

1   Hilton, Tim (2004) *One More Kilometre and We're in the Showers* pp. 81–6.

2   Hilton, Tim (2004) *One More Kilometre and We're in the Showers* p. 81.

3   It made the back page of the *News Chronicle* of 7 August 1956. There were a few small paragraphs elsewhere.

4   Oakley, William (1977) *The Winged Wheel* p. 66.

5   *Cycling*, 24 January 1941. Similar predictions occurred regularly for most of the 1940s.

6   Lloyd-Jones and Lewis (2000) *Raleigh and the British Bicycle Industry* p. 202.

7   See, for example, Thompson, Hawkins, Dar and Taylor (2012) *Olympic Britain: Social and Economic Changes Since the 1908 and 1948 Olympic Games* published by the House of Commons Library p. 137.

8   Department for Transport table TRA0101, *Road Traffic (Vehicle Miles) by Vehicle Type in Great Britain*.

9   See, for example, Camm, F. J. (1936) *Every Cyclist's Handbook* pp. 28 *et seq*, and the *Cycling Manual* of 1919, published by *Cycling* magazine, pp. 41–2.

10 Oakley, William (1977) *The Winged Wheel* p. 85.

11   Buchanan Report *Traffic in Towns* (1963) see Oakley, William (1977) *The Winged Wheel* p. 180.

13 1960–1990: An Ugley Situation

1   For an account of the Ugley Huts, see *Cycling Weekly*, 28 August 2014.
2   Private interview with David Taylor, who joined the staff in 1982.
3   Private interview with Ian Emmerson OBE.
4   Private interview with David Taylor.
5   Henderson, N. G. (1977) *Centenary '78, the story of 100 years of Organised British Cycle Racing* p. 105.
6   Henderson, N. G. (1977) *Centenary '78, the story of 100 years of Organised British Cycle Racing* p. 111.
7   Bacon, Ellis (2014) *Great British Cycling: the History of British Bike Racing, 1868–2014* p. 166.
8   Fotheringham, William (2003) *Put Me Back on My Bike: in Search of Tom Simpson* pp. 59–60.
9   Fotheringham, William (2010) *Roule Britannia: a History of Britons in the Tour de France* p. 151.
10   McGurn, James (1987) *On Your Bicycle* p. 165.
11   Private interview with Peter Hopkins.
12   Berto, Frank (1990) *The Great American Bicycle Boom* in *Proceedings of the 10th International Cycling History Conference.*
13   Ritchie, Andrew (1977) *King of the Road* p. 12.
14   Ballantine, Richard (1972) *Richard's Bicycle Book.*

14 1992–2016: The Life of Lottery

1   Statistics from British Cycling, Cycling UK and the Department for Transport's annual Road Traffic Statistics.

2   Private interview with Robert Garbutt.

3   Private interview with Chris Boardman.

4   Boardman, Chris (2016) *Triumphs and Turbulence: My Autobiography* p. 171. Also, private interview with Ian Emmerson OBE.

5   *Guardian*, 18 September 2000.

6   *Guardian*, 17 August 2016.

7   On the early years of the team, see generally Moore, Richard (2012) *Sky's the Limit*.

8   Private interview with Chris Boardman.

9   *Cambridge News*, 30 August 2013.

10 Oakley, William (1977) *The Winged Wheel* p. 31.

11 *Cycling Weekly*, 9 August 2007.

12 Figures supplied by British Cycling.

15 Towards a Cycling Tomorrow

1   *Guardian*, 1 July 2015.

Acknowledgements

Cyclists have lent me old bicycles, answered question after question, found me eccentric old documents and photographs from club archives and family albums, and suggested new avenues to explore. Their interest in what I was doing was a constant encouragement.

In particular, I need to say thank you to Keith Bingham, Chris Boardman MBE, Scott Dougal, Ian Emmerson OBE, Robert Garbutt, Peter Hopkins, Kati Jagger, Ray Miller, Simon Mottram, Ken Platts, Tony Pickering, Dave Preece, Hannah Reynolds, David Taylor, Paul Tuohy and Peter Underwood. And also to the many riders on the Benson vintage cycle run who gave me such a warm welcome.

I'm grateful to Simon Richardson and the staff at *Cycling Weekly* for access to their archive, and for making me many, many more cups of tea than I ever made them in return. I'm also indebted to the staff of the University Library in Cambridge.

In the final spurt for the finish line, Ian Preece did a very fine job of copy-editing the manuscript.

Without my agent David Godwin and his colleagues at David Godwin Associates it seems unlikely that the book would ever have been started, and without Charlotte Atyeo, my excellent editor at Bloomsbury, it is clear to me that it would never have been finished.

Index

ALSO AVAILABLE BY MICHAEL HUTCHINSON

**FASTER: THE OBSESSION, SCIENCE AND LUCK
BEHIND THE WORLD'S FASTEST CYCLISTS**

'What is it about me that makes me faster than the vast majority of bike riders? Is it innate, or something I achieved by training? Why are a lucky few faster than me? Is it just more of the same thing that makes me faster than everyone else? Most importantly, what can I do to catch them? These questions have had a hold over me for more than a decade – most of my adult life. It's no sensible preoccupation for a grown man. I know that. But I can't help it.'

In *Faster*, Michael Hutchinson investigates what makes a fast bike rider – the extraordinary physiology, the mental resilience and how they must give over their whole existence to chasing a perfection they may only experience once or twice in their lives.

'A unique and funny writer with a true understanding of what it takes to make it as an elite cyclist' CHRIS BOARDMAN

'Michael Hutchinson takes an inhuman sport and makes it deliciously, wonderfully, wickedly human' NED BOULTING

'Michael Hutchinson is not only faster than you, he can explain why in sharp and funny prose' GARY IMLACH

Pb: 978-1-4088-3777-1
Ebook: 978-1-4088-4374-1

WWW.BLOOMSBURY.COM